W9-AIR-415

Emily,
Hope you enjoy.
Best, [signature]

CEO
CAPITAL

CEO
CAPITAL

A GUIDE TO BUILDING CEO REPUTATION AND COMPANY SUCCESS

LESLIE GAINES-ROSS

John Wiley & Sons, Inc.

To Dan, my compass

CONTENTS

PREFACE

WHY THIS BOOK?

For me, it all began at home. *Fortune* magazine would arrive in the afternoon mail, and my dad would scurry off to another room, not to be seen for an hour or two. When dinner was about to be served, he would emerge and join the rest of the family around our kitchen table. Conversation began with a review of the day's minutiae. Who needed help with homework? Who needed a drive from here to there? After 10 minutes or so of such domestic queries, my dad—by now more than a little bored with the practicalities of child rearing and domestic science—would inevitably interject some business-related non sequitur: "Hey, did you know that AT&T now has telephones in different colors that can match your room?" Or perhaps, "Get this, GE's considered the best. Notice how quickly they came to fix the fridge?"

One of us children would, sure enough, take the bait and soon start complaining about why such-and-such company was not "smart enough" to make a better product or ask its customers what they really wanted ("Why can't girls get a pair of Levis that are soft?"). It didn't take long before my dad was into some tale about a company that was working on a new product that we'd like or explaining why another company could not make money from our half-baked ideas. He would recite all these facts and figures, mention CEOs by name, competitors by industry, plans to expand, plans to contract, importing, exporting, brands to be launched, and problems to be solved. As the years went by, CEO names such as Watson, Sloan, McGowan, and Warner made their appearance at our dinner table. The CEOs and companies were soon familiar dinner guests and, even as a young girl, I found their triumphs and tribulations spellbinding.

My dad was a CEO himself. He and my uncle built Atlantic Wire & Cable, their wire manufacturing company, from scratch, working up from a company of two employees to a company of 200. He always believed that by reading about CEOs in *Fortune* and by studying how they approached problems, he would learn important business lessons that, if properly applied, would make his business steadily improve. And it did until the end of my high school years, when the business hit a particularly bad patch.

I can't say I fully understood at the time what all the fuss was about, but now I do. When he had to appear in court to face his creditors, my dad, as an owner of his company, was for all intents and purposes a CEO just like Jack Welch or Bill Ford. It mattered little that Wall Street analysts had never questioned him about his corporate strategy. He was the company. He was Atlantic Wire & Cable. He felt that way in court and while standing before his disappointed and angry vendors. Thankfully, he would eventually bring his company back to life, and, in time, restore his good name. Yet, for me, this trying incident ignited a lifelong fascination with building and losing reputations.

Ironically, more than two decades later, I found myself at *Fortune*, the magazine that my dad so assiduously studied, heading up their marketing and communications department. During my years at *Fortune*, I often received calls seeking advice on how company reputations fared during times of crisis and economic downturns, or in the face of fierce competition, or otherwise. Where else to turn for guidance but the *Fortune* "Most Admired Companies" rankings and the accompanying articles? Religiously I scrutinized *Fortune*'s "Most Admired" issues to see how some of the most highly regarded companies such as IBM, Eastman Kodak Company, DuPont, and Exxon Corporation were holding up. Some were up in the rankings; some down; and some down for the count. The rankings of many of the companies, including some that had been led by my former childhood dinner guests, remained relatively stable over the years, but not all. For some companies the business environment had changed. New market forces such as globalization, mergers and acquisitions, individual investing, technology, and the Internet were rewriting the rules. Company reputations were neither given nor guaranteed.

My habitual, in-depth examination of *Fortune*'s Most Admired Companies surveys revealed to me a dearth of information and analysis about how a CEO's reputation influenced a company's reputation. As I pondered this revelation, while continuing to study *Fortune*, four realizations coalesced:

1. The *Fortune* rankings suggested that the perceived quality of a company's management directly and unalterably related to the company's success. Although *Fortune* did not specifically focus on CEOs, it did analyze management reputation. If good management directly and positively affected a company's success, surely the reputation of its most senior executive officer would have a similar, if not far greater, effect.

2. The *Fortune* covers almost always featured the sagacious visages—not the corporate logos—of the chief executive officers, from the late Roberto Goizueta (The Coca-Cola Company) and Michael Dell (Dell Computer Corporation) to Herbert Kelleher (Southwest Airlines) and Jeffrey Immelt (General Electric Company). This remained true even when

the featured story had little to do with the company's chief executive. Didn't this focus on individual leaders rather than on their company logos or other company symbols amount to the editors' instinctive understanding that chief executive officers in some way embodied the souls of their companies—that CEOs were the paramount corporate symbol?

3. *Fortune*'s analysis of those companies that rose or fell most extensively in rank typically dwelled at great length on what their CEOs did or did not do to deserve either collective admiration and repute or criticism and disrepute. Once again, the focus seemed to be the CEO and not just the company.

4. The business and general media, not just *Fortune*, increasingly seemed to concentrate on, if not extol, what amounted to a new class of chieftains of enterprise. Such coverage, with its emphasis on how individuals turned around companies or otherwise led companies to financial greatness, clearly captivated not just the media but their target audiences as well, including professionals, analysts, investors, people like myself, and even the general public.

These four factors added up to one undeniable fact—the chief executive officer's reputation influenced a company's image and its destiny. The people who were deciding where to work, where to invest, and where to place their trust were all profoundly interested in the chief executive officer. Bill Gates, Andy Grove, Jack Welch, and Warren Buffet mattered to America.

Having concluded that the well-being of a company and the reputation of its CEO were deeply and inextricably intertwined, I needed to know in what ways and for what reasons CEOs mattered so much. The naturally ensuing question was: How can companies better capitalize on their executives' reputations?

In 1997, I joined Burson-Marsteller as chief knowledge and

research officer. I was thrilled to learn that Burson-Marsteller was more than willing to have me explore the answers to these questions. Burson-Marsteller decided to conduct, for the first time, proprietary CEO reputation research. The more we learned, the more sophisticated our inquiries became. This led us in new directions and expanded our knowledge until we may now announce with confidence that we have established an entirely new body of business inquiry: What is the relationship between the CEO's reputation and the success of his or her company?

In writing this book, I relied heavily on Burson-Marsteller's research. I also analyzed related publicly available market research as well as the field research and writings of leadership experts: in particular, Harvard Business School Professor John Gabarro's seminal work[1] on how new executives take charge of their responsibilities, and the work of former Columbia University professors Donald Hamrick and Gregory Fukutomi[2] on the seasons of a CEO. They were all instrumental to my conceptualizing a CEO Capital model. The media's heightened interest in CEOs' right- and wrong-doing reflected the mounting recognition of the importance of CEOs and also a source of considerable information.

Our CEO reputation research brought us into many corner offices. Not surprisingly, CEOs were keenly interested in obtaining a "secret sauce" to brew a finer reputation and, concomitantly, a higher share price. CEOs nodded their heads knowingly when we discussed today's tendency toward lionization (and at times, demonization) of CEOs. They were aware of the heightened interest in and distrust of CEOs since the Enron, WorldCom, Global Crossing, and Tyco International debacles and wanted to know how to rebuild confidence in the executive office. They were also eager to hear how they rated vis-à-vis other CEOs and were curious to know which CEO in their industry earned the highest marks. Moreover, they wanted their direct reports to join the discussion. Several CEOs expressed unconcealed pleasure that for the first time they could now justify with figures and studies what they had always known instinctively. They now had a strategic and financially driven reason to utilize their communications, public affairs, investor relations, and human resource departments to support building CEO reputation and credibility. The easy part was telling CEOs that their reputations mattered—they already knew this. The more challenging part was describing which steps they could take to build a sustainable reputation for themselves and for their companies. These steps would take time and require focused attention, two items that most CEOs do not typically have in great supply.

THE BOOK'S OBJECTIVES

CEO Capital has four objectives:

1. To explain how important a CEO's reputation is to a company's reputation, well-being, and support
2. To identify the determinants of CEO reputation
3. To offer a model for building CEO reputation and bringing success to a company
4. To describe how CEOs master the stages of their tenure to leverage their company's standing and ultimate destiny

FOR WHOM THIS BOOK WAS WRITTEN

I wrote *CEO Capital* primarily for CEOs and professionals in the business of CEO leadership such as corporate communications executives, public affairs and marketing officers, advertising officials, public relations agencies, executive search professionals, and management consultants. This book provides guidance and suggests best practices for executives aspiring to become CEOs, CEOs in transition, new CEOs, interim CEOs, returning CEOs, and CEOs in midtenure. *CEO Capital*, however, also has meaning for students, academics, managers, and others who are looking to take charge of and rise to the apex of their careers. And the book has relevance for entrepreneurs or small business owners dreaming about or building their own companies.

CEO Capital is not about impression management or building personality cults. Nor is it a simple 1-2-3 recipe for assembling a chief executive's reputation. It is for the serious business professional who recognizes and honors the immensity of the chief executive's job, especially in today's ever more complex business environment. To quote Xerox PARC guru John Seely Brown, "The job of leadership today is not just to make money. It's to make meaning."[3] *CEO Capital* is meant for the CEO and professional who understand that benefiting from a CEO's reputation takes careful and thoughtful planning from the first hundred days to the last hundred hours. It is for those who understand that, yes, financial performance is important, but that a CEO's reputation is also built on qualities such as credibility, honesty, and engagement.

CEOs and other executives frequently ask, "What happens to a company after a revered chairman and CEO such as Richard Branson of Virgin Atlantic Airways, Jack Welch of General Electric, or Herb Kelleher of Southwest Airlines departs?" Implicit in this query is the notion that for the fortunes of a company to be too closely tied to the CEO is dangerous—but it need not be if done right. As more extensively discussed in Chapter 6, well-respected CEOs impart value to their companies that lasts beyond their tenure. A CEO's reputation is an asset of the company, not just of the individual who happens to be a CEO. To build a CEO's reputation to benefit a company is to capitalize on a reputation, to build CEO capital. Moreover, the best CEOs take succession planning seriously, building competent, efficient organizations that are more than capable of either developing or locating the best leaders. Finally, top CEOs—those who deserve to be revered—build value-driven, confident corporate cultures that will continue to flourish in the absence of any executive, even the luminary.

CEOs who carefully follow the blueprint laid out in these pages may well come through their first hundred days or even their first year with reputations intact and scratch-free. But the rapid pace of technology and the unpredictability of global economic, market, and political forces are all too likely to suddenly interrupt a CEO's best-laid plans even after a year or two of easy sailing, threatening to capsize the most stable reputation. For example, at the end of the 1990s, Jeffrey Bezos of Amazon.com was *Time*'s person of the year. Shortly after, however, he was billed as the antihero.

What I've learned while CEO-watching and writing this book is that there is no golden rule for avoiding all uncertainty, turmoil, and surprise; however, I firmly believe that CEOs are far more likely to navigate successfully through the uncharted, white-capped, and often stormy seas of business today if they follow the basic principles described in these pages.

THE CONTENT

CEO Capital is organized into three parts. The first part explains why CEO reputation deserves our undivided attention and can no longer be ignored. This section also lays the groundwork for how CEO capital can be built.

The second part, Chapters 4 through 8, takes the reader through the mindset and behavior of CEOs as five stages of the CEO Capital model unfold. Some CEOs skip over stages and some spend more time in one stage than another. Each stage includes numerous best practices. These best practices can be reordered and customized to suit the individual, the company, and the situation. Nothing is set in stone. Yet, the best practices cannot be ignored.

The final part, Chapter 9, discusses various corporate trends that will affect twenty-first century CEOs. As new CEOs assume leadership positions in our modern society, a society characterized by almost instantaneous and ever-accelerating change, the challenges and expectations facing CEOs will become even greater. Some rules of the road will stay the same, but many will change. Chapter 9 anticipates what will matter most for CEOs and what might lie ahead as they proceed through the second millennium.

CAVEATS

Before moving on to Part I, a few caveats are necessary. The CEOs mentioned in this book are not necessarily clients of Burson-Marsteller, nor have they necessarily sought Burson-Marsteller's or anyone else's assistance in building CEO awareness, positioning, and platforms. The copyright to all "CEO Reputation" materials is owned by Burson-Marsteller. All interpretations, impressions, opinions, or comments about or concerning the "CEO Reputation" materials are solely my own.

I drew on the expertise of my colleagues, interviews with CEOs, Burson-Marsteller's proprietary research, publicly available sources of information, and my own experiences to write this book. To those who have made these abundant sources available to me, I am immensely grateful. Without them, this book would not, could not, have been written.

OBSERVATION ON THE ENRON CRISIS

Recent events in 2002 have made *CEO Capital* more important than ever. The Enron crisis and its aftermath engulfed a number of

America's largest corporations—Global Crossing, Tyco International, Adelphia Communications, Arthur Andersen, and World-Com. As Americans found their hard–earned pensions and investments reduced to mere pittances of their former value, confidence in American business withered. Whether confidence will in time return is unclear. What is certain, however, is that the CEO of each troubled company stands at the center of each crisis, drawing the ire of many Americans. This is as it should be. One of the premises of this book is, after all, that ultimate responsibility for a company's successes as well as its failures rests with the CEO.

As one CEO's reputation after another loses its luster, who is chosen as a successor, who remains at the helm, and how each manages his or her tenure, matters more than ever. The new CEOs at Tyco and WorldCom, and even at AOL TimeWarner and Vivendi Universal, are being carefully watched to see if they can turn the tide.

This book sets forth the substantive steps a CEO should take to build an enduring and lasting company. Today's CEOs should take to heart the lessons in these pages and once again regain America's confidence.

August 2002
Brooklyn, New York

ACKNOWLEDGMENTS

As I put the final touches on my manuscript, I have found that expressing gratitude to the many people who stood by me during the bittersweet process of writing this book has become of the utmost importance to me. To show my appreciation in the most meaningful way possible, I have been drawn to bookstores, where I have scrutinized the acknowledgments of my favorite authors. After reading scores of these acknowledgments, I've come to the conclusion that there is no better way to express gratitude than simply by saying "thank you."

Many people at work, too numerous to name, deserve my most sincere gratitude for their extremely generous support: Harold Burson, Christopher Komisarjevsky, Chet Burchett, Judi Mackey, Carol Ballock, Peter Himler, Kathleen McGraw, as well as so many other colleagues at Burson-Marsteller. Little did I realize when I first joined Burson-Marsteller that it would be a hot house for fermenting ideas and taking risks.

Particular thanks to my colleague Per Heggenes, who keeps surprising me with his boundless encouragement, guidance, and good cheer. Enormous thanks to the Knowledge Development team with whom I work every day: Idil Cakim, Sarah Dietz, Melanie Driscoll, Steve Einhorn, Iris Harris, Sandra Clark, and Traci Nagy. Their personal and professional friendship has kept my head above the choppy waters. Extra thanks to Melanie Driscoll for her assistance with the tables, Linda Hersh for her pro bono help, and Jennifer Femia and Bobby Schrott for their always successful efforts at information retrieval.

An additional thank you to Jon Low at the Cap Gemini Ernst & Young Center for Business Innovation for his unfailing advice, confidence in my work, and all-around, ever-available collegiality. Also to Adina Genn, my thanks for her sharp editorial eye rendered on short notice and under time pressure. Thank you to my editor, Tim Burgard, at John Wiley & Sons, for believing that this book would meaningfully contribute to the literature on reputation and leadership.

I've also been fortunate to have a few angels hovering above me during the past several years—people who watched over me from afar and sometimes nearby, prodding me along the way. They include big-hearted, editor supreme Mark Murray, unflappable counselor and friend John LaSage, and the indefatigable Gabriela Clough. They have each been a ray of sunlight shining through a break in the clouds after a summer rain.

A handful of souls deserve special mention for their unwavering friendship as weekend after weekend passed by in a seemingly endless stream of writing. They were my fan club. I am much richer for having them in my life: my forever pal Marilyn Platzer and my loyal friend whom I met when I first arrived at Burson-Marsteller, Erin Rice-Mills. I hold them both very dear.

Thank you to the CEOs and communications directors who shared with me—notwithstanding very busy schedules—their thoughts on the challenges facing them, such as Phil Condit and Judith Mulhberg of the Boeing Company, Miles White and Cathy Babington of Abbott Laboratories, and David Pottruck and Joanne Cuthbertson of Charles Schwab. Also to be included are all those CEOs who met with me but whose names, for various reasons, cannot be mentioned here as well as the numerous unnamed CEOs and communications professionals who I meet every day in the course of my professional duties.

I owe infinite gratitude to my husband Dan. His love, patience, and support sustain me. To our children, Allison, Emma, and Hudson, I owe you many lost Saturdays and Sundays. I intend to make them up to you.

And loving thanks go to my parents, Howard and Muriel Friedman, who instilled in me an early thirst for business, and to my close-knit family of aunts, uncles, and cousins—a family of entrepreneurs, merchants, and builders—all of whom together awakened in me the wonders of commerce.

CEO
CAPITAL

CHAPTER I

THE CEO EFFECT

Thousands of employees know me only by reputation, so in a real sense, my reputation is everything.[1]

—David S. Pottruck, president and co-CEO,
The Charles Schwab Corporation

The fact is inescapable: These choices of single human beings [CEOs] exert enormous influence over entire enterprises. In the aggregate, they determine the prosperity of the nation.[2]

—Ram Charan and Geoffrey Colvin, *Fortune*

Imagine this. In April 1985, Coca-Cola CEO Roberto Goizueta removed from the grocery shelves all cans and bottles of the world's favorite soft drink. In its place came New Coke, a sweeter version of the all-time classic and a sure-fire kid magnet, accompanied by a marketing strategy designed to deal a blow to the growing popularity of Coca-Cola's arch rival Pepsi.

Goizueta had every reason to be confident that New Coke would be a success. He had already successfully introduced Diet Coke in 1982, turning it, within only one year, into the best-selling diet soft drink in the United States. He had conducted extensive market research before launching New Coke, finding that it prevailed over Pepsi in taste tests every time. Having done his homework and duly confident because of past successes, Goizueta gave the go-ahead for Coca-Cola to introduce New Coke—with great fanfare—on April 23, 1985.

A consumer revolt of epic proportions ensued, including threats of class action lawsuits, threats to employees, and a flood of telephone calls to headquarters.[3] As it would become clear, consumers were not only protesting against the taste of New Coke. New Coke had its admirers. Rather, they were also protesting against the removal of the old Coke, the classic version that they had been drinking for years and to which they remained obstinately loyal. Three months later, Goizueta had Coca-Cola resume remanufacturing the old Coke. Renamed "Classic Coke," the old formulation was back on the shelves.

Goizueta chose wisely and Coca-Cola not only survived the crisis, but emerged stronger than ever. How did one of the so-called largest marketing blunders of the 1980s not cost Goizueta his job or seriously undermine the strength of one of the world's best known brands? Clearly, far more was undoubtedly involved in resolving the crisis than Goizueta's reputation. Yet, had the CEO of Coca-Cola not had such a well-respected reputation, a positive outcome would have been far less likely.

The good will and credibility developed over the first years of Goizueta's tenure were instrumental in maintaining confidence in his leadership. As Goizueta reacted to the New Coke turmoil, the confidence that others had in him allowed Goizueta to transform a seeming negative into a positive. From early in his tenure, his successful introduction of Diet Coke, approximately five fiscal quarters after taking office, boded well for the future. There were other steps of which to be proud since assuming office in 1981. Goizueta had strengthened the Board by changing bylaws and bringing in new directors. He established management credibility by communicating clearly and candidly with Wall Street and by setting a firm strategic plan for the company's future.[4]

Goizueta became the change agent and dealmaker that successfully reawakened the tradition-oriented and sleepy Southern company. Working hand-in-hand with his strong number two, President Donald Keogh, Goizueta acquired Columbia Pictures in 1982, sold Coca-Cola's wine enterprises, consolidated bottlers into larger entities, and perhaps most important, boosted shareholder value based on economic performance.

Although not all his actions were successful, Goizueta had early on earned the support of his employees, shareholders, and the board. They were willing to accept risk-taking and even an unsuccessful step or two in expectation that Coca-Cola, under Goizueta's leadership, would ultimately flourish. Rightly so. Notwithstanding all the noise about the New Coke fiasco, Coca-Cola emerged a stronger company. Eventually the clamor for Classic Coke made evident that the public's bond with the Coca-Cola brand was all but unseverable. The New Coke/Old Coke controversy reawakened the public's loyalty and sales increased for all of Coca-Cola's soft drinks.

Goizueta's handling of New Coke's introduction and Classic Coke's reintroduction clearly demonstrates a direct link between a CEO's standing, in short his or her reputation, and a company's success or failure. This link has received surprisingly little or no attention among business scholars. On the surface, it seems so obvious that the CEO's reputation and a company's success would intertwine. Yet, if that is so, why have there been nearly no books and only a mere handful of articles, generally of the popular celebrity CEO type, written on the topic? Why have scholars overlooked the key role of CEO reputation in the literature on corporate reputation and branding? Why are there 9,940[5] books on "leadership," but only 249 on topics related to "CEO" (e.g., *The Five Temptations of a CEO* and *How To Think Like a CEO*), none of which directly discuss the importance of the CEO's reputation to a company's welfare? Three reasons come to mind for this utter lack of attention, a deficiency so palpable as to demonstrate beyond question why a book such as this is so urgently needed and so revolutionary.

A REVOLUTIONARY APPROACH TO CEO REPUTATION AND CORPORATE EXCELLENCE

Until now, little if any data has arisen indicating that CEO reputation matters as much as it does. Burson-Marsteller's research on CEO reputation is the first of its kind to define and deeply probe the drivers of CEO reputation and how CEO reputation affects the way that a company's stakeholders—that is, the company's most important constituents, those who have a stake in the company—perceive the company. No other research examines what stakeholders want from CEOs and to what ends they will go in pledging support to favored CEOs. Such support includes investing in their companies, recommending their companies as good employers, supporting them in a crisis, or giving their companies the benefit of the doubt when less generous interpretations are plausible. No other research looks at CEO reputation from the vantage points of different stakeholder groups, ranging from fellow CEOs to financial analysts to the media.

For the first time, CEOs will have a guide, securely grounded in research, upon which to rely from their first to last days of their tenures. Prior CEO research primarily dwelled on the challenges CEOs face—namely, "What keeps them up at night?" PriceWaterhouseCoopers, the global management consultancy, annually surveys CEOs at the World Economic Forum, which is typically held in Davos, Switzerland, but was held in New York in 2002 to ensure security and show solidarity after September 11. CEOs are asked about their midnight awakenings—their outlook on the economy, growth, technology, corporate citizenship, and competitiveness. PriceWaterhouseCoopers has published several books on these CEO nocturnal musings: *Straight From the CEO*[6] and *Wisdom of the CEO.*[7] But no book specifically focuses on what constitutes a favorable CEO reputation, why a favorable reputation is important, how a CEO earns a favorable reputation, and how a CEO can capitalize on reputation to best benefit a company.

Moreover, for the first time, it is possible to use factual evidence to dispel the arguments of those who would prefer to cast the primary role of CEOs in an unfavorable light. Both political correctness and current standards of polite business behavior discourage open discussion about the chief executive's importance. Hence, all too common are those who dismiss successful CEOs, especially those who have sought or, more often, have been forced into the limelight, as mere Celebrity CEOs—as if a prominent public standing taints everything a CEO does. Also common are those who refuse to acknowledge the importance of other successful CEOs who, although not well known among the general public, "lead quietly"[8] after having built strong reputations in their industry or among important business influentials. Far more acceptable in our egalitarian society is to focus on the contributions of a company's employees. It has been easier to view the company's success as the combined product of numerous workers or teams of managers rather than to attribute such successes in any material way to a single leader. In the old and post-dot.com economies, and perhaps not as much in the dot.com years, professionals steered clear of any hint of hero worship or adoration. Instead, the greater part of the business literature published in the 1990s stressed the more publicly palatable contributions of teams at the top, flattened hierarchies, distributed decision making, knowledge sharing, and employee empowerment. The CEO certainly figures into these discussions, but a tacit understanding appears to have coalesced among some that we are all too rational and sophisticated today to idolize, iconize, or lionize our leaders. This trend to discredit the role that CEOs play in their companies' successes has unfortunately become so fashionably overstated as to discourage giving CEOs any credit at all. When it comes to ceding importance to CEOs, some people almost wish it weren't true.

Finally, armed with this book, we can now remove the CEO's role from the amorphous region of the unmeasurable to a more concrete research-based realm. Scholars ignored the link between CEO reputation and corporate performance for historical reasons. The value of a company's worth historically depended primarily on concrete or *tangible* assets—assets associated with finance and manufacturing, buildings, equipment, and product inventories. Largely excluded from the balance sheet or other financial statements were *intangible* assets such as established relationships with customers, company or brand reputation, human capital, marketing savvy, and company know-how. Although scholars sometimes gave a perfunctory nod to acknowledge the value of intangibles, they considered such value, in the absence of factually based research to the contrary, to be relatively modest compared to the total value of the firm's capital. To expect scholars to focus on such seemingly minimally valued assets and to then delve deeper into the components of intangibles, in particular CEO reputation, was unrealistic. The CEO's reputation appeared to be no more than a derivative of more obvious intangible assets whose value scholars had only recently and reluctantly accepted. Not surprisingly, these same scholars typically gave short shrift to a CEO's reputation or incorporated it unthinkingly into another component of a company's overall reputation and goodwill. Modern business scholars today, however, do recognize intangibles such as intellectual property, innovation, relationships, and talent as the bedrock of the world's knowledge-enhanced economies. Now that the value of intangibles is recognized, the importance of the CEO as a significant intangible asset in its own right has also become more acceptable. In light of the research underlying this book, the CEO's role in unlocking and leveraging a company's assets has become even more evident, if not inescapably obvious.

CHAPTER 2

CEO REPUTATION: A CAPITAL INVESTMENT

But I say, by God, in 9 cases out of 10, you show me a truly great company with a great culture that consistently outmaneuvers its competition and is agile and has a high level of morale and retention, and people coming out of universities want to work for that company, then I say: Look at the top guy.[1]

—Robert "Bob" Lutz, former president of
Chrysler Corp.; current development chief
of General Motors

CEO *capital.* By this term, I mean the asset created by a CEO's reputation (not mere public acclaim) when it is harnessed to advance a company's success. It is the collective esteem that significant others, inside and outside a company, hold for the company's chief executive officer and, as a consequence, for the company. CEO capital is the composite of perceptions about a CEO that a company's stakeholders hold, whether these constituents are employees, Wall Street analysts or investors, customers, the media, government regulators, community leaders, or other business influentials.

CEO capital might plausibly fall under any number of components constituting intangible assets such as customer relationships, talent, and brand strength. Yet CEO capital, because of its impact on stakeholders, market capitalization, and other elements of corporate success, is far too significant to warrant anything but a separate and distinct classification. Just like any other wealth-creating asset, CEO capital needs to be invested in, managed, and leveraged over the long term to reap enduring benefits. Companies can utilize the equity that accrues from developing CEO capital to attract more investors, more partners, more customers, more job applicants, and more trust in corporate decisions. To emphasize just how important CEO reputation is to a company's success, to stress its value as a wealth-creating asset, the title of this book is *CEO Capital*, not *CEO Reputation*. I discuss a CEO's reputation, not as a frivolous exercise to feed executive egos, but because CEO reputations have a significant impact on a company's success and viability. CEO reputation, when harnessed on behalf of corporate goals, is a capital asset.

Every company today must acknowledge the importance of its CEO's reputation, and every company must spend the time to isolate the components of developing CEO capital, understand its underpinnings, and manage this highly important corporate asset. When accumulated, CEO capital

- Has a direct positive impact on a company's reputation and success
- Produces clear, discernible, and valuable payoffs
- Matters to an unprecedented number of influential constituencies
- Affords more time to develop long-term solutions in a fast-paced business climate

CEO CAPITAL HAS A DIRECT POSITIVE IMPACT ON A COMPANY'S REPUTATION AND SUCCESS

According to Burson-Marsteller's research, CEO capital contributes heavily to how companies are perceived today. This landmark CEO reputation research was initiated in 1997 and updated in 1999 and 2001. Burson-Marsteller solicited responses from five different stakeholder groups in the United States: CEOs and chairpersons; vice presidents and other senior executives; financial analysts and institutional investors; the business media; and government officials. These varied and essential audiences—from CEOs to media to government officials—all agree that CEO capital contributes greatly to a company's reputation. The impact of CEO capital is no minor sideshow to the main event. Rather, it occupies center stage.

In 1997, when Burson-Marsteller first polled U.S. business influentials, the CEO's average estimated contribution to a company's reputation stood at 40 percent. In 2001, this figure jumped to 48 percent, an impressive 20 percent increase.[2] If nearly half of a company's reputation is attributed to the standing of the CEO, common sense dictates that CEO capital is a currency worth investing in, accumulating, and cultivating.

The great importance attached to CEO reputation reaches far and wide. In 2001, Burson-Marsteller's research obtained similar results among business opinion shapers in the United Kingdom (48 percent of a company's reputation is attributed to the CEO), Australia (54 percent), and Germany (64 percent). Even among consumers, a segment often considered less informed about business matters, the CEO effect remains strong. In both the United States and United Kingdom, a 1998 poll of the general public indicated that a CEO's reputation accounted for 48 percent of a company's reputation.[3,4] At first perusal, the similarity of these trans-Atlantic results appear surprising. In 1997, the typical response outside the

United States indicated that the significant role played by CEO reputation was strictly an American phenomenon. This is evidently no longer the case. CEO capital now matters the world over.

CEO CAPITAL PRODUCES CLEAR, DISCERNIBLE, AND VALUABLE PAYOFFS

Building CEO capital is an investment well worth making. As seen in Exhibit 2.1, the payoffs are clear and on the rise. CEOs with highly developed capital reap significant rewards for their companies: decision makers are (1) more likely to buy or recommend the company's stock, (2) give CEOs the benefit of the doubt in a crisis or when share price is lagging, (3) consider companies of well-

EXHIBIT 2.1 *Payoffs of a Favorable CEO Reputation*

More Likely to	1997	1999	2001
Purchase stock in company	77%	88%	95%
Believe company if under pressure from the media	78	81	94
Recommend company as good alliance/ merger partner	80	87	93
Maintain confidence in company when share price is lagging	NA	NA	92
Recommend company stock	NA	84	90
Recommend as good place to work	73	80	88
Pay attention to company in media	68	75	80
Pay premium for products/services	24	24	52
Visit company Web site	NA	NA	38

NA = Not asked

Sources: Burson-Marsteller, *Maximizing CEO Reputation*, 1997, 1999; *Building CEO Capital*, 2001.

respected CEOs good alliance or merger partners, (4) recommend such companies as good places to work, (5) consider these companies worthy of tracking in the media, and (6) offer support when catastrophe strikes. Such support is critical to companies, especially during times when financing is scarce and companies find it nearly impossible to maintain the confidence of the media or Wall Street. As shown in Exhibit 2.2, payoffs cross stakeholder lines.

EXHIBIT 2.2   *Payoffs of a Favorable CEO Reputation by Stakeholder Group*

More Likely to	CEOs	Execs.	Wall St.	Gov't.	Media
Purchase stock in company	96%	94%	95%	90%	91%
Believe company if under pressure from the media	93	93	95	93	91
Recommend company as good alliance/merger partner	93	93	93	90	93
Maintain confidence in company when share price is lagging	95	91	92	89	89
Recommend company stock	92	89	92	87	89
Recommend as good place to work	91	87	77	95	87
Pay attention to company in media	81	82	74	80	76
Pay premium for products/services	51	53	52	64	42
Visit company Web site	40	35	35	56	44

Note: Sample consists of CEOs, senior business executives (Execs.), financial analysts/institutional investors (Wall St.), government officials (Gov't.), and business media (Media).

Source: Burson-Marsteller, *Building CEO Capital*, 2001.

Regardless of stakeholder group, support for a highly admired CEO is priceless. Peer CEOs, the media, Wall Street, and other business influentials will all go to the mat for a highly regarded CEO. Business influentials may be reluctant to pay a premium for a company's products and services or make a visit to a company website, but on matters more crucial to the institutional health of a company—for example, financial backing and confidence— business influentials support companies whose CEOs they trust and admire. The message rings loud and clear: Building CEO capital pays and provides immeasurable benefits to companies and their respective stakeholders and shareholders.

The payoffs for amassing CEO capital can also be measured in more objective, economic terms. According to David Larcker, professor of accounting at the Wharton School of the University of Pennsylvania, a 10 percent positive change in a CEO's reputation among CEOs studied in the 1999 Burson-Marsteller study resulted in a 24 percent increase in the company's market capitalization.[5] Additionally, Burson-Marsteller found that the top 10 CEOs identified in the 2001 study achieved a median compound annual stock return of 13 percent over a three-year period (July 31, 1998 to July 31, 2001), compared to a compound annual return of –7 percent for the bottom 10 CEOs.[6] Perhaps more significantly, admiration for some of these CEOs existed irrespective of company performance. For example, Michael Dell maintained a strong reputation as chairperson and CEO of Dell Computer in Burson-Marsteller's 2001 survey despite his company's lower compound annual return compared to the median return over the three-year period.[7] Collectively, these findings underscore the direct link between positive CEO capital and shareholder return. Although it may at times seem unclear whether an increase in CEO reputation causes an increase in market capitalization or the other way around, or perhaps whether a dynamic exists where both interrelate with each other, the correlation between the two remains firm. Companies with favored CEOs are more likely to be wealth builders, and those with less favored CEOs are not.

Further evidence of payoffs comes from research conducted by senior research fellow Jon Low of the Cap Gemini Ernst & Young Center for Business Innovation (CBI). Although the CBI research did not specifically address CEO reputation, it is nevertheless helpful. CBI researchers surveyed buy-side and sell-side analysts—the ultimate market makers—about how they arrive at their investment decisions. They found that nonfinancial factors drive a startling 35 percent of buy-sell-hold decisions[8]—an extraordinary admission from such a hard-nosed group. Among the top intangibles valued most were strategy execution, management credibility, and management quality—all factors highly correlated with elements of CEO capital. If the reputation of a company's management can move capital markets so extensively, surely the reputation of that most important of managers, the chief executive, does no less and, it stands to reason, undoubtedly does more— much, much more.

Thus proper management of CEO capital not only enhances a company's good name but also further strengthens the bottom line. If companies take charge of their CEO capital and leverage it strategically, the rewards can be deep and long lasting.

CEO CAPITAL MATTERS TO AN UNPRECEDENTED NUMBER OF INFLUENTIAL CONSTITUENCIES

From chat rooms to board rooms to the floor of the stock exchange, all eyes are on CEOs. Numerous and diverse constituencies are scrutinizing what CEOs do and say. These powerful constituencies include traditional stakeholder groups such as Wall

Street, the media, and special interest groups such as Greenpeace and The Sierra Club. With the recent rash of corporate scandals, these constituencies are increasing and now include among others the SEC, the Business Roundtable, and even the presidency.

Recent advances in technology have further empowered all these groups. The Internet, for example, has created a channel for fast and inexpensive dissemination of information as well as a similarly efficient means for developing grassroots organizations. The ubiquity of cable television stations (e.g., CNN, FOX, CNBC, and Bloomberg) and a surge in the types of business magazines not only increase the access of these constituencies to information, but also extend the reach of these groups to every corner of a company's business. The corporate world and the life of a CEO have become a fishbowl.

CEOs have always viewed certain influential stakeholders as requiring their attention. However, Burson-Marsteller's research has shown for the first time that these groups of influentials assign immense weight to the CEO and to the manner in which the CEO embodies the corporate brand. As shown in Exhibit 2.3, business influentials readily accept a CEO as a powerful surrogate for the company. For each of these influential groups, the CEO's reputation contributes to nearly half of the company's total reputation.

Business Executives

CEOs and executives believe that CEO reputation constitutes, respectively, 49 percent and 47 percent of a company's reputation. When considering a merger, fellow CEOs gauge their potential partner's credibility and integrity. CEOs seeking alliances do not mind benefiting from association with a well-regarded partner. In the same vein, senior business executives believe working for admired CEOs elevates their standing. Senior business executives

EXHIBIT **2.3**   *What Percentage of a Company's Reputation Is Attributable to the Reputation of the CEO?*

	Total	CEOs	Execs.	Wall St.	Gov't.	Media
1997	40%	38%	40%	39%	35%	46%
1999	45	46	44	47	46	52
2001	48	49	47	43	52	52

Note: Sample consists of CEOs, senior business executives (Execs.), financial analysts/institutional investors (Wall St.), government officials (Gov't.), and business media (Media).

Sources: Burson-Marsteller, *Maximizing CEO Reputation*, 1997, 1999; *Building CEO Capital*, 2001.

monitor their industry's most admired leaders, using them as yardsticks to rate themselves and other CEOs and as models from which to learn. Especially in light of recent business events, board members too are being pressured to be more hands-on and to critically evaluate the chief executives they hire.

Wall Street

Financial analysts questioned in the Burson-Marsteller survey indicated that CEO reputation constituted 43 percent of a company's image. They recommend "buys" or "sells" based on their perceptions of how well a CEO leads. Michael Useem, management professor at the Wharton School, predicts that in the years ahead, nearly one-third of a CEO's time will be spent wooing capital markets.[9] When Pharmacia acquired Monsanto in December 1999, the share price of both companies dropped precipitously. Pharmacia CEO Fred Hassan and his management team knew that they needed to be upfront, close, and personal. They hit the road, traveling to 14 cities in 10 days, hosting investor conference calls, and explaining the rationale behind the merger. The result was a rise in share price. Pharmacia became one of Wall Street's most highly rated companies by the end of 2000, and two years later attracted the pharmaceutical giant Pfizer as a suitor.

Media

Our research indicates that the business media view CEOs as contributing to 52 percent of a company's image. The media has the power to beatify or crucify. Accordingly, a CEO with substantive CEO capital will have an advantage over less established peers. A charismatic and inspiring chief executive such as former CEO Herb Kelleher of Southwest Airlines or Steve Jobs of Apple Computer makes good copy, drawing more readers than one who is less engaging as a communicator. In the absence of significant leadership failures or corporate disasters, the media inevitably sings their praises. Considering the power of the business media and its abiding interest in CEOs, the media is perhaps one of a CEO's most crucial stakeholders.

Government

Similarly, government officials believe that CEOs contribute a whopping 52 percent to corporate reputation. According to Burson-Marsteller,[10] legislators, in particular, readily concede that they are influenced by a CEO's image: Of the legislators surveyed, 55 percent said they were influenced a great deal, 39 percent said to some extent, and only 6 percent said to a small extent. Not a single legislator responded "no impact at all."

Bill Gates, head of Microsoft, practically ignored lobbying and relationship building with beltway politicos before 1999, making no political donation at all in the mid-1990s. As the antitrust suit began to solidify, however, Microsoft stepped up its grassroots efforts and, by the end of the year 2000, it was the third-largest corporate contributor of political donations.[11] Governmental lobbying is no guarantee that a company will get its way, but having a good reputation and being known as a contributor (as long as any such lobbying is legal and is openly disclosed) earns companies greater access to members of Congress and agencies, and greater attention for their side of an issue.

With the expansion of business worldwide and the ascent of the multinational company, foreign regulators—not just domestic officials—must also be considered. Foreign governments and agencies come into play when two companies merge or one is being acquired and either is formed under a foreign jurisdiction or has extensive non-American business requiring compliance with foreign regulations. Being on the good side of foreign governments can shield companies from—or at least give them advance warning of—unfavorable regulations, antitrust scrutiny, or any barriers to their acquisition strategy. After the proposed merger of GE and Honeywell International unexpectedly fell apart at the hands of European Union authorities, the new GE CEO, Jeffrey Immelt, indicated that he would not allow GE to be similarly surprised again. In an obvious attempt to strengthen ties with European governmental officials, he has moved GE's European headquarters to Brussels, the seat of the newly unified European community.[12]

Special Interest Groups

Regardless of whether the goals of special interest groups are worthy, they harbor a singlemindedness of purpose that makes them formidable. Special interest groups have unprecedented power to tarnish CEO and corporate reputations through consumer boy-cotts, protests, labor strikes, chat room campaigns, class-action lawsuits, and whistle blowing. These special interest groups can be creators of controversy and criticism. Therefore, Group Executive Lord Browne of British Petroleum (BP) was the first BP executive to speak before a Greenpeace Annual Conference on October 7, 1997, building a bridge to an organization that the oil industry in-stinctively had viewed as a natural opponent. As Browne later re-marked: "Everything we do, and the way we do it, has become a subject for dissection and analysis in the cockpit theatre of public opinion."[13]

CEO CAPITAL AFFORDS MORE TIME TO DEVELOP LONG-TERM SOLUTIONS IN A FAST-PACED BUSINESS CLIMATE

The CEO chamber is a revolving door today. For better or worse, there is little forgiveness for mistakes. A well-regarded and trusted reputation is perhaps a CEO's best bulwark against rash action that could cost the CEO his or her job—a doorstop inserted at the doorsill. For this reason alone, exploring and mastering the para-meters of building and maintaining CEO capital—allowing CEOs to earn the tolerance and patience of their boards, shareholders, and others as corporate struggles are worked out over the long term—is more important than ever.

In the past five years, nearly two-thirds of all major companies replaced their CEOs.[14] Outplacement experts Challenger, Gray & Christmas report that 2,045 CEOs left their jobs between Novem-ber 1999 and October 2001, approximately three *per day*.[15] Even more sobering, more than half of all current CEOs have held their position for fewer than six years. This shortened tenure is far greater than what it was in 1980.[16] Turnover among European CEOs occurs twice as often as U.S. CEOs.[17] So common are CEO hirings and firings that recruiting logjams are now the norm. Compaq and Hewlett-Packard, who later merged, both looked for CEOs at the same time during the spring of 1999, as did the top three retailer rivals soon after—J.C. Penney, Kmart, and Sears. In 2001 Lucent and Nortel also joined the hunt for replacement CEOs.

What is the reason for this high rate of dissatisfaction with CEOs over the past decade? Simply put, the increasing pace and impatience of the modern business world leaves little time to build CEO capital. Because of advances in technology and the rapid spread of information, news about CEOs and their companies are available 24/7. Privacy is no longer an option. With the Internet's pervasive presence, information about CEOs—their past performance, history, and personal information—is readily available to all. Add to this the recent scandals regarding CEOs and charges of financial irregularities—CEOs can run but cannot hide.

Because of this situation, the time period available to CEOs to perform and to perform well is now exceedingly short. Business influentials give CEOs only five poor earnings quarters on average before their jobs are in jeopardy—that's about 15 months![18] Only CEOs of substantial repute can be expected to relax this five-quarter rule and obtain additional time to produce results.

With stakes this high, CEOs need to move swiftly, smartly, and strategically. Speed is necessary so that a CEO might avoid the sword of Damocles, which every board holds over a CEO's head. Slowing the pace and adding flexibility to the five-quarter rule by amassing CEO capital and allowing the CEO to buy extra time is a benefit not to be scoffed at. The welfare of companies demands no less. Rome was not built in a day, nor was Microsoft or General

Electric built in five quarters. CEOs must build CEO capital, moving quickly on their companies' behalf to produce at least a semblance of results, thereby sidestepping short-term pressures in order to pursue corporate matters requiring long-term solutions. CEOs have no time to waste.

CHAPTER 3

HOW CEO
CAPITAL IS BUILT

Managing image and company reputation is one of the more obvious jobs of the CEO.[1]

—Jack Welch, former chairman and CEO,
General Electric

Great CEO reputations are not accidental. They are planned, reflected on, and nurtured. They can be built. The CEO Capital model incorporates what we know about the drivers of CEO reputation, the builders of CEO capital, and how these drivers can serve as a compass for CEOs. The model guides them through the various stages of their tenure—from the first 100 days to the last 100 minutes. For the first time, this model gives structure to a process that, in the past, was too often summarily dismissed with superficial categorizations such as charisma or celebrity, rather than scrutinized carefully and diligently, rooting out the complexities of building CEO capital. To set the stage for a discussion of the CEO Capital model, we must first isolate and review those elements that drive CEO reputation and amass CEO capital.

WHAT DRIVES CEO REPUTATION AND BUILDS CEO CAPITAL?

Burson-Marsteller has spent the past five years studying the factors that build equity in a CEO's name. The most recent wave of research shows that five factors contribute to CEO reputation. From day one—if not before—every CEO must carefully consider these factors, the CM factors.

The "C" Factors

The first three highest-rated determinants constitute the "C" component of these CM factors. These determinants are typically critical to establishing a favorable CEO reputation. These "C" factors comprise:

1. Credibility
2. Code of ethics
3. Communicating internally

The "M" Factors

The remaining two characteristics, the "M" factors, are:

4. Attracting and retaining a quality Management team
5. Motivating and inspiring employees

Stakeholders look to see how CEOs manage their organizations and put operating and social systems into place to build bench strength and keep employees loyal and productive. For example, the reputation of CEO Larry Ellison of Oracle Systems lost a notch or two when his widely admired Chief Operating Officer (COO), Ray Lane resigned. Ellison's inability to retain several senior team members over the years has cost him dearly, diminishing his supply of CEO capital.

Collectively, these top-tier drivers of CEO capital must *all* be in place for a CEO to earn top honors. With even one CM factor missing or insufficiently developed, a CEO courts disaster. All of the CM factors share one essential characteristic: They are soft qualities that must be built as soon as possible and nurtured constantly. Although these factors are effective and useful as soon as established, the longer a CEO holds them and nurtures them, the more firmly established, full bodied, and richer they become. Critically, a chief executive's words and actions must reinforce the CM factors day in and day out.

So important are the CM factors that each one surpassed even wealth creation in importance according to the 2001 Burson-Marsteller study. Of the 16 CEO characteristics included in the 2001 survey and shown in Exhibit 3.1, the harder financially driven characteristic of "increasing shareholder wealth" showed up as a less important driver than any of the CM factors. In what would appear to be a counterintuitive result, at least according to the historical emphasis on tangible assets, wealth creation did not surpass even one CM factor in any of the three waves of Burson-Marsteller's research. Thus, the CM factors are more important in shaping perceptions of CEOs than even shareholder gains. Evidently, financial performance is important, but simply not enough.

Being Credible

CEOs earn credibility by being consistently truthful and delivering on their promises. They also earn it by matching behavior with the values they espouse. A CEO of a well-known financially strapped company appeared in Burson-Marsteller offices with bloodshot eyes and a tired look on his face. He said that the hardest part of his job was traveling from office to office and customer to customer. When I asked why he did not use his company's corporate

EXHIBIT 3.1   *Drivers of CEO Reputation*

Top-Tier Drivers

Is believable	C factors
Demands high ethical standards	
Communicates clear vision *inside* the company	
Attracts/retains quality senior management team	M factors
Motivates and inspires employees	

Second-Tier Drivers

Cares about customers

Manages crises or business downturns effectively

Communicates clear vision *outside* the company

Increases shareholder wealth

Executes well on strategic vision

Third-Tier Drivers

Understands global markets

Is leader in industry

Breaks new ground/innovative

Embraces corporate citizenship

Has well-defined Internet strategy

Source: Burson-Marsteller, *Building CEO Capital*, 2001.

jet, he said that he could not justify such an expense in light of his company's cutbacks and layoffs. Despite his obvious exhaustion, he felt that flying on a private jet was inconsistent with the sacrifices employees were making on behalf of the company's recovery. To do otherwise would risk his credibility and discredit his and the company's reputation.

At the end of July 2000, an Air France Concorde crashed into a hotel and restaurant in Gonesse, north of Paris, with the loss of no less than 113 lives. Into this heart-rending human and corporate catastrophe walked Jean-Cyril Spinetta, CEO of Air France. As reported in the *Financial Times*,[2] Spinetta visited the crash site immediately, taking personal responsibility for handling Air France's response to the disaster. Evidencing Air France's clear preference for the well being of its passengers over profits, he also promptly grounded all Concorde flights until such time as they could be shown to be safe. His rapid response and decisiveness enhanced his credibility, the result of having experienced a similar tragedy as chairman of Air Inter, a previous domestic arm of Air France.

Later, Spinetta attended services in France and Germany for victims, provided complimentary flights for relatives, and did not quibble over compensating surviving family members. Furthermore, he seemed to always find the right words to sincerely express sympathy. According to crisis expert, Dean Emeritus Rory Knight of Templeton College, Oxford, there was a clear financial value to Spinneta's "honesty, transparency and effective communication."[3] Spinneta's behavior was "impeccable" and marked him as a "recoverer" likely to have his company "emerge [from a disaster] with an enhanced reputation and value."[4] Spinetta's credibility was never questioned; his sincerity never doubted.

Establishing a Code of Ethics

Setting and abiding by higher standards make a marked impression. Consultant Charles Farkas of Bain & Company and Suzy Wetlaufer, former editor of the *Harvard Business Review*, contend in their study of CEO leadership styles that CEOs are ultimately responsible for the actions and decisions of each member of their organizations, whether known to the CEO or not.[5] The importance of ethical conduct as a determinant of favorable CEO reputation rose from sixth place in 1997 to the top of the chart in 2001. For example, the previously sterling reputation of John Gutfreund, chairman and CEO of Salomon Inc., became severely tarnished because of the illegal bidding of Paul Mozer, a single bond trader. Gutfreund's delayed attention to Mozer's unethical behavior forced Gutfreund's resignation and resulted in his lifelong ban from ever serving again as chairman or CEO of a securities firm.[6]

Following the testimony of former Enron Chairman Kenneth Lay and CEO Jeffrey Skilling before Congress, ethical leadership is much at issue in the business community and general public. Questions have arisen about the ethical behavior of not only Enron executives, but also those of all major companies. A backlash against the integrity of CEOs has surfaced. Even Suzy Wetlaufer as editor-in-chief of the *Harvard Business Review* was forced to abide by her own precept that leaders are ultimately responsible for ethical conduct when she ran afoul of ethical rules while interviewing Jack Welch for an article and ultimately resigned. The general public expects ethical behavior. CEOs must heed the warning. Ethical issues are, of course, rarely black and white. Even so, CEOs must act in good faith according to ethical guidelines, establish and consistently abide by these guidelines, and be able to demonstrate that their actions, whether right or wrong, are based on ethical justifications.

Communicating Well Internally

Most CEOs are surprised to learn how much time, effort and resources must be spent communicating internally. The importance of external communications seems obvious to most. *The Wall*

Street Journal, analysts' calls, and trade publications all require attention. However, internal communications, directed toward the organization's managers and employees, demand far more of a CEO's time than do high-visibility contacts with outside audiences. According to Burson-Marsteller research, executives recommend that CEOs allocate no less than 53 percent of their time communicating internally.[7] Among other things, communicating well internally keeps employees informed of where the company is headed, how it is getting there, and how each employee can contribute. Moreover, when handled well, internal communications provide employees with an unambiguous roadmap guiding day-to-day decisions affecting customers, colleagues, and the company's reputation. Poor internal CEO communications leave employees questioning whether the company has a future and how they should commit their time and energies. Perhaps most dangerously, inadequate CEO internal communications allow too much leeway for unethical conduct. Without clearly expressed policies, procedures, and standards, employees may, accidentally or intentionally, engage in unethical behavior that can detrimentally affect them, the company, and stakeholders.

One good example of the value of communicating well internally comes from a new CEO of a $1 billion diversified services company. While reviewing with me his first nine months at the helm, he sheepishly related how at a meeting of top management he made much to-do about his vision of creating a world-class company. He was initially so proud of the impact of his vision speech that he had notes of the meeting distributed throughout the company in a rare companywide e-mail. Thereafter he succumbed to the position's daily pressures and did not further consider his vision until a meeting with his salespeople for which he had little opportunity to prepare. This new CEO was taken by surprise when one of the salespeople asked him what he had meant by world-class. Much embarrassed, he admitted to me that he had been unable to articulate a coherent answer. Here he had succeeded in gaining the attention of his employees but failed to take advantage of this obvious opportunity to gather their continuing support. He had made no plan for communicating internally and had let slip through his grasp a clear chance to engage employees.

Weak communications with stakeholders, particularly employees, is one reason why attempts to reinvent and revitalize companies fail. According to leadership expert John P. Kotter:

> *Transformation is impossible unless hundreds or thousands of people are willing to help, often to the point of making short-term sacrifices. Without credible communications, and a lot of it, the hearts and minds of the troops are never captured.*[8]

Unless CEOs communicate "change and direction," hundreds—even thousands—of employees will never know why and how they are being asked to lend their hands, hearts, and minds. To build CEO capital, CEOs must be tireless internal communicators.

Securing a Quality Management Team

Having a top-quality senior management team signals to stakeholders that the CEO has a strategy worth following and commands loyalty from some of the best professionals in the business. A top-notch, highly regarded senior team also signals that the CEO not only has the right people to execute his or her vision but also has prepared well for succession, should and when the need arises. Bill Gates of Microsoft knows about the value of "bench strength," of being rich in executive talent. "Take our 20 best people away," he said, "and I can tell you that Microsoft would become an unimportant company."[9]

Motivating and Inspiring Employees

The flip side of communicating well internally is that CEOs must be their organization's Pied Pipers, serving as masters of ceremony at town hall meetings, leading anchors on global webcasts and teleconferences, hosts at breakfast meetings, and even—as Intel's Andy Grove has been known to do—performing as a "Dear CEO" advice columnist. Many of the most celebrated CEOs repeatedly relate how much time is required to motivate employees. Jack Welch says that he spent between 40 to 50 percent of his time on leadership and employee communications. John Chambers of Cisco Systems says he spends about 70 percent of his time with customers and employees.

Dick Kovacevich of Wells Fargo, who is one of the most lionized CEO bankers in the United States, readily promotes employee appreciation. "The way I see it is, when you take care of your employees, they take care of your customers. And your shareholders wind up winning anyway."[10] When CEOs inspire their employees, they build a better corporate culture, leading to increased shareholder value. Everyone is a winner.

IMPLEMENTING THE CEO CAPITAL MODEL

The CEO Capital model of reputation reflects predictable stages through which each CEO passes during the course of holding office. Although the stages inevitably vary in one or more regards depending on the leader and the company, some elements are common to all. Some CEOs pass through the stages one at a time in sequence, combine stages, or others reverse the order entirely. Other CEOs may alter the stage sequence, but they should not neglect learning the lessons, embodied in each stage, that are needed to build CEO capital. Each lesson builds on another, strengthening the foundation of leadership. Whatever the sequence, the goal is the same—leveraging the wealth embedded in a CEO's capital to enhance a company's reputation and well-being, increasing its economic valuation, and differentiating a company from its competition. As a CEO builds capital, the CEO builds a company.

In the late 1980s, John A. Gabarro, a Harvard Business School professor, conducted research among a group of general managers in the United States and Europe.[11] When Gabarro plotted the organizational and structural changes that accompanied these managers as they took charge of their responsibilities, he discovered that these organizational changes, which he categorized into various stages, were essentially the same for all, whether insider, outsider, or even turnaround agent. Gabarro's stages thus laid the groundwork for the CEO Capital model, encouraging me to apply a similar approach to CEOs. If a recognizable and predictable pattern governed senior managers, why not chief executive officers?

Time Parameters

Burson-Marsteller's 2001 CEO research provides evidence for the first time that the business community expects CEOs to reach specific business goals within established time frames. The presence of these generally accepted time limits leads inexorably to the conclusion that a CEO's tenure can be organized according to defined stages.

According to the research, as shown in Exhibit 3.2, CEOs do not have much time to prove themselves. Business influentials expect results and expect them fast. Within the first 12 months, a new CEO must nail down a strategic vision and win employee support. Before year two ends, CEOs must install their senior team, stage a turnaround, and reinvent how business gets done. Even more alarming are the tight deadlines for earning Wall Street's favor and lifting

EXHIBIT **3.2** *Amount of Time for New CEOs to Accomplish Goals*

To develop strategic vision	8 months
To win support of employees	9 months
To develop quality management team	14 months
To earn credibility with Wall Street	17 months
To increase share price	19 months
To turn company around	21 months
To reinvent how company does business	22 months

Source: Burson-Marsteller, *Building CEO Capital*, 2001.

share price—17 months and 19 months, respectively. This is a tall order for any new CEO, Jack Welch wannabes included. This high-speed timetable highlights the urgency with which CEOs must take charge quickly, strategically, and methodically.

Stages of the CEO Capital Model

Exhibit 3.3 presents a timeline that briefly sets forth the five stages of the CEO Capital model in accordance with the CEO timetable shown in Exhibit 3.2.

Countdown. CEOs who have the time before officially taking office must plan and prepare. This Countdown sets the tone for and foreshadows the First Hundred Days, which, in turn, will set the stage for the duration of the CEO's leadership. During the Countdown, the CEO should assemble the transition team, develop sea legs, and be ready to explain what will remain and what will change after the transition. There is no standard time frame for this phase and, in some cases, CEOs have little opportunity to plan and are forced to hit the ground running.

EXHIBIT 3.3 *CEO Capital Model Timeline*

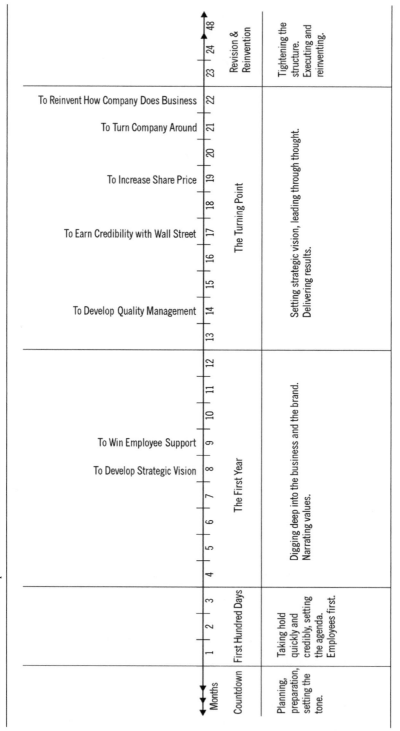

Months	1 2 3	4	5 6 7 8 9 10 11 12	13 14 15 16 17 18 19 20 21 22	23 24 48
	Countdown	First Hundred Days	The First Year	The Turning Point	Revision & Reinvention
	Planning, preparation, setting the tone.	Taking hold quickly and credibly, setting the agenda. Employees first.	Digging deep into the business and the brand. Narrating values.	Setting strategic vision, leading through thought. Delivering results.	Tightening the structure. Executing and reinventing.

To Reinvent How Company Does Business — 22
To Turn Company Around — 21
To Increase Share Price — 19
To Earn Credibility with Wall Street — 17
To Develop Quality Management — 14
To Win Employee Support — 9
To Develop Strategic Vision — 8

The First Hundred Days. The new CEO must take hold of the organization quickly and credibly. The CEO must focus internally, build momentum, and keep eyes wide open and ears to the ground, ever vigilant for warning signs and signals. The CEO must set an agenda, tend to the board, build a team, and declare what matters most, both personally and professionally.

The First Year. The remaining 265 days of the first year are crucial in developing the new CEO's capital and, in particular, persona. Today reputations are typically either established or undermined within a mere one year's time. The one-year anniversary is a generally accepted milestone, a time for evaluation. By the first anniversary, it is hoped that the CEO has successfully become immersed in the business, learned quickly, listened to new voices, and cultivated a CEO persona. The CEO should have amassed sufficiently substantial capital, won the necessary employee support to persevere through pitfalls, and become adept at continuing to address the considerable, unfinished business that undoubtedly remains.

The Turning Point. At this pivotal point, the CEO commits to a strategic vision and is taking meaningful steps to transform the organization for the better. This stage, which generally consumes most of the second year, requires putting stakeholders at ease by delivering results, confirming members of the senior team, and seeking input from special interest groups both inside and outside the company. During this stage, the CEO embarks on a plan for the future, leading with thought. Business influentials will evaluate the CEO, as will the media and the board.

Revision and Reinvention. The CEO's strategic vision should now be in place. However, visions need to be flexible, capable of evolving over time to accommodate the ever-changing marketplace forces and innumerable, incalculable influences that will affect the company. The CEO's vision requires continual alteration. The vision's principles need to be repeatedly communicated and reworked to meet the organization's needs and to reinvigorate its role as a motivating force. During this time the CEO must refine and consolidate strategies and actions. As vision adapts to need, the direction of the company alters. As the altered direction becomes more pronounced, the CEO must repeatedly modify and restate the vision. Typically, the CEO has in effect reinvented a new vision, usually a requirement every three or four years. With each new successful vision, both the CEO's and the company's reputations are enhanced. Successively reinvented visions, accompanied by repeated journeys through the CEO Capital model, represent the apex of a well-developed CEO reputation—the most concentrated form of CEO capital.

One final note: We have spoken at length about the research performed by Burson-Marsteller and other organizations, which we believe is essential in understanding the role CEOs play in the successful company, and in documenting why the CEO Capital model has taken the form that it has. As much as we respect this research and are willing to benefit from the analysis of such studies, there comes a time to leave the rarefied theories of factors and drivers and get practical. In the final analysis, no theory can help a CEO unless it can be applied to the day-to-day requirements of running a company. What better way to determine tried-and-true ways of running a company than to consult CEOs who have actually led them?

This I have done. To demonstrate every stage of the CEO Capital model, I have isolated techniques used by CEOs whom I have either spoken to in person or have studied. I have used these techniques—successful tools of the trade—to demonstrate the practical application of the principles espoused in this book. Accordingly, in the discussions of each stage, I have intentionally devoted an entire section to CEO best practices in the hope of modeling helpful and realistic ways of applying what I preach. Following a discussion of best practices, I devote a concluding section in each stage to reflections. This section is an in-depth analysis of significant topics or issues of general applicability to each stage. Additionally, each stage's discussion features a chart summarizing how the best practices link to the CM Factors that are so important to building CEO capital.

Not surprisingly, after reviewing all five stages of the CEO Capital model, the reader may be left with the impression that the stages read almost like a manual on how to lead a company. This perception is quite acceptable and entirely reasonable because nothing is more conducive to building CEO capital than building a strong, high-performing company. Any similarity between the two is entirely intentional.

APPEAL TO ALL CEOS

Before embarking on the CEO Capital model of building reputation, one critical factor must be in place: The CEO must buy into the importance of amassing CEO capital. The CEO must come to terms with the idea of being the ultimate spokesperson for the organization, the embodiment of the brand, and the official storyteller who knits together the company's past, present, and future. The same goes for the board of directors. Does the board agree that the CEO should spend a fair portion of time building trust, setting standards, and openly communicating to stakeholders and shareholders alike?

The business of building CEO capital is not uncontroversial. Some CEOs balk at what they consider a mere makeover. Some claim they do not harbor a big enough ego to recast a company in their image. Others dismiss the notion on the grounds that the board did not hire them to engage in personal image building. Some decline, pointing to particularly visible CEOs in their industry and disparaging these celebrity CEOs as being starstruck and shameless.

If CEOs do not believe that enhancing their reputations materially benefits their companies or acknowledge that their reputations are as valuable as any other corporate asset, then the company's commitment to building its CEO's reputation and well-being is doomed to failure. A half-hearted attempt to follow this book's guidance will simply not work. The CEO's unabashed commitment is a salient, unavoidable prerequisite.

Fortunately, despite initial defensiveness and resistance from some CEOs, most eventually become aware that their words and actions strengthen and sustain a company's reputation and add value. The vast majority of CEOs inevitably pay a great deal of attention to their positioning and reputation. Burson-Marsteller's research found that most CEOs and their stewards acknowledge paying substantial attention to capital building. As shown in Exhibit 3.4, nearly 8 of 10 CEOs reported paying disproportionate

EXHIBIT 3.4   *How Much Attention Do CEOs Pay to Their Own Image?*

	CEOs	*Execs.*	*Wall St.*	*Gov't.*	*Media*
Very/fairly much	79%	85%	93%	83%	82%
Not too much/not at all	19	13	6	14	16
Don't know	2	2	1	3	2

Note: Sample consists of CEOs, senior business executives (Execs.), financial analysts/institutional investors (Wall St.), government officials (Gov't.), and business media (Media).

Source: Burson–Marsteller, *Maximizing CEO Reputation*, 1997.

attention to their reputations. Wall Street, too, expects no less and assumes that CEOs devote even more time and resources on reputation building.

Most CEOs have too many fires to put out, not enough time, and too many important bottom-line responsibilities awaiting attention. However, CEOs must make the time to nurture their reputation and build CEO capital. Noncommitment will not suffice. Effort is required. It will be time well spent. CEOs need only pay homage to the words of CEO Warren Buffet, who succinctly noted when discussing CEO reputation and its relationship to furthering corporate ends: "People are voting for the artist, not the painting."[12]

APPEAL TO READERS

The CEO Is Not Dead

As this book goes to print, the media is much abuzz about how the concept of the celebrity CEO is dead, the implication being that the current economic downturn, fraudulent balance sheets, and the hypercompensation paid to CEOs has somehow undermined the important leadership role of chief executives. Don't believe one word of it. Leadership has always been—and will always be—important. Does anyone seriously believe that organizations of any stripe will succeed long without stalwart leadership? If anything, the economic downturn has increased the importance of leadership in business, and the leaders in business are of course none other than CEOs.

Where the media and pundits go wrong is to confuse the recently much maligned, media-hyped big "C" Celebrity CEO with the small "c" celebrated CEOs who by dint of strong leadership, discriminating vision, force of character, and other admirable traits become celebrated by their employees, their industry, their peers, and occasionally even the media for jobs well done. Celebrity CEOs are a fashion statement, going in and out of favor as the winds of popularity blow this way and that, to be praised when things go right, to be condemned when things go wrong. They are easy to idolize. They are easy to demonize. They make good stories. They are high drama. This book is about celebrated CEOs, some of whom may find themselves to be media icons as a natural result of their accomplishments, many of whom you may never hear about, but all of whom do their jobs well.

CEOs Are Not Perfect—Just Like the Rest of Us

A CEO's job is difficult, highly complex, and pressured. In this book, I refer to many CEOs, some of whom may be out of favor or perhaps jobless by the time the reader peruses these pages. Do not believe even for a moment that if a CEO has on some level not succeeded that he or she does not have valuable lessons to offer. For the most part, CEOs are highly accomplished, talented people with much to teach us, regardless of their prevailing circumstances. They deserve our attention and usually our respect. As this book points out in Chapter 8, it is almost inevitable that leadership skills may begin to wane after four or five years in office. Errors are to be expected, but these errors do not negate the successes. Remember that even the New York Yankees and the Atlanta Braves, baseball's most winning teams, are not always World Series champions.

Best Practices Are Cumulative

The CEO Capital model is divided into five stages that we discuss separately. During each stage we isolate various best practices to serve as a guide for the CEO. These practices are not intended to be exclusive to each stage. For the most part, we have assigned them to a particular stage because the practices they illustrate are most commonly attributed to that interval of a CEO's development. Perhaps most important is the fact that the beginning of a succeeding stage does not mean that the best practices of prior stages are automatically irrelevant. Each new best practice should be added to previous ones and institutionalized before the next set arrives. All best practices are cumulative.

PART II

BUILDING CEO CAPITAL

CHAPTER 4

THE COUNTDOWN: BEWARE THE TWO-HEADED MONSTER

In my first 90 days [as CEO-elect], I haven't gotten that fully articulated. But I can tell you this: There is going to be a next new thing.[1]

—GE CEO-elect Jeffrey Immelt's response to an
analyst asking about his strategy, March 2001

I don't have any retirement plans. I work harder than anyone else around here. I know more. And there's a shortage of good talent. So why should I deprive the company of my experience and ability?[2]

—W.R. Grace and Co. CEO Peter Grace, age 75,
after firing several heirs apparent

The period immediately before a CEO takes office, the Countdown, is a time to cherish—a time when a CEO may quietly plan for the future, contact key stakeholders, research the company, and do all those innumerable tasks for which there will be so little time later. Unfortunately, not all CEOs-elect have an opportunity to participate in this preparatory stage. The rapid departure of a predecessor, by reason of dismissal or otherwise, often permits only the briefest of Countdown stages, if any at all. But if a Countdown is available, the incoming CEO should make good use of it, rather than simply rushing head-on and headstrong in an impatient charge toward power. The Countdown is the calm before the storm. It is a rare moment for reflection and will be sorely missed once the rain clouds burst and lightning illuminates the sky.

No standard time period exists for the Countdown, although the period from the public announcement of a CEO's appointment to the transfer of power has an optimal length, neither too short nor too long. A publicly announced transition period of anything less than 60 days would be so short that it might create the appearance of an internal problem requiring a too-prompt transfer of power. Anything more than 18 months, an exceptionally long training period, might communicate a lack of confidence in the incoming CEO's leadership ability. For this reason, many companies delay any public announcement of a CEO's appointment in an attempt to provide its CEO-elect with more pre-announcement planning time. This time is unhampered by the pressures of public scrutiny and still permits a public countdown of acceptable length. Although the official Countdown might appear to be only a few months, the preparatory period for the new CEO is actually much longer.

The announcement of the CEO's appointment sets the public timer ticking. Once made, the announcement has many significant effects with a real impact on corporate behavior. No sooner is the announcement made than the presiding CEO becomes a lame duck. With the outgoing CEO deprived of long-term future consequence, the authority and prestige of the outgoing CEO's pronouncements will wane as business influentials turn their attention away from the old and await the new. How will the soon-to-be betrothed couple, the new CEO and company, interact? Will theirs be a marriage made in heaven or one made in hell? Once the board announces the anticipated transfer of power, answers to these questions become paramount, and the outgoing CEO is all but forgotten.

The period between the announcement and the date that the new CEO takes office is unique in still other ways. Although stakeholders will undoubtedly attribute various positive or negative qualities to a new CEO as soon as they learn of the aspirant's identity, these amount to little more than top-of-mind associations. Stakeholders generally avoid opinions until the CEO-elect actually takes office. Once the CEO begins to wield the reins of power, however, opinions will begin to form. These opinions will continue to coalesce at a quickening pace until typically a year later, when they solidify into a more definitive judgment. The Countdown is analogous to an engagement, a precursor to a planned wedding, not to be taken all that seriously until rings are actually exchanged.

Accordingly, the Countdown affords the new CEO a grace period, during which time the CEO may plan and coordinate without the accelerating scrutiny that looms ahead. Although not technically in power and not yet outwardly responsible, the CEO-elect will find that this stage provides a rare opportunity to reach out to stakeholders. During this relatively halcyon period, CEOs-elect will find themselves in a perfect position to calm stakeholder fears, to provide assurance that a well-performing company will continue to perform well, if not better, or in the alternative, that a poorly performing company will soon be reformed and regenerated. The Countdown, if available, should not be wasted.

This chapter reviews the challenges facing CEOs-elect and establishes guidelines for managing the steps leading to the first day in office. The quiet leadership often associated with this stage should not be confused with ineffectualness. CEOs-elect often find that the actions they take and the statements they make during this stage reverberate rapidly throughout the organization. If managed properly, the Countdown phase can set the tone for the CEO's first hundred days and first year.

BEST PRACTICES FOR THE COUNTDOWN

Following the rules of the road can help minimize bumps and avoid potholes. Here are best practices that, if followed, can keep CEOs and their companies moving in the right direction. Exhibit 4.1 outlines these practices and shows how they generate CM factors.

Get Your Transition Team on Board

The insider CEO-elect should tap an inner circle of trusted players, presumably a team of well-established colleagues, and have them begin planning the transition. For the outsider CEO-elect who is unfamiliar with the company's workforce, this task is somewhat more difficult. The outsider CEO must first interview various managers and executives, selecting from them a core group of advisers to act as the transition team. Both kinds of CEOs keep membership of this core group flexible, adding to or subtracting from it as needs arise and as each member's capabilities become more defined. The CEO should observe how well team members work individually and with others, remaining ever aware that one or more may qualify for additional duties once the transition concludes.

Transition team membership is in no way sacrosanct. The CEO should never hesitate to vary the circle or to seek assistance from others outside the team. The expertise of the Chief Financial Officer (CFO) and Chief Operating Officer (COO), for example, is almost always helpful and should be tapped into when needed. The same rule applies to anyone else who has a specific contribution to make, even if the person comes from the outgoing CEO's inner circle.

One *Fortune* 500 chief executive newcomer, who was committed to maintaining good relations with the outgoing CEO, sought the guidance of the outgoing CEO's assistant. The incoming CEO encouraged this assistant to speak up about any plan of action that she felt might not sit well with her outgoing boss. In this way, the incoming CEO tamed from the very start the two-headed monster—the often turbulent relationship (more fully described later in this chapter) between the new and outgoing CEOs. Other officers typically asked to weigh in are directors of human resources, investor relations, and communications or public affairs; however, every business is different. What works well at one company may not at another. For example, one chief executive of a large conglomerate thought it essential to seek the advice of an employee responsible for the company's Web operations, but not every CEO would find this worthwhile.

The CEO-elect should initially form a small transition group as one means of getting up to speed as quickly as possible. Miles White of Abbott Labs started with such a small team, but eventually enlarged the group as circumstances required. "I wanted my organization to begin quickly, to ready itself promptly. So we did have a small group that began to think about our agenda and in that way pursue my vision and strategy from the very start."[3] By the time the outgoing CEO retired six months later, the group had grown to 40 people.

Regardless of who is on the Countdown team, the incoming CEO must guard against setting overly ambitious goals. There is no worse way to start than by failing to meet initial goals. The

EXHIBIT 4.1 *CM Factor Analysis: The Countdown*

			RESULTS		
Action	*Credibility*	*Conduct*	*Communication*	*Motivation*	*Mgmt.*
Get transition team on board.	X				
Emphasize orderly transition.	X		X		
Address why CEO was chosen.		X			
Describe what will change/remain the same.	X		X		
Be patient. Develop sea legs.			X		
Draw up CEO constellation chart.		X			
Communicate.	X	X	X		
Establish clear division of labor.		X			
(Beware the Two-Headed Monster.)					

Credibility: In this early transition phase, credibility is built by taking charge—tapping the transition team to plan the first 100 days, articulating that succession is a result of the company's thorough planning, making sure it is known that the CEO-elect comes with needed strengths and skills, and quietly signaling what will stay the same and change.

Conduct: A clear division of duties between incoming and outgoing CEO is noticed and promotes productivity. The CEO-elect's respect for the outgoing CEO and his or her legacy provides cues to the new CEO's integrity. Discussions about which stakeholders to address first and last signal the new CEO's understanding of the role as the guardian of the company's assets.

Communicating internally: Listening to small groups of employees is critical. The incoming CEO might also listen to key customers and financial and industry analysts. Communications should be kept largely out of the public eye to provide opportunities for transitioning CEOs to rehearse and test emerging theories.

Motivating employees and building a management team: These are on the radar screen but not acted on just yet. Time to begin watching the senior team in action and considering who should stay, leave, or assume different responsibilities. In some cases, new senior appointments are made to signal the CEO-elect's priorities.

transition plan should also conform to the CEO's style, incorporating an approach with which the CEO feels comfortable. If the CEO-elect performs better in small groups, hold meetings that are one-on-one or in small group settings. If the CEO is unfamiliar with the financial analysts covering the company or its industry, arrange introductory conference calls with select analysts. Above all, the CEO-elect must allocate time for frequent meetings with the transition team, thereby remaining aware of the plans being devised. Such meetings also ensure that these plans reflect the incoming CEO's wants, needs, abilities, and style. The meetings also serve as a way to confirm that the plans are consistent with the principles that will eventually govern the CEO's tenure and that in time will coalesce into the company's vision.

Make It Known That an Orderly Transition Plan Is in Place

Harvey Golub of American Express first announced the 2001 ascension of Kenneth Chenault to CEO in 1997, four years ahead of schedule. Although as previously noted lengthy time periods between announcement and taking office are usually frowned on, Golub believed that special circumstances outweighed any countervailing drawbacks. Golub explained that the early announcement eliminated any doubt that the future of the company would be hampered by the absence of succession planning. Golub claimed that this long-term, public method of succession was the best way to "clarify our plans for you [employees] and the external world and to allow Ken to increase the range of his responsibilities."[4] Over the course of this unusually long transition period, confidence in American Express's future remained high, demonstrating that the mere existence of an orderly transition period, even an excessively long one, can instill confidence.

Proclaiming that a well-planned, thorough transition is in place can be more important than even announcing the selection of the successor. Let us say, for example, that a company wants to maintain the privacy of a designated CEO for as long as possible. A delayed announcement of the CEO's designation is a possible way of accomplishing this aim, but only if the company makes abundantly clear that a thoughtful transition process has been and is currently in the works. Without clarifying the existence of such a process, the company runs the risk of losing the confidence of its employees, customers, shareholders, and other influentials.

CEO Herb Kelleher of Southwest Airlines, for example, caused such a dip in confidence over the airline's future. Although Kelleher's health had become an issue, neither he nor the company's board assured the business community that a succession process was in place. In November 2000, *Fortune* interviewed Kelleher and Gordon Bethune, the chairman and CEO of rival Continental Airlines. In response to an inquiry regarding succession at Southwest, Kelleher, with tongue in cheek, said that for all he cared, Bethune could take over: "I am planning to have Gordon succeed me. With Southwest it's no problem! What's going to happen to Continental?"[5] Kelleher's lack of seriousness about succession planning raised reasonable concerns about Southwest's future. Not until 2001, when James F. Parker was announced the designated successor to Kelleher, were these concerns allayed.

Another way to show continuity and order in leadership transitions is through joint appearances of the outgoing and incoming chief executives. Thus James A. Johnson and Franklin D. Raines, outgoing and incoming Fannie Mae CEOs, respectively, visited investors around the globe in what the company dubbed a "Hello Goodbye" tour. For similar reasons, at Hewlett-Packard (HP), Lewis Platt frequently accompanied new CEO Carleton (Carly)

Fiorina on her "Travels with Carly" visits to 20 HP sites in 10 countries. While still chairman, Platt generously made himself available to reinforce Fiorina's statements about respecting company tradition and culture, thereby signaling to all a smooth, natural changing of the guard.

Address Why You Were Chosen

One of the more obvious questions that any business influential would ask upon first learning of a new CEO appointment is "Why him?" or "Why her?" Although the reasons for choosing a chief executive may be obvious to the board of directors and even, perhaps, to senior management, it is not always obvious to others. Consequently, those qualities of a CEO-elect that attracted the board need to be publicized consistently and as often as possible, building the CEO's credibility among internal and external constituencies.

General Electric (GE) succeeded in communicating its reasons for choosing Jeffrey Immelt as CEO. Media coverage dwelled on the keys to Immelt's success: his effective implementation of Welch's Six Sigma program and his infusion of Internet technology into GE Medical Systems. Based at least in part on GE-supplied information, news coverage also noted Immelt's people orientation, an important quality for 21st-century CEOs as well as one of the CM factors.

Describe What Will Remain and What Will Be Different

Something more than avuncular reassurance will be necessary to calm employees' anxieties, who naturally often feel themselves floating adrift during the initial stages of any changing of the guard. Honoring the successes of the outgoing CEO's tenure or promising a new dawn when the company has been less than successful is all well and good; but to be truly effective, something more is necessary.

At the very least, the incoming CEO should isolate a few broad changes needed to move the company forward. For instance, one *Fortune* 500 incoming CEO spoke about speed and simplicity, two qualities that every employee knew the company sorely lacked. GE's Immelt honored the management culture built by the near-legendary Welch, but wisely hinted that changes were nevertheless on the horizon. At the quarterly executive council meeting religiously attended by GE's top executives, CEO-elect Immelt made a point of beginning every discussion from the customer's point of view.[6] His message was abundantly clear: On his watch, the company would more strongly focus and improve on customer service.

Be Patient: Give Yourself Time to Develop Sea Legs

The Countdown presents the incoming CEO with the valuable opportunity to practice being chief executive—to role play, make behind-the-scenes decisions, and get acquainted with the board—all in the absence of real-world scrutiny and consequences. Rather than learning on the job after taking office, the CEO-elect can use this extra time to visit plant sites, customers, and employees. Through media training, introductions to several major stakeholders such as key analysts and customers, and a gradual shift in public speaking duties, a CEO can ease into the job smoothly and effectively without becoming overwhelmed.

On-the-job training, although inevitable to some degree, should be minimized to the extent possible. As pointed out in the following section, the CEO-elect can better prepare for new responsibilities if both the outgoing and incoming CEO cooperate in the spirit of a smooth transition; however, even without such cooperation the incoming CEO should prepare, and thus avoid surprises. Becoming immersed in the company's operational details is one way to prepare. Another is to talk with outside consultants, management gurus or other CEOs who have witnessed successful and unsuccessful transitions and can offer objective, independent advice. The incoming CEO should do whatever is necessary to shorten the learning curve.

Draw Up a CEO Constellation Chart to Prioritize Stakeholders and Executive Appointees

The CEO-elect and the transition team should develop a chart similar to the one in Exhibit 4.2. This chart identifies a company's key stakeholders and serves as a tool for evaluating and prioritizing the groups that require a CEO's attention. This simple task helps focus attention and promote the efficient use of the CEO's time. These stakeholders need to be managed one by one according to their unique needs.

Who is included in this chart and who is excluded matters. In his first three days as New York City's mayor-elect, Michael R. Bloomberg met with his nonsupporters. He met with the head of the city's most powerful union, attended a business dinner hosted by 100 Black Men, and shook hands with activist Reverend Al Sharpton. By meeting with these diverse groups who had been at odds with his predecessor, Rudy Giuliani, Bloomberg made clear that his administration would be inclusive and that more voices would be heard in City Hall. On the other hand, Bloomberg did not make overtures to the city's traditionally conservative alliances,[7] giving a more middle-of-the-road flavor to a Republican government in an overwhelmingly Democratic city.

A caution for CEOs: Avoid unintentionally slighting stakeholders. Not paying a courtesy call during Countdown to a stakeholder

EXHIBIT 4.2 *CEO Constellation Chart*

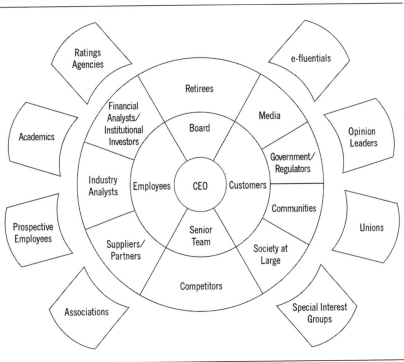

who expects such a call may forever cause resentment or at least create negative feelings that could be difficult to reverse. More serious adverse consequences are also possible. Neglecting an audience can sometimes derail a CEO's mission. Although this lapse occurred during Bill Gates's tenure as CEO and not during a Countdown, consider the negative consequences of his having neglected the Washington, D.C., beltway politicos in the years before the Microsoft antitrust suit. Compare this misstep with Andy Grove's attention this audience and Intel's relatively smooth sailing through the threatening seas of antitrust regulation. Paying attention to important stakeholders pays dividends, while ignoring them during Countdown or at other times can be disastrous.

What is true externally is also true internally. For similar reasons of prioritization and efficiency, the CEO-elect should craft a similar constellation chart of possible executive appointments, breaking down the executive team component in Exhibit 4.2 to begin making up the long-term senior management team. The incoming CEO must learn as much as possible about the organization's most talented employees. Although several members of the long-term team will also have been on the transition team, the teams are not identical. Functions and commitments are radically different, their respective tasks qualitatively different.

The selection process takes time. First impressions need to be sifted and sorted. The CEO-elect must lessen the anxieties of keepers and, where necessary, make commitments to ensure their support and continued availability. The new CEO must also deal with one of the more sensitive problems: how to handle former competitors, runners-up for the CEO title. Many employees will have a deep emotional interest in the company's treatment of their former colleagues, and they will scrutinize how the CEO-elect addresses this particularly sensitive task. Thus one of the most critical jobs of an incoming CEO is to assemble the long-term team, set aside the maybes, identify who is not going to make the cut, and deal with the also-rans.

Communicate, Communicate, Communicate

A CEO must communicate effectively. Secondary channels such as company memos, voice mail, e-mail, interviews for in-house publications, the company intranet, and company newsletters are all excellent conduits for clear, consistent, frequent, transition-related messages. Although the board of directors will be familiar with the succession process, other important constituents such as employees, customers, vendors, communities, and investors are not. They must not be left uninformed.

Frequent communication keeps people in the loop, conveys and instills confidence, motivates, and clarifies. Home Depot was instinctively aware of the importance of communicating during moments of change and took advantage of every opportunity to do so. Their 1997 annual report was one such vehicle. It included a joint Letter to Stockholders from Bernard Marcus and Arthur Blank, the company's co-founders. Chairperson Marcus intended to transition leadership to President and COO Blank. Although the letter did not explicitly address the transition, the mere fact that it was jointly composed indicated cooperation and shared power. The letter also set the stage for the succession announcement, proclaiming Blank as the CEO-elect, shortly after the annual report was published. The introduction to the following year's report included a one-page statement written by Marcus as well as a three-page Letter to Shareholders written by Blank. Marcus praised Blank's first full year as CEO, showing confidence in the company's future. "My partner from day one, Arthur Blank," wrote Marcus, "has made terrific strides in moving our shared vision for the Company closer to fruition during his first full year as CEO."[8] When Blank formally took full control, no stakeholder was surprised because it was apparent that Blank had been part of the decision-making process for months before taking office. Marcus's praise one year later was the icing on the cake. It reconfirmed the smoothness of the transition and reinforced the confidence that the joint communication during the Countdown had instilled.

One final note about communicating during the Countdown. The tone is often the message: *How* you say it is often as, if not more, important than *what* you say. Enthusiasm can carry the day. How much excitement and emotion accompanies the baton passing makes a deep impression on employees, board members, customers, and other key stakeholders. Who could forget Jack Welch and Jeff Immelt, smiling side by side on the day Welch announced Immelt as his successor?

REFLECTIONS: BEWARE THE TWO-HEADED MONSTER

Unique to the Countdown process is the peculiar circumstance of a company having in effect two leaders: one du jour, one de facto. The departing CEO is a lame duck but has actual authority. The other is a rising star without actual authority, but whose power nevertheless increases as day one closes in. The situation is awkward, to say the least. During this tense period, the natural tendency is for the board either to put an end to the pain by shortening the Countdown or, even worse, to succumb to the tension by taking umbrage and allowing conflict to simmer. Far better for all is if the two heads of this monster resist self-defeating behavior, put aside personal frustration, and choose the high road of cooperation.

When cooperation prevails, the Countdown can be a time of extreme optimism, productivity, and celebration. Take the yearlong transition period at SmithKline Beecham during which Jan Leschly prepared to assume leadership from Robert Bauman. The two worked together on the Vision 2000 transition team, jointly setting strategic goals for the organization. As recounted in *From Promise to Performance,* a book on SmithKline Beecham's transformation, serious Countdown work began almost immediately and was a joint project from the start:

> *The two men agreed that Jan would start working with what would be Jan's team to develop the SB of the future, while Bob focused on the day-to-day operations.*

This was highly unusual for an outgoing chief executive; usually the roles are reversed during the last year of a chief executive's tenure. . . . In another effort to ease the chief executive transition both inside and outside the organization, Jan began to accompany Bob to the sector and corporate staff meetings and went with him when he visited with the press and analysts. By autumn 1993 the roles had been reversed, with Bob attending in support of Jan. Hardly a beat had been missed.[9]

From Jan Leschly's point of view, "Bob was involved but knew he was not going to be implementing the results." The key was that Leschly "had a wonderful period working with Bob," in part because as the incoming chief executive, he was able to be involved without yet being held accountable. "I can certainly recommend this to any CEO," Leschly said. "The key is to have a proper transition."[10]

No one says, however, that cooperation is easy. Lack of cooperation between CEOs is perhaps the primary reason why a startling number of prospective CEOs have transitions that fail, and like Peter Grace's heirs apparent, sometimes even have their appointments renounced as a result. In research by transition experts Dan Ciampa and Michael Watkins, no less than one-half of insiders who are being groomed as successor CEOs and an almost incomprehensible three-quarters of those who come from outside the company do not make it to the corner office.[11] Among the reasons for this astonishingly high failure rate, say consultant Ciampa and Harvard professor Watkins, is the failure of the incumbent CEO to relinquish power gracefully, compounded by the incoming CEO's frustration over being number two. As the highly cooperative Chairman and CEO Harvey Golub of American Express explained after voluntarily handing over his responsibilities to Kenneth Chenault, the tendency of most CEOs is not to cooperate:

"Some CEOs won't let the successor expand responsibility very much before the changeover and therefore don't have an opportunity to provide at least some level of guidance."[12]

Miles White, chairman and CEO of Abbott Laboratories, succeeded a CEO who officially handed over power several months after White's appointment. White recounts:

> *I think a long transition is a terribly awkward thing. The typical organization will turn its compass needle very quickly to the new leader. A new CEO will not wish to appear in conflict philosophically with the outgoing CEO and will carefully measure any agenda or decision going forward.*[13]

The situation for the new CEO and outgoing CEO can indeed be awkward until the new CEO takes full reign. For White, whose perceptions about the transition process served him well, the transition worked smoothly and without a hitch.

Staples, the office supply retailer, carefully managed a succession even though Staples' founder and CEO, Thomas G. Stemberg, and Ronald L. Sargent, president and COO, shared a Countdown lasting one year. To avoid missteps, the two men sought the advice of other chief executives who successfully had passed the baton and adopted many of their suggestions, including, in particular, establishing a cooperative and lengthy Countdown. From Microsoft's Steve Ballmer, successor to Bill Gates, they learned the importance of communicating with employees, and from Arthur Blank, former CEO and chairman of Home Depot, they learned about the need to define roles.[14] Finally, Stemberg granted Sargent the right to approve or disapprove Stemberg's budget, which covered a period after Stemberg would have relinquished his title.[15]

The lynchpin of a successful, collaborative CEO transition centers on establishing early in the Countdown stage a clear understanding of leadership responsibilities and then maintaining each CEO's respective duties. The outgoing and incoming CEOs of one *Fortune* 500 company, for example, wrote down the responsibilities they would each assume during the transition period. After exchanging notes and discussing division of labor, they were able to jointly lead the company, reducing confusion and personal conflict. In another case, a CEO-elect maintained a constant flow of communication with the outgoing CEO. The two executives established a rule that allowed any decision to remain open to challenge within 24 hours of being made in the hope that any contentious issues could be amicably resolved in private. Both CEOs kept the other informed of all decisions, reviewing them with each other on a daily basis. Moreover, the outgoing CEO, like Staples' Stemberg, committed to not making any operating decisions that would have an impact beyond the changeover date. There is a lesson to be learned from these examples: A specific, carefully drawn division of labor, seasoned with respect, contributes mightily to taming the two-headed monster.

Keeping these guidelines in mind helps plant the seeds from which a promising beginning to a CEO's reign will grow. This reign, in turn, will ideally mature, and with a little loving care, become a highly successful tenure. If the Countdown period is handled adeptly, the incoming CEO can set the right expectations and help lay the groundwork for fully developing CEO capital. The pace will quicken as day one approaches. CEO-elects should make sure that all the right thank-you's are handed out to those who helped make the process positive and smooth. For the incoming CEO, it is best to remember one thing about the changing of the guard: "It's not a coronation."[16]

During the final few days before day one, the incomer will have had an opportunity to see some teammates in action; to meet with key customers; to listen to employees' hopes, dreams, and concerns; to honor the predecessor's legacy; and to raise expectations for a new beginning. The stakeholders, in turn, will have had an opportunity to bond with and form a first impression of the soon-to-be chief executive officer. However, as the Countdown rehearsal draws to a close and the curtain begins to rise on the first act, the hardest work is just about to begin.

CHAPTER 5

THE FIRST HUNDRED DAYS: CEOS UNDER THE MAGNIFYING GLASS

There is no training to be a CEO; it's an extraordinary thing.[1]

—Gerald M. Levin, former CEO,
AOL Time Warner

Everything is under a magnifying glass.[2]

—G. Richard Wagoner, Jr., president and CEO,
General Motors

The First Hundred Days could hardly be more different from the Countdown. As discussed in Chapter 4, the Countdown, this stage is the calm before the storm, affording the CEO-elect a period of reflection relatively free from the prying eyes and judgments of others. Once the CEO takes office, however, the storm hits, with winds that will increase in velocity through the First Hundred Days and the remaining stages of his or her tenure.

The new CEO will not feel the full brunt of the storm during the First Hundred Days; he or she will still have a grace period to prepare for the future, to coalesce ideas, to solidify a game plan, and to develop a vision. However, the new CEO will undoubtedly feel as if he or she has been slammed with hurricane-strength winds, especially the CEO who is occupying the chief executive's seat for the first time. So shocking is the difference between being a mere senior executive and being the executive in chief.

Miles White, chairman and CEO of Abbott Labs, aptly describes the shock a CEO experiences when facing the storm, and for the first time bearing the weight of increased visibility and heightened scrutiny to which all new CEOs are subject. "Now in that first 100 days, the new CEO is under intense scrutiny from everybody."[3] As White knows firsthand, the CEO must contend with the often nascent, half-developed points of view of critics, who may or may not have sufficient information to form such opinions. White adds: "They don't have [the CEO's] rhythm or his or her personality. They don't have a sense of how he or she is like or unlike the previous CEO. Does he or she have an agenda? Is there a hidden agenda? If so, do they even know what that agenda is?"[4]

Compounding the psychological impact of feeling watched is the burden of ultimate responsibility that is borne by all leaders— what former President Harry Truman meant when he said, "The buck stops here." With the office of chief executive comes final responsibility for the company's welfare. There is no one else to whom responsibility shifts. Final authority and final responsibility rests with the CEO. Even for newly appointed CEOs who have served as chief operating officers or chief financial officers, or otherwise bring extensive experience from within their industry, the office of chief executive looks different when the buck stops at their door. For example, Phil Condit, chairman and CEO of The

Boeing Company, marveled on how different and even isolating the world looked when seated behind the CEO's desk:

> *The fact was that there used to always be somebody down the hall and you would wander in and say, "Hey boss, this is what I am thinking about doing, what do you think?" And all of a sudden, you get to this place and you turn around and there is nobody to say, "Yes, I think that is a good idea," to confirm your idea, to make it okay. You are the one.[5]*

This sense of responsibility, combined with the increased scrutiny of influentials, can become overwhelming. No wonder CEO Rick Wagoner of General Motors observed that during the First Hundred Days most CEOs feel as if they are living life under a magnifying glass.

In a way, the First Hundred Days is an artificial construct. Nothing about the First Hundred Days requires that a CEO's performance be evaluated at just that moment. Nothing about the chief executive's job requires that any specific task be completed within that time frame, other than tradition and the sense that 100 is a nice round number. Some chief executives believe that establishing their legitimacy takes more time. Some say less. Lou Gerstner of IBM told a friend that he expected to spend his first 120 days sizing up the situation at IBM.[6] President George W. Bush, no less a CEO than any other, gave himself 180 instead of the traditional 100 days to acclimate himself to his job. Most, but not all, of his constituents seem to have granted him the extension.

Whether the First Hundred Days is an appropriate milestone, it has developed a meaning of its own. One hundred days is a traditional milestone at which most CEOs can expect to be evaluated. Stakeholders will ask, perhaps for the first time: How is the enterprise faring? Where is it heading? So, whether or not the First Hundred Days should be a milestone, Burson-Marsteller's research demonstrates beyond question that business influentials consider it to be one. If influentials treat it as a milestone, then that is what it is.

The first hundred days originated when President Franklin Delano Roosevelt took office on March 4, 1933 and successfully kicked off the New Deal. In 100 days from the date of his inauguration, FDR sent Congress several historic bills that paved the way for the creation of the Federal Emergency Relief Administration, the Civilian Conservation Corps, the Reconstruction Finance Corporation, and the Tennessee Valley Authority. In his first hundred days, FDR also devised a plan with Congress to provide the Federal Trade Commission with new regulatory authority. By these early actions, the president reassured concerned Americans suffering under the Depression that someone was doing something to help them. One hundred days was an easily remembered number— the perfect call to action.

Presidential advisor David Gergen researched for Ronald Reagan the first hundred days of several previous presidents. He determined that the first hundred days, as a traditional milestone and time for evaluation, was important for at least three reasons.[7] First, all incoming chief executives are evaluated from day one. The fact that the president had won an election mattered little—to be a candidate was one thing, to be a president another. Second, chief executives had an opportunity to use the first hundred days to establish a thematic stamp to their presidency, such as FDR's New Deal or Eisenhower's search for peace in Korea. Thus, if used correctly, the first days of a leader's tenure afford the opportunity to frame one's future actions. And third, haste should be avoided in the early stages of the presidency because premature action can lead to significant controversy, such as Kennedy's Bay of Pigs, Ford's pardon of Nixon, and Clinton's "don't ask, don't tell" policy on gays in the military. In short, all chief executives should beware of taking premature action.

This last point regarding premature decisions requires special attention. CEOs will be somewhat stunned by the scope of their responsibilities and the scrutiny that they will endure from day one of taking office. Yet, the pressure to perform should not cause them to act in haste. Far better to get one's house in order first by following this chapter's best practices. There is time to act. CEOs should remind themselves that the company and stakeholders have a high tolerance for change during this period and will not judge them harshly fresh out of the gate. No one will be waiting at the end of the First Hundred Days to hand the CEO a diploma for successfully completing CEO 101. Once the company house is in order, if there is time left, the First Hundred Days may be used to get a head start on management goals such as winning selective stakeholders' support.

BEST PRACTICES: NAVIGATING THE FIRST HUNDRED DAYS

Most successful CEOs first focus inward during their First Hundred Days. Establishing a relationship with employees and then organizing the top brass should receive priority status. Dealing with Wall Street or the media during the early stages, although considered useful, clearly takes a back seat to setting matters right within the company.

Exhibit 5.1 outlines the best practices of the First Hundred Days and describes how they coexist with the CM factors, the necessary qualities inherent in building CEO capital.

Put Employees First

At one time, CEOs seemed almost to forget that their company had any employees other than their direct reports. When Mort Meyerson

EXHIBIT 5.1 *CM Factor Analysis: The First Hundred Days*

			RESULTS		
Action	*Credibility*	*Conduct*	*Communication*	*Motivation*	*Mgmt.*
Put employees first.	X	X	X	X	X
Reconstitute the senior team.	X	X			X
Set your own agenda.	X	X			
Tend to your board.			X		
Declare what matters.	X	X	X	X	X
Identify short-term wins.	X			X	
Communicate personally, symbolically.			X	X	
Gather ye promises.	X	X			
Touch base with select stakeholders.	X	X			

Credibility: New CEOs' first job is to get their house in order, establishing a relationship with employees and evaluating the senior team. CEOs must focus on priorities, establish parameters for goals in the months ahead, and gather momentum to dampen opposition and signal progress. Be careful what you promise—delivery will be noted. Select stakeholders need contacting.

Conduct: The spotlight will be intense, and each action and personal nod will reflect on the CEO's internal compass. Perceptions of the CEO's fairness and moral judgment will hinge on early signs of change in the senior team.

Communicating internally: A variety of communication methods—broadly and personally communicated—should be used to motivate employees to buy into the CEO's emerging program. An explicit and implicit declaration of values is recommended. Straightforward communications with the board is required.

Motivating employees: Employees are the most important audience in the First Hundred Days. CEOs must reach out and pay close attention to off-the-record conversations. Legitimacy depends on employees' willingness to follow.

Building a management team: The CEO is vulnerable until the team is in place. Act swiftly. This is the hardest work of this early stage.

73

led Electronic Data Systems (EDS) in the 1980s, he communicated with his employees from a distance—a very long distance—just as other CEOs did at that time. According to Meyerson, at most he went on stage at a management meeting twice a year to deliver a pep rally speech. Otherwise, he wrote memos to at most a dozen or so top executives, many of whom were his direct reports.[8] Lawrence A. Bossidy, former chairman and CEO of AlliedSignal before it merged with Honeywell International, had similar recollections: "I mean, you could be C.E.O. 10 years ago and never have talked to your employees. You talk to them every day now."[9]

Bossidy is right. Twenty-first century CEOs communicate directly with their employees. As seen in Exhibit 5.2, a vast majority of senior managers (75 percent) believe that among the responsibilities facing a CEO within the first three months on the job, communicating with and focusing on employees is extremely important. A CEO who had an opportunity to experience a Countdown may well have already started communicating with employees, as is entirely appropriate; however, relating to employees as a

EXHIBIT 5.2 *Stakeholder Priority in First Hundred Days*

	Extremely Important To Communicate To
Employees	75%
Financial community	44
Customers	38
Media	5
Other (government, partners, etc.)	3

Source: Burson-Marsteller Executive Omnibus, Wirthlin Worldwide, April 1999.

prospective CEO is one thing, but relating to them as a CEO in power is quite another. It would seem unrealistic to expect full candor from all employees, including many with previous loyalties still intact, while a predecessor CEO remains in control.

Even if a CEO has spent time and effort reaching out to employees before assuming leadership, more communication, especially of the bidirectional type—talking as well as listening—is needed once in office. Understanding employees and the way work gets done often transcends institutional structure and is not readily apparent without first obtaining a feel for it. Transition experts Dan Ciampa and Michael Watkins describe such structural fuzziness in *Right From the Start*: ". . . the new leader must understand the 'shadow organization'—the informal processes and alliances that exist in the shadow of the organization's formal structure and strongly influence how work actually gets done."[10]

For CEOs of multinational *Fortune* 500 companies, reaching out to employees and understanding them is no small task and can include, among other things, extensive travel, repeated town meetings, webcasts, frequent face-to-face conversations, and one or more offsite retreats for senior managers. Only with such effort will a CEO be able to focus on the elusive social network that constitutes a company's social structure. Only in this way will the CEO be able to discern why work that should be getting done is not getting done.

The methods of relating to and learning from one's employees are almost infinitely varied. Listening and listening well is perhaps the most obvious way, although not necessarily the easiest. Raymond Gilmartin, chairman, president, and CEO of Merck & Co., speaks about being an outsider and his first meeting with the top 50 employees. He asked them point blank: "If you had my job, what would you do?"[11] The best CEOs listen carefully to the answers and above all, make a point of not shooting the messenger.

Gilmartin cautions CEOs that if an employee criticizes how the business has been run and the new CEO hastily disagrees, word will quickly spread through the grapevine that the CEO is not receptive to new ideas or change. CEOs must remember that each encounter will leave an impression, and the aggregate of these impressions will in time coalesce, forming what amounts to a general, organizationwide opinion of the CEO. Best to start from day one earning that trust and building CEO capital.

A wise CEO will also make arrangements to allow employees to speak freely without fear of reprisal from their immediate superiors. During his first 60 days at AlliedSignal, Larry Bossidy spoke with more than 5,000 employees. One way he chose to listen was by holding "skip-level lunches," inviting small groups of employees to attend without nametags and without their supervisors. Bossidy knew that under these conditions, employees would be ruthlessly honest and not worry about retribution.[12]

Listening is important, but relating to employees entails much more. CEOs can motivate employees by connecting with them in other ways. Fred Hassan of Pharmacia made this realization during his first meetings with employees when he made a point of taking notes. Upon becoming CEO of the recently merged Pharmacia & Upjohn (now Pharmacia Corporation) in 1997, he immediately flew to Stockholm, Milan, London, and Kalamazoo—all corporate centers—to seek out and attend to company employees. By taking copious notes during these meetings, Hassan communicated nonverbally that he was sincerely interested in what people had to say. Many of these early meetings were one-on-one and had a personal touch appropriate to Hassan's style. These meetings allowed him to better understand the distrust and tension that had developed following the cross-cultural union of the two multinational drug companies—one Swedish, the other American. By taking notes, Hassan demonstrated, visually and irrefutably, that he was really listening and that he had heard something so worthwhile that he wanted to ensure it was addressed. He not only communicated the value that he placed on employee comments and opinions, but he also motivated employees. Hassan left employees with the clear impression that they had participated in a company decision and helped make a difference.

Carleton (Carly) S. Fiorina, who became president and CEO of Hewlett-Packard (HP) in 1999, was a firm believer in communing with employees from the get-go. As one of the few women to have risen to the highest levels in the corporate world, Fiorina's beginning was very public. The press had a field day with her appointment. Fiorina graciously granted interviews and was receptive to the ensuing media frenzy. In this way she acquiesced to her board's desire that HP become a more outspoken, publicly visible company. After a few days of attending to journalists, however, Fiorina exited the public stage.[13] For the remainder of her First Hundred Days, Fiorina turned inward, wisely focusing on HP's employees, among other things.

Fiorina gets high marks for those First Hundred Days, even though she has subsequently endured a hailstorm of criticism for more controversial actions later in her tenure. She focused on employees by conducting a Listening Tour. She visited many HP locations in several countries and made extensive use of the company's internal communications network. She sent en masse monthly voice mails and e-mails and used streaming video on the company's intranet. Fiorina also penned a letter in HP's quarterly in-house magazine, read all her e-mails (and more important, answered them), and made clear that she wanted to hear from HP's 90,000 employees about anything that had gone or was going wrong. Fiorina told employees to send her a list of the "10 stupidest things" that HP was doing. Communicating internally among employees is a critical driver of building CEO capital. Fiorina built her early reputation by modeling this behavior and making internal communications a signature of her early efforts to build CEO capital.

In addition to listening and taking notes, Fiorina acted on what employees told her. During her first month as CEO, she followed up on her Listening Tour with a senior management offsite meeting. At the meeting, she spoke about her early plans to reorganize HP around customers and detailed what she had learned from listening to employees.

Reconstitute the Senior Team

All that has been said about a CEO's attending to employees also applies to senior management. After all, senior managers are employees too. Yet, they are also a different category of employee given their direct contact with the CEO, high level of compensation, and decision-making authority. Accordingly, they require separate consideration.

One of the first steps taken by nearly all new CEOs is restructuring senior management, remaking the company's senior leadership in the CEO's image, and building the team. No less than 80 percent of senior managers anticipate radical changes in senior management after a leadership change.[14] When asked what was the single most important action he undertook during his First Hundred Days, Rana S. Talwar, former CEO of Standard Charter, emphasized "changing people."[15] He observed that this was also the most difficult part of the job. Changes in the senior team or structure of the office of the CEO are clear evidence to all that the CEO has taken charge.

Moreover, because executives expect movement in the senior team early on, CEOs should take advantage of this early high tolerance for change and make changes immediately, even if the need for prompt action means they must rely on their instincts. Most

CEOs rue their initial hesitancy, wishing they had acted more swiftly in rearranging the team at the top. Change in the senior team never seems to progress as fast as a CEO would like. As one CEO replied, "I wish I had moved faster to eliminate the dead wood among the executive ranks—those responsible for the previous poor results."[16]

If there is an optimal time during which to wield the hatchet, that time is during the First Hundred Days and perhaps a few months thereafter. Employee terminations are always difficult and heart-rending decisions. Making terminations promptly upon taking office, however, will minimize any demoralizing effect on the organization. Companies expect new leaders to bring in or surround themselves with their own people. To be replaced in the course of such a transition is far more acceptable than after time has passed when people are more likely to attribute termination to poor performance than to organic change. Prompt change upon taking office is the wise and humane thing to do. Indecision only makes matters worse.

When James "Jamie" Dimon became chairman and CEO of Bank One Corporation in March 2000, he immediately began cleaning house. Confident that his board supported him, Dimon was able to move fast. He was committed to making room for former colleagues from Citicorp and even found it necessary to terminate a 37-year Bank One veteran who had served as acting CEO before Dimon's appointment. Bringing in people whom the CEO knows, has confidence in, and can work with comfortably undoubtedly helps the first months pass more smoothly. These familiar faces know how the CEO makes decisions, what the CEO expects, and most important, what the CEO wants to achieve and how to achieve it.

The order in which CEOs hire or fire senior employees is not without significance. Timing can amount to a conspicuous signal, highlighting a particular aspect of the new CEO's philosophy. GE's Jeff Immelt's early selection of Yoshiaki Fujimori as the new chief of GE Plastics sent the signal that diversity would be a cornerstone of the new GE. Similarly, CEOs may use first appointments to emphasize other aspects of a program (e.g., accountability and merit-based promotions).

CEOs are particularly vulnerable to missteps and misperceptions until they solidify their top team. Most management scholars agree that a chief executive will not be able to function smoothly and effectively until the senior team is up and running and a consensus exists among team members to move in one direction.[17] When first coming into office, the last things a CEO wants to be concerned with are unspoken loyalties, hidden agendas, and silent enemies. No better way exists to eliminate such uncertainty than to bring in, as core members of the senior team, executives whose loyalty and abilities are known quantities.

Set Your Own Agenda

With so much to do, so much to change, and so much to learn, the CEO must focus on the forest and not get lost among the trees. CEOs should not allow daily demands to undermine their long-term goals and priorities. Tom Bell, former CEO of Young & Rubicam before WPP acquired the company, cautions chief executives not to be sidetracked by their job's immediate requirements. Instead, CEOs must focus on long-term goals and see the big picture rather than waste valuable time extinguishing localized fires.[18] A common complaint among new CEOs is that they all too quickly become overbooked with and overwhelmed by requests. New CEOs need to set their own agenda, prioritize their audiences, and learn as much as they can as soon as they can about the organization. If they don't and they act under pressure and in haste, they run the risk, which former presidential advisor Gergen warned against, of taking premature measures that all too frequently lead to serious missteps.

During the Countdown, the CEO needed to be patient, so as to take advantage of a rare opportunity for reflection and planning, free of scrutiny and day-to-day pressures. This time, however, patience is necessary precisely because the new CEO is subject to increasing daily demands. New CEOs must resist the urge to give in to these everyday demands and remember that CEOs answer to a higher authority, in particular the board of directors under whose gaze they take responsibility for the company's long-term welfare. The CEO must either delegate day-to-day problems to others or defer action on these matters in favor of concentrating on more far-reaching structural and strategic issues. These long-term issues will set the tone for the CEO's tenure.

Alan G. Lafley became president and CEO of The Procter & Gamble Company (P&G) on June 8, 2000. He assumed office after Durk I. Jager's brief 17-month reign. In his first interview with analysts, investors, and reporters, Lafley firmly stated that he intended to immerse himself in the company's business and stabilize the corporate ship. No less than six weeks of in-depth learning and analysis was necessary.[19] Lafley had kept his word. He resisted those who wished to write his agenda for him. He wrote his own and then followed it. Near the end of Lafley's second year, P&G's share price had risen. The board showed its confidence by giving him the additional title of chairman.

Tend to Your Board

We often act as if the CEO is the final authority on corporate matters. In many regards this is true, but as indicated previously, even the CEO must answer to a higher authority: the board of directors.

The board appointed the new chief executive for a purpose, and the CEO must respond to that mandate. Building relationships with each board member is therefore critical. The CEO's authority emanates from them. Without their support, the CEO is out of a job. As governance expert Ira M. Millstein advises: "There is nothing more important than getting to know the people who can fire you."[20] Accordingly, CEOs generally cite the board as their most critical constituency—the one constituency that must be appeased and without which achievement is impossible.

Michael Armstrong, chairman and CEO of AT&T, echoes this advice, noting that a CEO should as a practical matter not only talk up the wisdom of any particular policy, but also forewarn the board of any possible risks:

> *If you haven't educated that board and brought them along so that the risks as well as the things that aren't going to go well are in front of them and they are with you on those risks, obviously they are going to have a short trigger when [things] go wrong.*[21]

Thus, a crucial aspect of managing up, according to Armstrong, is educating the board. By keeping their boards aware of financial progress and considerations behind policies, CEOs justify certain risk-taking, thereby obtaining sufficient freedom of action to pursue their vision.

Nothing is wrong with making a CEO's relationship with the board upfront and personal. Some CEOs make a point to visit board members on their home turf, and some organize retreats that mix business and pleasure. CEOs often invite board members' spouses to these retreats so members may get to know one another in an informal setting. When chief executives and boards know each other well, the CEO becomes more attuned to the board's thinking and the board less likely to misunderstand the CEO.

Cementing a relationship with the board takes time. Miles White, CEO of Abbott Labs, espouses this long-term view: "The board has to get comfortable with your management and leadership of the company. I think a board that is doing its job properly must give a lot of oversight in the first two years to the new CEO. I don't think you just hand him the keys and say 'call us in June.'"[22] So the sooner the CEO begins establishing a working rapport, the better. Otherwise, the CEO may not have the opportunity to work further on cementing the relationship and building CEO capital, especially in times like these when boards are hardly shy about directing ineffective CEOs to the exit sign.

Declare What Matters

The new chief executive must come up with a few clear ideals or themes that guide the organization within the First Hundred Days. Foreshadowing a CEO's themes during the Countdown helps because it serves as a peg on which to hang the CEO-elect's hat, hinting at the future and assuring employees and others that the CEO-elect has matters well in hand. Yet mere suggestions during the Countdown of what the future holds typically are not enough once a CEO takes office. As Gergen indicated, it is important during the First Hundred Days to establish an executive's "thematic stamp." Suggestions may suffice during the Countdown, but a firm theme is required during the First Hundred Days. Detailing how one's theme is to be put into practice (i.e., promulgating an operational game plan) is not yet necessary. What is required is a definite, articulate expression of values so related as to compose a theme or themes. This thematic stamp sets before employees a roadmap of desirable actions and attitudes, conveying that the company is in good hands with a well-charted future course.

At his first town meeting with employees, Brian Kelley, former president of Ford's Lincoln Mercury division and now CEO of SIRVA, laid out his expectation that the company should put people first and seek ways to lessen bureaucracy or create less structure. As seen in Exhibit 5.3, Kelley itemized 13 factors in minute detail for all to see and hear. No mistaking it: Kelley had laid out a roadmap. The company would be moving forward with clarity.

A prime example of articulating ideals occurred when Lawrence A. Weinbach took office as Unisys Corporation's chairman, president, and CEO. After one month on the job, Weinbach met with his group of top 100 managers and laid down the law. Every manager, Weinbach included, was to be responsible for two customers.

EXHIBIT 5.3   *Brian Kelley Believes in . . .*

More . . .	*Less . . .*
People First	Organizational Structure
Proactive Empowerment	Waiting to be Empowered
Results	Visions
Personal Accountability	Assigned Accountability
Execution	Strategies
Proud Craftsmanship	A Job
Products	Concepts
Detail	Generalizations
Passion	Rationalization
Straight Talk with Respect	Polite Talk with Hidden Meaning
Real Teams	Corporate Teams
Show Me	Tell Me
The Answer is in the Market	. . . Not in Meetings

Town Hall Meeting, Irvine, California, January 7, 2002.

"It became very clear," Weinbach later observed, "that I had to change that culture and change it quickly."[23] This two-customer rule simply and efficiently communicated the company's need to become more customer oriented. As time went by, Unisys continued to build on its customer-centric theme until it became a well-recognized pillar of the company's culture.

Sears, Roebuck Chairman and CEO Alan J. Lacy provides another effective approach to declaring intentions and guiding employees. At Lacy's first presentation to his most senior executives, he outlined principles, itemized in Exhibit 5.4, that constituted his management philosophy. He also detailed the type of management style he thought appropriate for executives. Lacy offered this directive: Manage your time well, and if you are not sure if the CEO said something or not, just ask him!

Identify Short-Term Wins

In these early months, CEOs should, whenever possible, call attention to initial successes that align with and reinforce the CEO's first initiatives, such as a new marketing plan, an innovative customer solution, a sought-after hire, a boost in share price, or a significant new business win or product launch. Proclaiming early wins motivates employees and demonstrates that effective change is progressing according to plan. Early wins create momentum. Momentum, in turn, constitutes a call to action for believers in the CEO's program, while at the same time diminishing opposition and stonewalling. Moreover, documenting and lauding successes help establish the CEO's authority. Although the board may have given the new CEO the power to reign, the new CEO must earn employees' respect. Success does that. It legitimizes the board's choice of chief executive and solidifies the CEO's standing among peers and subordinates, thereby building CEO capital.

EXHIBIT 5.4   *What To Expect From Your New CEO, Alan Lacy, CEO of Sears, Roebuck and Co.*

AJL Management Philosophy

Build a Very Good Organization
Operate as a Team—Everyone Equal
Let Good People Do Their Jobs
Emphasize Getting Things Done and Done Well
Maintain a Brisk, But Sustainable Pace
Communicate More Rather Than Less—Builds Perspective, Alignment
Continuously Improve—People, Product, Process
Fact-Based Decisions
No BS Allowed
Note: Watch Out For "Alan Said . . ."

AJL Desired Personal Style

Always Have the Company's Best Interests at Heart
Take Ownership
Be Positive
Be Constructive
Be Resilient
Be Flexible
Be Approachable
   My Name is Alan
Anticipate
Work Hard, But Have Fun at It
Act as Coach
Note: Pet Peeve—Time Management

For this reason, Steve Jobs sought high and low for an early win to legitimize his return to Apple Computer and to confirm that he was the right chief to rejuvenate the company. After shuttering Apple's PC cloning business and discontinuing extraneous projects such as Newton, Jobs focused on the iMac, the company's best chance for survival. With iMac's success, Jobs had the proof he needed, a win to trumpet, proving to Apple's critics and employees that he and the company were back.

Weinbach of Unisys also made good use of short-term wins, or more accurately, the prospect of short-term wins, to communicate a theme of his management philosophy and to motivate. He addressed employees on day one and promised them that if they helped him achieve a positive financial turnaround within the first year of his tenure, he would reinstate certain benefits that had been cut during leaner times. Weinbach was true to his word, and after his employees met management goals, he reinstated the company's 401(k) matching program.[24]

Thus, the smart new CEO should be on the lookout for early achievements that can be celebrated and incorporated into the fabric of the company's culture. Publicly honoring and calling attention to significant milestones focus the organization on desired priorities. Chairman, President, and CEO Keith E. Bailey of The Williams Companies touted the company's success in increasing share price. When Tulsa-based Williams reached $50 per share, Bailey, like Weinbach at Unisys, coupled celebrating the win with a reward. Each employee received a $50 bill as a bonus. In this way, Bailey caused the entire company to focus on increasing share price. He solidified his standing among employees, reinforced good performance, and made abundantly clear that at least during this phase of his tenure (prior to the company's financial problems), his program led to success.

Identifying short-term wins that are consistent with management policies, especially if the win can be attributed to employee efforts, goes a long way in securing confidence in new management. Such successes are win–win situations for everybody, highly memorable and motivating, and indicative of progress toward a new future.

Communicate Personally; Use Symbolic Gestures

Once a CEO is on the job, communication within the organization is qualitatively different from internal communication during the Countdown. The major concern of the CEO-elect is to assure employees that the transition is progressing well, that the two-headed monster will not get out of control, and that continuity will be maintained. During the First Hundred Days, communication assumes additional functions. The CEO must now reach out to employees, attempting to establish a dialogue from which to learn as well as to project the new management philosophy. Perhaps most important, the CEO can use communication to motivate employees to buy into the new program.

For these reasons, new CEOs should do their best from day one to reach out to employees on as personal a level as possible. David S. Pottruck, co-CEO of Charles Schwab, says that without the sense that the CEO has a personal interest in them, employees cannot fully appreciate the intent and meaning behind management pronouncements, even messages left on voice mails or in electronic in-boxes. "The leader is the message,"[25] says Pottruck. This powerful concept should be taken to heart.

Traditional in-person presentations, for example, are a good way to introduce large numbers of employees to the CEO. Not all CEOs, however, are comfortable espousing from auditorium lecterns. David Pottruck, for example, discovered the perfect forum for his well-known co-CEO and founder, Charles Schwab:

> *We stumbled across this notion that I would interview Charles Schwab on stage where I would ask him questions. It wasn't a speech, it was an interview. And we actually stumbled upon this because when Chuck and I would give a speech, Chuck would give a very short speech and I would give this much longer speech. Then we would go to Town Hall to answer questions. Chuck*

was great at answering questions because that was Chuck. He would just blossom. In answering these questions, he would reveal his passion, his thinking and his perspective, and everybody loved that.[26]

If delivering formal, prepared speeches before large groups is not a CEO's forte, the CEO should insist on a more personal format, such as small groups with question-and-answer sessions. Although not all formal speeches can be avoided, CEOs can bypass many of them in favor of other more effective forums.

Another way to communicate broadly is through e-mail. Richard H. Brown joined EDS in early 1999 from Cable & Wireless and began sending e-mails to employees. Brown used e-mail to emphasize his management philosophy, adopting a personal style. One such personalized e-mail unequivocally pronounced that the ends would no longer justify the means:

Before closing, I have one more subject to share with you. Recently, we had a talented leader whose personal values represented a serious departure from our own code of conduct and, therefore, the values of this enterprise. Despite good performance, we asked this leader to resign. He did so. Requesting his resignation, while difficult, was the right thing to do. EDS has a long tradition of high values and is viewed publicly as a company with unquestioned integrity and character. Each of us has a responsibility to behave in a manner aligned to and consistent with the principles outlined in our code of business conduct. Good results can never be a substitute for ethical leadership. The code is the code. Read it, understand it and always conduct business by it.[27]

In this manner, the EDS CEO talked often about "intense candor" and "filterless" dialogue. What better way to communicate candidly than through an e-mail message, a personal form of communication, with each e-mail addressed "To the EDS Worldwide Team."

Because of advances in technology, other effective ways are also available to reach large groups of employees, while retaining a personal touch. Richard Wagoner, CEO of General Motors, uses quarterly telecasts accompanied by simultaneous e-mail translations and frequent teleconferences among his top managers worldwide.[28] Within days of his appointment as CEO of Accenture, Joe Forehand used a global satellite broadcast to 39 different locations to conduct question-and-answer sessions.

CEOs can also use symbolic gestures to communicate at a personal level. The poetry and power of symbols forge a firm understanding between leaders and those they lead. After just a few days at AT&T, Michael Armstrong toured the company's western facilities and learned that the company was having problems servicing customers. At one customer service center, he sat down at an operator's station, put on a headset, and fielded customer orders. The image of the CEO doing the work of a service operator spread throughout the company. This symbol conveyed to all that Armstrong would be an engaged CEO, that each employee, whether service operator or senior manager, made an important contribution to the company, and that, above all, customers mattered.

Symbolic acts are powerful signals. During the first days of their tenure, new CEOs must be careful—employees are likely to probe their every word and nuance for significance. Symbolic gestures, large and small, carry weight far greater than their face value during this period. Stakeholders too are more likely to notice and read meaning into them. Given the disproportionate impact of such symbolic acts, they can, when carefully crafted, be highly effective tools for reaching out to employees.

Following are examples of particularly effective symbolic acts taken during CEOs' First Hundred Days. Notice how the importance of each is immediately apparent, some when placed in context and others without any explanation at all:

- *Casual dress day.* One *Fortune* 500 CEO, wanting a more open and collaborative work environment, declared casual dress day on his first day in office.
- *No limousines for the boss.* Michael Armstrong of AT&T decided to eliminate chauffeur-driven cars for top executives.
- *No investment art.* Mark Willes, previously of *Times Mirror*, removed Picassos from the executive dining room, replacing them with *Times Mirror* photography.
- *Group athletic facilities.* Miles White, chairman and CEO of Abbott Laboratories, installed volleyball courts and soccer fields at the company's headquarters to encourage open interaction and communication among different divisions and staff levels.
- *No charts.* To underscore the elimination of bureaucracy, Louis Gerstner, Jr. of IBM banned organizational charts.[29]
- *Executive march.* To motivate and excite employees about the business transformation underway, David Pottruck, co-CEO of Charles Schwab, marched his senior managers, nearly 100 in all, across the Golden Gate Bridge wearing jackets labeled with "Crossing the Chasm."[30] The march symbolized how the company was going to collectively make the leap to integrating people and technology.
- *Meeting abroad.* Doug Daft, CEO of Coca-Cola, wanted to ensure that his managers think globally. He invited executives in offices worldwide to London to deliver their midyear reports. This was the first time that U.S. division heads had delivered such reports outside of the Atlanta headquarters.
- *One-on-one contact.* On his first day as CEO, Chris Komisarjevsky, president and CEO of Burson-Marsteller

Worldwide, went to the basement of worldwide headquarters in New York City, then shook the hands of each employee until he reached the executive floor—13 floors above.

- *Employee manual destroyed.* Gordon Bethune, CEO of Continental Airlines, burned the employee manual in the company parking lot.[31] The employee manual was symptomatic of all the rules and regulations that kept employees from servicing customers.

- *Doorless office.* Lord John Browne of BP took the door off his office. He replaced it with a sliding-glass panel.

Gather Ye Promises, a Prophylactic Measure

On day one, the CEO should mark down the 365th day on the calendar. As discussed more fully in Chapter 6, other influential constituencies will have this day staked out too and will be reviewing all prior promises to see which ones have been kept. It is far better to make a few promises that are kept than to make many that are not. During these First Hundred Days, any goals or timelines that have been articulated will be measured against performance during later stages.

If goals are set forth in the First Hundred Days, a new CEO should maintain an inventory of proof points or deliverables with respect to each. The CEO should designate a senior executive as keeper of this inventory. Having these proof points on hand for the media and other stakeholders will prove invaluable when the phone rings one year later with a reporter from *The Wall Street Journal* or *Business Week* on the line.

Touch Base with Select Stakeholders

After putting the corporate house in order, the CEO should attend to selected external stakeholders if time allows. During the Countdown, the CEO may have already established contact on an individual basis with various crucial stakeholders. This effort now needs to be extended to the vast array of stakeholders on a priority basis according to the CEO's constellation chart and the level of contact expanded and developed. Typically, the stakeholders of greatest concern at this stage are Wall Street, customers, and the media (as seen in Exhibit 5.2).

Wall Street.   After employees and senior teams, CEOs must next turn their focus to the financial community.

Engineering a strong relationship with the financial community at the earliest stage is critical. Both Burson-Marsteller's proprietary research and Cap Gemini Ernst & Young's Center for Business Innovation's research, *Measures that Matter*, confirm that analysts place great weight on how they perceive the quality of a company's management.[32] Setting the right tone and being personally acquainted with analysts at the outset are essential.

In those early conversations with key analysts and institutional investors, CEOs should feel free to acknowledge that problems exist in all companies, that time is of the essence, and that the first few months require burrowing deeply into the organization. As James B. Adamson, Kmart's new chairman, CEO, and turnaround expert stated on a conference call made the day former CEO Charles Conaway resigned: "It's going to take some time to analyze where the business is today. I hope we will have the strategy complete by end of this year. I want to make sure it's very thoughtful and that we have something that works."[33]

Customers.   Customers should be the CEO's next focus when building CEO capital and furthering the interests of the company. Obtaining introductions to and establishing personal contact with the company's best customers, as well as making personal visits to any dissatisfied ones, should be the next priority. Soon after taking office, Gordon Bethune, chairman and CEO of Continental Airlines, and Greg Brenneman, Continental's president and COO at the time, called each dissatisfied customer, apologized for problems, and promised to work on repairing strained relationships.[34] They also invited the airline's 60 best customers to Bethune's house for cocktails and again expressed regret for poor performance.[35] Richard H. Brown, upon becoming chairman and CEO at EDS, visited the CEO of Blue Cross & Blue Shield of Massachusetts. His visit was the first time in seven years that an EDS CEO had approached the company's most important customer.[36]

The Media.   Granting media interviews is low on the list of must-dos for new CEOs (see Exhibit 5.2). Perhaps it is even a must-not-do. Maintaining a low media profile at the start is generally good counsel. As presidential advisor Gergen noted in his study of presidential terms, chief executives must avoid grievous errors during the First Hundred Days. Media exposure without full opportunity to gain a thorough understanding of corporate workings is an invitation to disaster. Even if CEOs grant an interview, they should be selective about to whom they grant interviews and certainly be selective about what they say. In any event, media training for chief executives, if not obtained during the Countdown, should be obtained before any media exposure and repeated periodically throughout their tenures.

Thus David Cote, when he first became CEO of Honeywell International in 2002, turned down an interview with *The Wall Street Journal* "until he became more familiar with the company."[37] While some introductory calls to major media might be helpful for the media-savvy chief executive, particularly to the trade media or local media, other interviews should be granted only with planned intent, for strategic reasons and, if necessary, with guidance from corporate communications specialists. Exposure to the media should not be left to serendipity.

Sometimes a business matter becomes legitimate news and the media cannot be avoided. After announcing its merger, Daimler-Chrysler's co-CEOs gave their only joint U.S. interview in *Fortune*.[38] With that done and their public responsibilities accomplished, they then fervently returned to work, dealing with internal issues. Although the media should be approached carefully, the press can be a powerful ally if managed properly. Not only can media interviews send positive messages to targeted audiences such as customers, vendors, and the community, they can also serve as an effective communications channel to employees.

Robert A. Eckert, new chairman and CEO of Mattel, had his first comprehensive interview with *The Wall Street Journal* at the close of his First Hundred Days. He broadly outlined his intentions to focus on his company's core business, renegotiate expensive licensing deals, increase international sales, and return the company to a focus on profits—not volume. In keeping with these broadly defined goals, and aware of the need to gather ye promises, Eckert cautiously set a flexible timetable for accomplishing results.[39] His reluctance to provide hard facts may have disappointed the media and a few analysts, but a new CEO must walk a fine line between announcing expected growth rates and being able to deliver. Not until nine months later did Eckert state that sales would increase moderately and earnings per share would rise over the next three to five years to reach low double-digits to mid-teens.

New CEOs should look ahead to that day when they will be referred to as a straight-talker by the media, as was WPP Chief Executive, Sir Martin Sorrell.[40]

REFLECTIONS: CEOS UNDER THE MAGNIFYING GLASS

During the First Hundred Days, scrutiny of CEOs begins in earnest. The new CEO will still have an opportunity to adjust and will still have wiggle room when interacting with stakeholders. Stakeholders are generally aware that the CEO is new on the job and needs time to settle in. Even though CEOs will have time to finalize plans, they are still the subject of heightened scrutiny. Only the rare CEO would not feel pressured. This pressure is largely caused by the inability of stakeholders to separate CEOs per se from the companies they run.

This tendency to treat chief executives as the embodiment of the company's soul has been described as an attribute of that most derided of business personalities, the celebrity CEO, more fully discussed in Chapter 6. Castigation of the CEO as the embodiment of a company on these grounds is a bit unfair because CEOs become alter egos by dint of their leadership position, not celebrity status. CEOs are stand-ins for their companies because they are company leaders, whether they are big "C" Celebrity CEOs with their names in headlines, small "c" celebrated CEOs unknown to the general public, or even CEOs who have not yet made their mark. We need not enter the current celebrity CEO debate at this point and determine whether celebrity for CEOs is beneficial or detrimental to a company. We do need, however, to recognize that the propensity to treat the CEO as the embodiment of the company exists, has existed for some time, and will exist more or less in the foreseeable future.

Having said this, the fact remains that on a local, national, and even global basis, stakeholders over the last decade or more are paying more attention to the comings and goings of CEOs than ever before. This attention starts on day one, as soon as the CEO takes office, and is perhaps the single most significant life change thrust on an executive once becoming CEO and commencing the First Hundred Days. CEO coverage in the major U.S. national media has increased seven-fold (73 percent) over the last decade.[41] In Europe, coverage of CEOs over the past five years has soared a whopping 127 percent.[42] The inclination for the spotlight to focus on a single human being rather than on the large institution that the CEO runs promises to continue as time compresses the flow of information and the need-to-know accelerates. There are several key reasons for this situation, discussed as follows.

A New World Order

As national boundaries melt away with the advent of the Internet, and as the speed of communications quickens, a new world order has emerged. Once national governments were the supreme regulator of how companies bought and sold goods and services across borders. This control has weakened in the face of the ever more powerful multinational company. Whereas the old world order was populated by political leaders such as Ronald Reagan, Margaret Thatcher, Mikhael Gorbachev, Deng Xiaoping, Fidel Castro, and Nelson Mandela, the new world order is also inhabited by captains of industry such as Bill Gates (Microsoft), Jack Welch and now Jeff Immelt (General Electric), Scott McNealy (Sun Microsystems), John Chambers (Cisco Systems), Bill Ford (The Ford Motor Company), Richard Branson (Virgin Atlantic), Lord John Browne (BP), Jürgen Schremp (DaimlerChrysler), Phil Condit (Boeing), and Idei Nobuyuki (Sony). In fact, *AsiaWeek*'s 2000 list of the most powerful people in Asia-Pacific, the "Power 50," led off with a Hong Kong tycoon—Li Ka-shing, chairman of Cheung Kong Holdings—rather than the more traditional politician.[43] For nearly a decade, CEOs, as well as world leaders, have been capturing our imaginations and investment dollars. Incredibly, within four months after 9/11, headlines regarding Enron's former chairman Kenneth Lay and CEO Jeffrey Skilling shared headlines with Osama Bin Laden. As the post-Enron corporate crisis continues, headlines periodically appear with articles on the newest demonized CEOs such as John Rigas of Adelphia Communications,

Martha Stewart of Omnimedia, Gary Winnick of Global Crossing, and Bernie Ebbers of WorldCom.

CEO Betting

Betting on CEOs has become a national pastime as stock ownership continues to expand beyond sophisticated institutional investors to the general public. CEO-driven investing accelerated in recent years as more people played the stock market. Many Americans saw the booming economy in the late 1990s as their one-time opportunity to share in the wealth of the technology age. According to the 1998 Survey of Consumer Finances, nearly 49 percent of American households hold stock in publicly traded companies.[44] This trend will rise as the baby boomers begin to inherit from their parents an astonishing estimate of more than $41 trillion, now considerably diminished since the economic downturn starting in March 2000.[45] As baby boomers invest this mighty sum as part of their retirement planning, more people will want to be increasingly knowledgeable about chief executives and the companies they run.

In the late 1980s, the stock market evidenced no propensity to focus on new CEOs[46], but this is no longer the case. Even financial sages have joined the trend. Herb Allen, the well-known financier, knows about the CEO effect on investing: "For a long-term investor—the only kind of investing I do at Allen & Co.—the CEO is absolutely the key to the whole thing. He's much more important to me than the business itself."[47]

Moreover, the rise of one particular SuperCEO had an electrifying impact on both the small and institutional investor. The charismatic Jack Welch, former chairman and CEO of General Electric, heavily influenced the appeal of the "great man" theory of corporate success. His amazing 20-year run as CEO and the astounding wealth he brought shareholders exemplifies the extraordinary impact a single leader can have on a company's value. Holman W. Jenkins, Jr. emphasized how important chief executives are to investors when he summed up what he called "The Jack Welch Way" in *The Wall Street Journal*:

> *So much of the market value of any company depends on the market's confidence in the person running it—and "market" these days means a small number of fund managers who are able to assess top management face-to-face. These investors don't necessarily know much about a company's products and processes, but they can readily judge whether the people in charge are likely to recognize opportunity and move quickly to exploit it.*[48]

Investors are always on the lookout for the next Jack Welch. For a while, John Chambers of Cisco earned that title. Now every new CEO is a prospect.

CEO Churn

The ephemeral nature of many CEOs' tenures also piques public interest. The CEO chamber today has been a revolving door. Given the attention on CEOs nowadays, the departure of the prior CEO and the arrival of the new CEO is both a business story and a public interest story—a soap opera that is played out in a boardroom. This avalanche of coverage serves to excite not just business news junkies but the general public as well. Nine CEOs out of the nation's largest 200 public companies lost their jobs in the first quarter of 2001.[49] Even more sobering, outplacement experts Challenger, Gray & Christmas report that 63 CEOs left their jobs in June 2002.[50] More than half of all current CEOs have held their position for fewer than six years.[51] Not surprisingly, poor financial performance as a reason for CEO departure has increased by 130 percent between 1995 and 2001.[52]

The CEO turnover rate is unprecedented. Prematurely shortened tenures are far greater than they were in 1980.[53] In recent years, CEOs were ousted from the following well-known companies: Xerox, Maytag, Avon, Procter & Gamble, The Gillette Company, Bertelsmann, Swiss Life, ABB, Toys 'R' Us, UAL, Coca-Cola, Zurich Financial Services, Vivendi Universal, Campbell Soup, Newell Rubbermaid, Lucent Technologies, and Mattel. The tally is even worse among the dot coms. The average tenure for dot-com CEOs stands at 26 months.[54]

The recent retirement of many business greats adds yet another layer of interest to CEO personalities. At the start of the 21st century, several high-profile CEOs retired, such as Jack Welch of General Electric, Charles Knight of Emerson Electric, Herb Kelleher of Southwest Airlines, Larry Bossidy of Honeywell International, Lou Gerstner of IBM, Harvey Golub of American Express, Alan "Ace" Greenberg of Bear Stearns, and Hans Becherer of Deere. The media attention surrounding Jack Welch's retirement and the appointment of his successor was perhaps the decade's lead business story.

SuperCEOs

A new super class of executive heroes has emerged. Jack Welch won a $7.1 million advance from Time Warner to publish his memoirs, a sum far greater than that awarded to Ronald Reagan, Colin Powell, and Pope John II. A survey conducted among Japanese women named Carlos Ghosn, CEO of Nissan, one of the men they would most want to father their children. Furthermore, according to survey research performed by Roper Starch Worldwide and *Fast Company*, college graduates reported that if they had to choose whom to sit next to on a cross-country flight, Bill Gates of Microsoft would triumph over Oprah Winfrey, the popular talk-show host. Equally amazing, even the inconsistently praised

Michael Eisner, chairman and CEO of The Walt Disney Company, easily prevailed over actor Bruce Willis.[55] Business even trumps Hollywood.

Bill Gates is another CEO who contributed disproportionately to the cult of the SuperCEO. Both his youth and nerdiness captured the imagination of the American people. His rise from Harvard dropout to software billionaire is legendary. Gates's meteoric rise to icon status was not, however, accidental. Although his recent antitrust troubles may have tarnished his image somewhat, from the start Gates was a brilliant promoter. David Kirkpatrick, a Board of Editors member at *Fortune*, finds that Gates's marketing skills outweighed even his technological skills:

> *[Microsoft is] a brilliant blend. It's as much a great marketing company as a great technology company. They've been very savvy in doling out Bill Gates's cooperation and presence to get cover stories at strategic moments for their marketing purposes. They have brilliantly used Gates as . . . the embodiment of Microsoft's marketing message.*[56]

Gates intuitively understood how to build a brand name. As evidence of his willingness to buff his image, daily press inquiries about Microsoft in 1993 and 1994 hit a whopping 1,200.[57]

Another factor influencing the SuperCEO trend is that many well-known companies have sprouted from charismatic founding entrepreneurs. To be a founder is part of the American Dream, part of the Horatio Algier attitude that with a bit of effort and a touch of will, you can accomplish anything in America. In recent years, of course, the opportunities to found a company were greater than ever, if only because of technological change, the rise of the computer, the hyper-capital markets, and the constant search for the next best thing. For this reason alone, the following modern folkloric champions of commerce are now forever fixed in our minds as synonymous with their companies: Bill Gates (Microsoft), Michael Dell (Dell Computer), Steve Jobs (Apple Computer), Larry Ellison (Oracle), Scott McNealy (Sun Microsystems), Steve Case (AOL), and Jerry Yang and David Filo (Yahoo!).

Unlike the magnates of the Industrial Revolution, these CEOs approached their public roles in a way that was not true even 10 years ago. They are more willing to market themselves. They might not be as gung-ho as Tom Peters counsels in his book, *Reinventing Work: The Brand You 50*[58]—"think of yourself as a package"— but they accept the need for visibility and public positioning. Until 1990, CEOs had their public relations staff issue press releases if they had something to say. In the early 20th century, Henry Ford succinctly summarized his view of publicity: "I am going to see that no man comes to know me."[59] In the 21st century, however, CEOs invite the public to know them or at least to know their carefully crafted images.

Different cultures react differently to SuperCEOs. In some cultures, such as the Netherlands and Australia, the public looks down on high achievers, criticizing them for having "tall poppy syndrome." The phrase refers to the tall poppies that absorb all the sun's rays to the exclusion of the needs of shorter poppies attempting to grow in their shadows.[60] The CEOs of several of the largest European companies, which struggled to penetrate the U.S. market, intentionally donned a U.S.–style image—overtly ambitious, media-savvy, and shareholder-driven—but at the same time opened themselves up to tall poppy criticism. One such criticized and now jobless CEO is Jean-Marie Messier, chairman of Vivendi Universal SA, who moved to New York from Paris to penetrate the U.S. market and became the target of jokes and anger among his fellow Frenchmen.[61] Messier clearly overdid the advice of Robert L. Crandall, the legendary and larger-than-life chairman, president, and CEO of American Airlines, who said of his public role:

"We were trying to transform the public image of American. A successful public position is in effect the equivalent of an advertising campaign."[62]

Media Obsession

We have come a long way from 1980 when there were only a few thousand business journalists; now there are more than 12,000.[63] In earlier days, CEOs were featured on page one or the evening news only when caught in some scandalous situation or after having suddenly died. Now activities in the regular course of business—not just mergers and acquisitions, but also new product launches and, of course, CEO successions—are as likely to get a CEO front-page billing as scandal, shame, and stigma.

A select few publications have always devoted pages to the captains of industry. *Fortune, Forbes,* and *Business Week* have been covering industry titans since commencing publication in the first part of the twentieth century. These magazines are now joined by other business chroniclers who report business news as it happens and who are not bound by weekly or biweekly deadlines (e.g., CNBC's Squawk Box, Bloomberg, Salon.com, and CNNMoney). The competition among these rival sources is fierce, and nothing sells better or more successfully scoops a competitor than reeling in the most sought-after story moments after events unfold, particularly if centered on a CEO who has some explaining to do.

Also helping to fuel this media mania was the overwhelming number of mergers and acquisitions that preceded the onset of the millennium. Corporate coupling was too titillating to ignore—the none-too-discreet romancing among commercial titans and multinationals occupied the front pages of newspapers, 24-hour news outlets, and Internet chat rooms. Attention paid to the CEO of each of the merging partners was unprecedented, almost as if each were jousting medieval champions, with the victor to earn the hand of the fair maiden of commerce bedecked with gauzelike streamers of blue-chip chiffon. The media dissected and inspected every detail of each CEO's leadership style and personality. We learned about their childhoods, their mothers' early tutelage, their first paper routes, their coaches, their first careers, marriages, and divorces.

Not atypical, for example, was the evident giddiness of Sandy Weill of Travelers and John Reed of Citicorp in photo after photo as they merged forces. A similarly big news item was Steve Case of AOL and Gerald Levin of Time Warner as they surprised everyone one Monday morning with their startling union of new and old economies. On a somewhat less blockbuster but nevertheless news-worthy level was the prenuptial disagreements and ultimate sepa-ration in 1998 of the planned marriage of Jan Leschly's Smithkline Beecham and Sir Richard Sykes's Glaxo-Wellcome. The unsuc-cessful merger seemed to be attributed not to a failure of business economics but to irreconcilable differences between CEOs. Head-lines and more headlines. All of this attention deifying leaders, placing them on pedestals, raising them to mythic status. Some ris-ing to great heights, others falling to great depths.

The ups and downs of CEOs continue to fascinate. The constant churning of chief executives adds sugar and spice to the daily ho-hum of business plans, pricing wars, commodization, and stock market gyrations. Timothy Koogle's resignation as CEO from Yahoo!, Jill Barad's ouster from Mattel, and Eckard Pfeiffer's dis-missal from Compaq were psychoanalyzed to death. More than 160 articles were devoted to Barad's long-overdue firing in the six months after her January 2000 ouster. The short tenures of Xerox's Richard Thoman, Procter & Gamble's Durk Jager, and Coca-Cola's Doug Ivester amounted in their own right to a dra-matic miniseries. Even Al Dunlap's teary fall from grace generated such big news that his story landed on the cover of *Business Week*. The article, based on a book by accomplished management writer John Byrne, was as good as any John Grisham thriller, with its bloodless stabs in the back and tales of betrayal.[64] Tyco's ex-CEO Dennis Kozlowki's spending spree, including a $6,000 shower curtain, made the front page of *The Wall Street Journal*.[65] Without a doubt, the CEO soaps will continue to transfix as fascination spreads for all things business. Such executive suite parables focus our attention on CEOs, whether we care or not, whether CEO deification (and demonization for that matter) is in the best interest of companies or not.

———————

If by the end of the First Hundred Days, the new CEO has focused on employees, set the agenda, begun building the team, catered to the board, identified short-term victories, communicated well, and declared what mattered most, things are off to a good start in building CEO capital. The job is probably harder than it seemed at first. The demands to be on all the time, combined with continuous scrutiny, never subside or diminish, and only intensify over the next 265 days. With a magnifying glass focused on their daily deeds, balance sheets, and share price, these men and women will need a healthy dose of confidence, stamina, and humanity to persevere in the months and years ahead.

CHAPTER 6

THE FIRST YEAR: FROM PUPIL TO CEO PERSONA

There was certainly a lot more to do than I envisioned. Every time you squeeze one side, something else popped up.[1]

> —Douglas N. Daft, chairman and CEO of Coca-Cola, commenting on his first year

I've got to immerse myself in this company. I want to see as much, hear as much, and feel as much as I can in the context of the ongoing business of this company.[2]

> —Remarks by Louis V. Gerstner, chairman and CEO of IBM Corporation, in his first year

To continue the marriage metaphor, if the Countdown is the engagement leading up to the wedding and if the First Hundred Days is the honeymoon, then the First Year should parallel the first year of marriage. And so it does—during the First Year, the CEO and the company behave like newlyweds after the glow of the honeymoon has worn off. A little less romantic, a bit more down to earth, and with in-laws to impress, CEOs at this stage still feel full of optimism for the future. Notwithstanding many fervent hopes and numerous sanguine expectations, reality lays before them. The time of truth has come. It is time to make the marriage work, to be fruitful and multiply, and to be successful. It is time for the CEO and the company to get down to the serious business of doing business and to demonstrate that the vows made to the board will be kept.

Although the stakes are now higher, CEOs do not necessarily have to obtain immediate results, although the time will soon come for that. The CEO and company are still newlyweds after all, and at least during the first year of life together, provided there is no catastrophe, stakeholders will be forgiving. Some CEO decisions may generate comments—even raise a few eyebrows—but by and large stakeholders will defer any seriously adverse judgments a while longer. As seen in Exhibit 6.1, a mere 10 percent of executives feel comfortable judging a CEO's effectiveness during the early months on the job.

An overwhelming 64 percent, however, say that they postpone evaluating CEOs until after the first year in office. Thus as discussed in Chapter 7, performance assessments become firmly entrenched only after the first anniversary. For now, life for our corporate couple, though tempered by the need to make a living, is still good, relatively free-wheeling, and filled with youthful exuberance and a hopeful future.

If during the First Year the CEO has been successful, the CEO will have built a storehouse of credibility—one of the most critical CM factors—and accrued substantial CEO capital. The CEO's reputation should buy confidence among employees and stakeholders, who by the end of the first year should view the CEO as a model for desirable traits, values, and appropriately industrious behavior. Usually such a fully developed reputation, what I call the *persona* of a CEO, is primarily an in-house affair. When success-

EXHIBIT 6.1   *When Can You Realistically Judge the Effectiveness of a New CEO?*

Within the first month	—%
In 2–3 months	3
In 4–6 months	7
In 7–11 months	14
In 1–2 years	64
3 years or more	10
Don't know	2

Source: Burson–Marsteller Executive Omnibus, Wirthlin Worldwide, April 1999.

fully developed, such persona is that of a celebrity CEO, with a lowercase "c," where celebrity is earned among employees and other business influentials who are closely related to the company rather than one that is promulgated publicly.

The notion of an uppercase "C" Celebrity CEO rarely passes muster with board members, employees, and most of all, CEOs themselves. Although an uppercase "C" Celebrity CEO may on occasion be appropriate, it is rarely sustainable in the absence of having first developed a firm foundation of lowercase "c" celebrity status. Meaningful CEO capital is built on performance, not fans. More is said on this later.

Exhibit 6.2 provides a snapshot of the best practices to come and explains the way in which each CM factor falls into place in this stage of CEO capital building.

BEST PRACTICES: THE FIRST YEAR

The wise CEO's approach toward the First Year, or more accurately the remainder of the First Year following expiration of the

EXHIBIT 6.2 *CM Factor Analysis: The First Year*

Action			RESULTS		
	Credibility	Conduct	Communication	Motivation	Mgmt.
Engage in Intense Learning					
Learn from customers, analysts, alumni, employees.	X	X	X		
Benchmark through research.	X				X
Cultivate a CEO Persona					
Be introspective, cultivate a folklore.					
Be a narrator CEO, use language of leadership. Make sure you are heard.	X	X	X	X	X
Organize and Plan					
Find your number two.					X
Choose your operational tenet.		X	X		
Articulate/embody ethical conduct.	X	X	X		X
Beware the close of the first year.	X				

110

Credibility: The CEO should dedicate the next 265 days to filling in the gaps by becoming immersed in the business. Making good use of competitive benchmarks will put the CEO in touch with the company's reality and help solidify the mission of the senior team. The effective CEO focuses internally, articulates the character of the company, and embodies its values and soul. The company will expect evidence that financial targets are being met. Surprises or uncertainty will damage credibility.

Conduct: "Walking the talk" and "talking the walk" is critical. The CEO must make ethical leadership visible, not only by verbalizing messages, but also by modeling appropriate ethical behavior.

Communicating internally and motivating employees: A positive CEO persona is built through two-way communications with stakeholders, narrative lessons, and emotional engagement. CEO persona that stands for something unique and deeply resonates throughout the organization will energize and bind employees. CEOs should create a specific and practical operating tenet that draws attention and makes clear how the company will succeed.

Building a management team: In year one, the senior team needs to be in place to meet the company's challenges. Cultivating a CEO persona by putting the company first will serve as a center of gravity for the senior team.

111

First Hundred Days, is three-pronged. First, the CEO who has used the prior stage(s) effectively should by now be more than familiar with the company's workings and at the very least realize what he or she does not know. The CEO should dedicate the remaining 265 days to filling in any remaining gaps in order to attain, by the end of the first year, a comprehensive practical and analytical understanding of the company. Harvard Business School Professor John Gabarro, who is cited in the Preface, refers to such a need for intense learning, as do Columbia University Professors Donald C. Hambrick and Gregory D. S. Fukutori, who refer to this period as the experimentation stage.[3]

Crucial to this learning process is putting aside preconceived notions, remaining open-minded, and listening to what others have to say, no matter how unpleasant. Establishing contacts within the organization who can provide information can also promote other worthwhile goals (e.g., identifying and motivating quality employees and winning over stakeholders). Still, the CEO should not be distracted from the prime directive—immersing oneself in the business so thoroughly and developing such an instinctive feel for the company that the CEO, so to speak, becomes one with the company. In turn, the CEO and company become, to the extent possible, alter egos of each other.

In addition, the CEO must establish a unique corporate persona in which the CEO's every action and deed reflects in some way the corporate values the CEO wishes to advance and the vision the CEO wishes to instill. This may be easier said than done. It also may require deep introspection and perhaps even adopting an increased sensitivity to the personal attributes and needs of employees and others. Granted, sensitivity is not commonly associated with the hard-driving, competitive personalities that typify many CEOs. CEOs, however, must develop personas uniquely balanced to take into account not only CEOs' personalities but also the companies' needs and well-being.

Finally, the First Year is by its nature the last opportunity to retain flexibility. By the end of the First Year, the CEO must commit to a plan of action. Accordingly, as part of the CEO's three-prong approach, the CEO should take advantage of stakeholders' continuing tolerance for change to select a second-in-command who can assume some of the burden and fine-tune plans further. In anticipation of the inevitable performance evaluations to come, the CEO must push hard to produce at least a few concrete results, some evidence demonstrating that the CEO's plan of action over the past year (and if there was a Countdown, even longer) will eventually bear fruit.

Engage in Intense Learning

Learning from Customers.   Michael Dell knows how to listen to customers. Every week, Dell's senior management team listens to taped recordings of customer telephone calls. Included in the listening mix are both satisfied and dissatisfied customers—the ultimate arbiters of a company's success. Dell's intent is to make attending to customer wants and needs an ingrained habit, business as usual.

After several months on the job as CEO, Larry Bossidy, former chairman and CEO of Allied Signal and Honeywell International, realized that something was seriously amiss. Not a single salesperson had sought his assistance in establishing or maintaining customer relationships. When Bossidy had worked at GE, customer contact was part and parcel of daily business activities:

> *In my former incarnation at GE, I spoke frequently at customer meetings of one sort or another. Why? Because customers have events and they need speakers and no*

one wants to speak. I raised my hand. Why? Because I'm Mario Cuomo? No. Because it gives me two hours to spend with a customer's organization. That's a chance of a lifetime.[4]

GE executives sought out every opportunity to have contact with customers, and as Bossidy points out, that is not an opportunity to be missed.

CEOs can tap into customers' psyches by stepping into their customers' shoes, a form of enforced empathy. David Sable, president and CEO of Wunderman New York, the world's largest integrated marketing solutions company, spends one day a month visiting the malls in different regions of the country.[5] He talks to clerks, cashiers, and managers about how products are selling, how consumers are feeling, and which items are hot. Sable learned his customer-focused approach early on as a young manager when his CEO would require that each new manager spend a day working at a customer's outlet. One year, for example, the CEO and Sable made a point to visit Kinney Shoes outlets in Los Angeles. They traveled back and forth between Anglo and Latino neighborhoods to identify and compare which shoe styles were popular in which neighborhood. At Wunderman, Sable lives the company's vision: "The customer, not the product, is our hero."

Learning from Analysts.   Now that the CEO is well settled in the saddle, contacts with Wall Street assume added importance. When the third and fourth quarter under the CEO's watch arrive, analysts will look to the CEO for an articulation of goals, target dates, and a strategic vision. Meeting with these analysts can be extremely helpful, albeit tricky. Before meeting with them, CEOs would be wise to arrange in-depth interviews ("soft soundings") with outside independent researchers to obtain insights into what Wall Street expects of the company and how it envisions the company's standing in its industry. From listening to and surveying analysts, the CEO can learn much about Wall Street's expectations and be prepared for the first several meetings. What do analysts view as industrywide problems? How does the company stack up against its competitors? What past problems need addressing? What is their current diagnosis of the company? Is the company answering Wall Street inquiries promptly and clearly? Is the company disclosing enough?

But beware: The CEO should not earn favor at the cost of setting overly precise targets and goals—details that the analysts inevitably try to elicit. The CEO will want some ambiguity and leeway. Once targets and goals are set, failure to meet them can devastate share price. All too often a successful year, even a very successful year, is viewed as a failure if the company does not meet stated goals. Rather than be trapped by fixed projections, the CEO must keep goals realistic to demonstrate credibility and control. It's better to underpromise and overdeliver than to overpromise and underdeliver.

One additional caution: The CEO should not attempt to wing it. Although CEOs in their first year are given substantial leeway as they adapt to their responsibilities, Wall Street nevertheless expects to hear thoughtful commentary from the CEO as well as the CFO. As one analyst said in a proprietary in-depth interview conducted at Burson-Marsteller regarding a CEO in the utilities industry, "If you're making a decision to invest, you know, a couple hundred million dollars, you'd usually like to hear from the top guy."[6] In the post-Enron era and in light of corporate accounting scandals, CEOs should expect even greater demands for disclosure and accountability. Accordingly, new CEOs must demonstrate that they have done their homework and show reasonable familiarity with the challenges facing their companies and their industries. Make no mistake about it, analysts will hold the CEO accountable. After all, one of the top indices, analysts say according to Burson-Marsteller's research, is the quality of top management.

When encountering financial audiences, CEOs should be realistic. In his first analyst discussion five months after being installed, Gillette's new CEO, James M. Kilts, made no specific predictions about earnings and revenue growth targets. In no uncertain terms, he insisted that his first year would be a transition year and that he could not, would not, provide a date by which the turnaround would occur. Kilts did, however, discuss his plans for cost cutting, increased advertising, and product reevaluation. Although analysts expressed disappointment—set targets and time frames are far easier to analyze—Kilts refused to succumb to the pressure, indicating that providing targets and deadlines created a "circle of doom" with which prior executives surrounded themselves, a practice that he did not want to repeat.[7]

By trimming expectations, CEOs give themselves breathing room. Overpromising and underdelivering will not go unnoticed. In his early tenure, CEO Peter Dolan of Bristol-Myers Squibb predicted that sales and earnings would double in five years.[8] He grew to regret his bold forecast one year later after a series of missteps and inventory problems apparently raised concern among directors.

Learning from Alumni—Former Employees, Former Executives. CEOs and senior management often overlook the wealth of information and talent to be found in former employees, in particular former executives and managers. Other than occasional glances at the visages of the company's founders or former company CEOs as they have been enshrined in oil paintings displayed on boardroom walls, rarely do thoughts of former executives and other managers intrude on the present. These images from the past, however, are not always mere reflections of some distant kin that is a part of history. Many former executives are alive, vital, and still engaged in thinking about the company's success. If only asked, they would have much to say about the company's future. They are an influential constituency whose support and institutional knowledge can be invaluable.

Miles White of Abbott Laboratories recognized the importance of these employees emeriti early on: "I think you have to pay attention to your retirees too because if they have built their wealth with the company stock, they are engaged shareholders. They tend to be vocal and carry an emotional edge because they helped build the company early on."[9] White notes that retirees are the first to get the message out if they do not like something. According to White, former executives should be regarded as company ambassadors with whom the company should maintain ties. "Our retirees have meetings around the nation, and we will send some of our top executives to speak at these meetings. We also e-mail retirees . . . we have a retiree newsletter and Web site."[10]

Learning from Prospective and Current Employees.   Until the end of the 1990s, when the war for talent became particularly heated, many companies failed to recognize the information inventory that stands ready to be elicited from prospective employees. In the first year of Bill Ford's tenure as chairman, the Ford Motor Company held a conference for MBAs only. Although these introductory meetings and other more overt job-fair events served a recruiting function, they also may help the company as a source of feedback. Prospective employees, typically young, represent the wave of the future, with new ideas and an instinctive awareness of current trends. As business school graduates, they are familiar with business needs and, even if inexperienced, are far from being commercially naïve. From these individuals, who are independent third parties with something worthwhile to say, a CEO can obtain considerable objective, fresh viewpoints about the state of the company, unfiltered and direct. Presumably cognizant of the insights gained from these meetings, as well as desirous of stepping up its recruiting efforts, Ford Motor has since extended these conferences to include college graduates.

Listening to and learning from employees one-on-one, an activity encouraged during previous stages of building CEO capital, should continue and, if not yet institutionalized, should at least be reduced to routine. Both systematic and spontaneous contact with employees should continue regularly not only to motivate and gather information, but also to prevent the ivory tower walls that surround most executive offices from rising too high. CEOs should schedule time each week to walk the halls as well as plan customer visits, make quarterly analyst calls, and attend town hall and division meetings. One CEO of a major high-technology company purposely leaves Tuesday mornings open to walk the halls and visit people in their offices. Phil Condit, chairman and CEO of The Boeing Company, similarly seeks access to his 198,000 employees by regularly walking through production lines. As Condit points out, direct employee contact can be eye opening:

> *I was up on the 747 production line walking through one section after another. I called out to the mechanic, "How's it going?" and he said, "Great, super." I then asked, "What's happening?" and he said, "Do you really want to know?" I replied, "Yep." He explained to me that no two airplanes were ever the same. The mechanic described how hard it is trying to assemble airplanes when each one is different. That short encounter affected our strategy on how we approach design. Now every airplane is identical. This has become part of our transformation. So . . . that mechanic had a real impact on where we are going. As CEO, you try to listen as carefully as you can.[11]*

Condit's encounter with the 747 mechanic lingers in his mind to this day.

Another technique for listening is to conduct annual employee surveys that are completed anonymously. An equally important source of feedback is exit interviews. One CEO, for example, noticed after reviewing such interviews that more women than men, with at least three years or more experience, were leaving the company. To determine if this highly troublesome talent drain revealed a problem that needed addressing, the CEO, working with the vice president of human resources, hired a well-known nonprofit research organization that concentrated on women in the workplace to explore this discrepancy. This independent organization contacted and interviewed a select sample of former female employees. The investigation revealed that working mothers and women planning families complained of long hours and inflexible work schedules. The company's ability to retain skilled, trained women increased two-fold once the CEO had identified that the problem existed and then had it remedied.

Learning through Research and Benchmarking. One *Forbes* 500 CEO offered this advice to new CEOs: "The first priority is to get in touch with the company's reality."[12] In year one, determining the company's standing in the industry and among stakeholders is important work.

Undertaking research to measure how key stakeholders (i.e., employees, customers, prospects, vendors, suppliers, partners, unions, local community groups, and even special interest groups) perceive the company and its strength and weaknesses vis-à-vis competitors is critical. Anecdotes will not do. Well-designed research, independently performed and statistically based, is essential. Once a CEO understands the company's relationship with stakeholders and has a feel for the company's standing within the industry, the CEO should marshal the senior team to study industry leaders. The study should include competitors within a company's industry and top and up-and-coming companies outside its industry. For example, how did a company outdistance itself from competitors? How did a company break out of its industry and emerge a world leader? How did Starbucks do it? How did Continental Airlines do it? How did Charles Schwab do it? How did Pfizer do it? These companies differ from each other and have different lessons to teach. Each has a CEO who has listened acutely to customers, understood the need for differentiation, and energized the workforce.

Typically, companies often have considerable, if not vast, quantities of information about how the company stands among its competitors. Companies, however, do not usually compile this information in a usable and accessible form. Reams of this data—a source of considerable intellectual wealth—are inevitably dispersed in truncated form across various divisions and regions. Marketing knows what customers think. Investor relations knows what financial analysts and institutional investors think. Human resources knows what employees think. Public relations knows what the media thinks. Public affairs knows what community leaders, legislators, and regulators think. Moreover, because business units usually conduct their research at different times of the year and ask different questions, drawing conclusions from such disparate materials is not easy. The CEO must seek to systematize and make all this data uniform and from it, generate a comprehensive analysis that is meaningful to not only one division but to the entire company. The sooner this task is accomplished, the better.

Reputation research such as *Fortune*'s Most Admired Companies[13] and the Reputation Institute's Reputation Quotient[14] may also be highly valuable. This primary research provides an independent picture of the competitive landscape along with a means to confirm, reject, or add to the company's internally generated sense of its image and industry standing.

Cultivate a CEO Persona

Be Introspective and Attuned to Others.   The unexpected and unimaginable days following September 11 elicited from CEOs a level of caring and sensitivity toward their employees that the public rarely observed with CEOs. The horrific event tapped a well of emotion and feeling to which CEOs never knew they had access. That such sensitivity constituted a model of human behavior well worth repeating was also not lost on the nation's chief executives. You didn't have to be based in New York City or Washington D.C., and you didn't have to be Howard Lutnick of Cantor Fitzgerald or Kenneth Chenault of American Express to realize that caring for and being emotionally involved with your employees was good business, personally and socially rewarding, and internally reassuring.

During the aftermath of the attack, CEOs became kinder and gentler for all to see. It is unfortunate, of course, that an event such as September 11 was required to elicit such a depth of emotional leadership. Yet the corporate response to September 11 did have the positive result of showing us CEOs being at their sensitive best, exhibiting a kind of emotional leadership with obvious applicability to other duties.

This type of leadership is known as "emotional intelligence." According to the esteemed Daniel Goleman's 1998 theory, emotional intelligence consists of self-awareness, self-regulation, motivation, empathy, and social skills, all of which revolve around a leader's ability to relate to others.[15] Mastering these five elements, switching seamlessly from one to the other when required, is one way to lead successfully. As Goleman points out, a CEO's emotional style is contagious, creating a chain reaction of improving interpersonal relationships throughout an organization. This progression of improving interactions energizes the company, which in turn, according to Goleman, improves employee performance, company efficiency, and financial results.[16] The key to becoming emotionally intelligent, states Goleman, is to be in touch with one's own motivations and psyche.

This is not to say that a CEO cannot lead successfully without emotional intelligence. Attila the Hun or Genghis Kahn were, as far as history reveals, successful leaders in that they accomplished much, even though no one would ever suggest that either was of a sensitive sort. The modern equivalent, say "Chainsaw" Al Dunlap, also had his successes at Scott Paper, despite being known as ruthless and unfeeling. Be that as it may, an awareness of and sensitivity to interpersonal relationships, even if not a requirement of effective leadership, undoubtedly can be a helpful trait for dealing with, organizing, and motivating people. Becoming more of a people-focused person, in short, won't hurt and is apt to make a highly positive contribution to an organization.

Not all CEOs are imbued with emotional intelligence, and some come to it the hard way. In 1992, Mort Meyerson took on the job of CEO of Perot Systems after seven successful years at EDS. He quickly came to realize that his leadership style had to be redefined. "What I realized after I left [EDS] was that I had also made a lot of people very unhappy. . . . The emphasis on profit-and-loss to the exclusion of other values was creating a culture of destructive contention."[17] Meyerson reinvented his notions of leadership: "When I returned to Perot Systems, my first job as a leader was to create a new understanding of myself."[18] He wrestled with not having to know everything, not having to control all customer contacts, and not having to make all decisions. Meyerson's newfound definition of leadership emphasized shared leadership and eliciting the abilities and talents of employees. He came to see himself less as a leader from whom all authority emanates and more as a coach who brings out the best in others.

David S. Pottruck, president and co-chief executive of Charles Schwab, wrote about his conversion to the softer side in his book with Terry Pearce, *Clicks and Mortar*.[19] Initially, Pottruck's leadership style was akin to that of a bulldozer. A former linebacker and heavyweight wrestler at the University of Pennsylvania, Pottruck's general approach when something needed to be done was to steamroll through. But then a sudden epiphany, similar to the one that occurred to Meyerson, caused him to consider whether he would be more effective if he changed. This he did, intentionally and systematically. After substantial soul searching, including experimenting with therapy and professional coaching, he replaced his hard-edged approach with an emotionally more intelligent one.

One of my CEO interviews was with David Pottruck. My experience that day demonstrates how incredibly effective his emotionally intelligent, softer approach can be. Notwithstanding my heavy preinterview preparation, I was taken aback almost immediately upon entering his office. After getting up from behind his desk, Pottruck directed me toward a small round table where, in this less intimidating setting, we began our interview. He spoke from the heart about many things—from being named president after the sudden heart attack of his predecessor, his partnership with his colleagues, the differing roles that he and Charles Schwab play, the role of leadership in a downturn economy, the company's vision and values, the diverse requirements of the CEO job, the advent of high-speed electronic communications, and his advice for new CEOs.

What he had to say was certainly substantial and informative, yet the impact of his comments seemed to transcend their content. Upon reflection, I realized that Pottruck had used the word *passion* nearly a dozen times. Perhaps even more important, his tone had been so reverential and respectful, his comments so deeply felt, that I could not dismiss from my thoughts the sounds and images of our meeting.

Pottruck's emotional intelligence is evident immediately—his manner and voice respectful and refined. His deeply felt bond with the company manifests itself in his frequent use of the word *we*. His remarks are effective almost irrespective of content simply because his manner and persona move those around him.

Cultivate a Personal Folklore.   Jeffrey Sonnenfeld, a long-time CEO scholar and author of *The Hero's Farewell*, realized that employees often view the CEO as a company folk hero because "he is capable of creating or transforming the firm's strategic purpose while shaping the culture of the membership."[20] The CEO as folk hero puts his or her reputation at risk and uses that reputation to build CEO capital for the glory of the company and its share price. The wise CEO must therefore always remain aware of how his or her particular folklore evolves and is perceived.

E-mails and corporate Internet chatrooms permeate the workplace. The CEO is inevitably a central topic in this in-house gossip. It need not be sophisticated talk. Where the CEO is, to whom the CEO spoke or did not speak, what the CEO did, and so on. Being the center of such communal chatter seems almost a natural offshoot of being the person in charge. The fuss in New York City, for example, about the weekend retreats of newly elected Mayor Bloomberg is just that type of buzz. It also adds an element of mystery and intrigue to his mayoralty: Billionaire mayor and man about town eschews business life for public service while using his previously amassed wealth, including private jets and helicopters, to elude media in pursuit of private life.

CEO legends grow exponentially as people attempt to read the tea leaves and then pass on their analysis of CEO attributes for others to discuss. When CEOs fail to offer up insights into their character or background and do not provide enough tidbits to feed the grapevine, they miss an important opportunity—using the CEO story to motivate and inspire. Politicians have known this since time immemorial. For instance, Lincoln's log cabin and Washington's cherry tree are folklore tales by which politicians conveyed selected positive aspects of each president's persona. As a result, CEOs should not overlook the office gossip, the company tattle, and the employee chatrooms. Far better to monitor folklore much like that of Lincoln and Washington. This lore can serve to enhance a CEO's persona, which if properly handled will be consistent with and reinforce the CEO's themes of leadership, thereby building CEO capital and furthering the organization.

Here are a few examples of the effective use of personal history and stories to develop a business-oriented folklore:

- *Teamwork.* Chris Komisarjevsky, president and CEO of Burson-Marsteller Worldwide, openly refers to his experiences as a Vietnam War pilot. His unit's missions were successful, he stresses, because each unit member was utterly dependent on each other, an attitude of interdependency that he instills at Burson-Marsteller.
- *Responsible corporate citizen.* John T. Dillon, chairman and CEO of International Paper Company, emphasizes ethical leadership. In the late 1990s, Dillon responded to the hate crimes directed toward Southern black churches by making an open-ended offer, without fanfare or publicity, to the National Council of Churches to rebuild fire-bombed houses of worship, donating enough finished wood products to rebuild

17 churches, amounting to more than $2 million.[21] Dillon's quiet sense of "right" immediately became part of company folklore, making employees proud to belong.

- *A product for the people.* Leonard Riggio, chairman and CEO of Barnes & Noble, grew up in a predominantly Italian, working-class neighborhood in Brooklyn. Riggio's family history stands in sharp contrast to the book industry's privileged history and reinforces the broader, more inclusive market that his company targets across such a wide swath of America.

Although primarily a matter for in-house promulgation, there are occasions when such folklore has uses beyond company walls. The media is one stakeholder that is particularly interested in CEO lore and anecdotes. The media will be looking for some way, especially during the first year after a leadership change, to forecast a company's future. In the absence of hard data, which is sorely difficult to come by given many a new CEO's lack of track record, journalists will search far and wide for autobiographical information to buttress their reports and commentaries. As Noel Tichy, professor at the University of Michigan Business School, says, "Leadership is autobiographical."[22] Moreover, biographical material has the added benefit of enlivening articles with a touch of human interest. Data such as birthplace, the occupations of a CEO's parents, a childhood description, a teacher's recollection of the CEO's school days, academic background, early signs of ambition, and significant job-related successes and failures will all be of interest.

Isolating and then promoting character traits, expertise, outside interests, values, or life-changing events, provided they are consistent with a CEO's business approach, will go a long way toward building an impressive image and CEO capital. Better for the CEO to reveal remembrances in desirable form and to direct a narrative toward a positive image, rather than to allow a journalist to play amateur sleuth and psychologist. Take for example the story of Jack Welch's mother. Although she doted on her son extensively, those writing about Jack Welch's childhood do not refer to her as having been overattentive to her child, to her having pampered her son, or to her having been overbearing. Instead, they refer to the unwavering support she provided that led to Welch's confident nature. How would his relationship with his mother have been reported had Welch not discussed his mother first, predefining the relationship before someone else did?

Be a Narrator CEO.   Elie Wiesel aptly put it: "God made man because he loves stories."[23] Just as the image of a treasured elder spinning a yarn before a dimming fireplace forms a Rockwellesque part of American culture, so too does the business leader who leaves an audience inspired and motivated. Storytelling is a powerful way to influence constituencies. Noted Harvard educator Howard Gardner describes in *Extraordinary Minds* the value of the narrative skill in which leaders "make [a] common bond with their followers; by describing goals they seek in common, obstacles that lie in the way, measures for dealing with these obstacles, milestones along the way, and promise that the desired utopia can eventually be achieved."[24] Stories, like legends, supply a living history, a glue that bestows on its audience membership in an organization where inclusion, shared values, common goals, and jointly held interests peacefully coexist.

Herein lies the strength of business storytelling. Narratives featuring lessons gleaned from the company's triumphs, catastrophes, and missteps convey to a company's employees and other stakeholders these values, goals, and interests. For this reason, the well-respected international corporation 3M trains its executives to become adept at storytelling. Business narratives in the 3M program contain three essential elements: (1) setting the stage (the situation that requires change), (2) the dramatic conflict (why the situation is untenable, what must improve), and (3) the resolution (how the company will improve).[25]

Raymond Gilmartin, chairman, president, and CEO of Merck & Co., describes how he arrived at Merck in 1994 during a period of uncertainty and turmoil for both the company and the pharmaceutical industry. On day two of his new job, Gilmartin says he was handed a speech given by founder and former CEO George Merck some 50 years earlier. One sentence of that speech encapsulated what Gilmartin believed should be the enduring code of the company: "Medicine is for people, not for profits." Gilmartin repeats this story with what a journalist once reported as irritating regularity. The job of an esteemed narrator CEO is to recite the company's core values and model desirable behavior so that it becomes a living credo to employees and customers alike. If repeating that credo with irritating regularity does the job, so be it. Gilmartin thus repeatedly reminds everyone of the company's unassailable core values. These values, which give meaning to action, guided the company's decision to price Crixivan, its new AIDS-fighting drug, 30 percent below competing products, guaranteeing that the drug would find its way to those who needed it.

Warren Buffet, chairman and CEO of Berkshire Hathaway, is also a master storyteller. If they were sold at retail stores, his annual reports might well become bestsellers. Consider the following tale appearing in the 1995 annual report that stressed Buffet's skepticism about acquisitions:

> [W]hy potential buyers even look at projections prepared by sellers baffles me. Charlie and I never give them a glance, but instead keep in mind the story of the man with an ailing horse. Visiting the vet, he said: "Can you help me? Sometimes my horse walks just fine and some-

*times he limps." The vet's reply was pointed: "No prob-
lem—when he's walking fine, sell him." In the world of
mergers and acquisitions, that horse would be peddled
as Secretariat.*[26]

Warren Buffet's gift for such storytelling is hard to imitate and not
for everyone. Stories told by CEOs that are even half as compelling
will still humanize business lessons. As Don Cohen and Larry
Prusak, authors of *In Good Company*, explained, these stories
"convey the norms, values, attitudes, and behaviors . . . probably
more fully—with more rounded context—than any other kind of
communication."[27]

Use the Language of Leadership.   CEOs need to find the right
words and analogies to inspire and command attention, words and
analogies that are passionate, persuasive, and full of purpose—in
short, meaning makers. U.S. presidents, for instance, received
higher ratings for charisma and greatness when they used positive
images and words such as *grow, journey, frontier, clamor, dream,
imagine, listen,* and *see* versus conceptually neutral words such as
source, commitment, produce, alternative, moderate, think, and
endeavor.[28] Thus word choice has a direct and tangible effect on a
leader's effectiveness.

Just as listening to a president is a memorable moment for most
Americans, so too is hearing their CEO speak—a touch of high
drama, less historical perhaps, but usually more personally meaningful for most employees. Peggy Noonan, columnist and former
speechwriter for Ronald Reagan, advised President George W.
Bush to invest in stagecraft to create a bolder sense of drama[29] to
build a more presidential persona. Only after the terrorists' attacks
on New York City and Washington, D.C. did President Bush find
a leadership voice, although he appears to struggle still. His use of
frontier imagery, calling Osama bin Laden wanted dead or alive,

and seeking to rally the United States and the world by referring to an Axis of Evil, was, at least rhetorically speaking, an improvement over prior generally lackluster speeches. Bush's words certainly had an impact, arousing vehement responses from not just Americans but from people around the world.

In using language and imagery, Carly Fiorina of HP is a virtuoso. In fact, some say that her fluency worked in her favor to convince reticent investors to vote positively for the HP–Compaq merger in the March 2002 proxy fight. Talking about the shifting business landscape early in her tenure, Fiorina draws an analogy to the Italian Renaissance:

> To find a parallel for the historical shift that we're undergoing, I have to go all the way back to the first Renaissance in Italy. Because when Copernicus and Galileo and Leeuwenhoek exploded the earth-centered universe and the old Greek theories of biology, they exploded religion, they exploded politics, they exploded commerce. . . . In that time 500 years ago, invention was the prime virtue. . . . I firmly believe we're at the beginning of a second Renaissance: the digital Renaissance.[30]

Such masterful communications skills were also in full bloom during her one-year anniversary speech to employees. She saw Hewlett-Packard as "a winning e-company with a shining soul."[31] She spoke of "aspirational performance" and "ennobling strategies" and reminded employees that HP "must be known as much for its strength of character as for the strength of results."[32] "A company is an organic, living, breathing thing," she explained, "not just an income sheet and balance sheet. You have to lead with that in mind."[33]

Persuasive CEO communication needs to connect on both rational and emotional levels. CEO communication is at its best, and CEO capital is best built, when chief executives express their goals through lively and engaging speech filled with genuine emotion.

Make Sure You Are Heard.   What Thomas H. Davenport calls the "attention industries"[34]—television, advertising, film, and print—have much to teach regarding gaining and keeping the attention of targeted audiences. The techniques learned from these various forms of media include using multiple media, issuing clear and concise messages or points, repeating these messages or points, communicating with regularity and emotion, and being thought inspiring, interesting, and personal.[35] In short, select a few significant messages and repeat them often and succinctly in various forms with emotion and in a meaningful, personal way to win the attention of the greatest number of people.

For a CEO to communicate through different mediums is perhaps the least obvious of these prescriptions. For example, those employees who are not typically office bound are likely to have less access to electronic messages than other employees. Posting hard copies at factories, plants, and other offsite locations helps the communications process, but there is no guarantee that such notices will be read. Similarly, younger employees, who have been brought up using computers with information delivered to them almost instantly may be more receptive to information transmitted in short sound bites rather than the companywide presentations that older employees might prefer. Not every audience is equally receptive to the same type of communications.

For these reasons, CEOs must cast a wide net when communicating with employees. In addition to in-person meetings and e-mail, companies should post executive speeches on their Intranet and company Web sites. Forward-thinking CEOs buttress these efforts with follow-up, hard-copy memos, audiotapes and videotapes, Webcasts, internal chats with the CEO, and mailings to the home when appropriate. Online chat sessions, such as those that Burson-Marsteller's Chris Komisarjevsky has with employees, allow for one-on-one interaction between employees and their CEO and are becoming a more common corporate communication technique. John Chambers, CEO of Cisco Systems, prefers voice mail because he believes it does a better job of capturing emotion than e-mail. He also considers to whom the message is being sent: "Now, if I'm communicating with an engineer, I'd better send an e-mail; if I'm communicating with a sales force, I probably should send it by voice mail."[36] Chet Burchett, CEO of Burson-Marsteller U.S., employs "CEO in the Hot Seat" open-door sessions in different offices during which employees can ask candid, unscripted questions. A toll-free telephone number is available to employees in regional offices who want to participate through teleconference.

Obtaining feedback on a regular basis to determine if corporate messages are being received and understood by the target audience is often overlooked. Three-quarters of the way into their first year, CEOs should perform a communications audit to evaluate whether their messages are resonating. Sears Roebuck surveys employees monthly and annually to determine whether management messages cascade through the organization.[37] The company sends surveys to the homes of employees who are not electronically connected and distributes them in work areas where employees meet and socialize.

Organize and Plan

Find Your Number Two; Seek Independent Counsel. For the new CEO, the first year may be lonely, socially isolating, and undoubtedly overwhelming. By the first anniversary, new CEOs should be able to determine whom among their direct reports they can trust. At this point, the astute CEO should, if at all possible, appoint an aide-de-camp, an alter ego, a business soulmate.

The chosen number two is often the chief operating officer or chief financial officer. Some of these CEO–COO or CEO–CFO partnerships have been immensely effective. Take for example Sun

Microsystem's Scott McNealy and recently retired Ed Zander, Staples' Tom Stemberg and Ronald Sargent, Disney's Michael Eisner and Robert Iger, or Coca-Cola's Roberto Goizueta and Don Keough back in the early 1990s. Today we see the pairing between President George W. Bush and Vice President Richard Cheney (at least in the beginning) and between PepsiCo's CEO Steven S. Reinemund and CFO Indra K. Nooyi. Boeing's Phil Condit and Harry Stonecipher are yet another accomplished pair, with respect to which Condit said: "I don't believe I could have done it without someone like Harry. He can see a hole in an operating plan from 50 yards. I, for whatever reason, can see around the corners."[38]

The chemistry between such pairs, however, all too often can go awry with disastrous results. Witness the surprise break between CEO Doug Daft of Coca-Cola and Jack L. Stahl, the company's former COO. The issue usually gets down to this: number two operates at number one's discretion and in number one's shadow—not sometimes, but always. As stated by Jeffrey Tarter, author of *Softletter*, a newsletter that focuses on business issues, number two's job is not an easy one:

> *There isn't much question about what a chief executive officer does for a living. Defining strategy, making decisions, shaping products, talking to the public, keeping the bank account full—in the end, the CEO is simply the one person who is responsible for a company's success and survival. But what about the chief operating officer? . . . the COO typically has to carve out a job by taking tasks and authority away from the CEO and from other top executives. Not surprisingly, the COO's job often ends up as a political battleground.[39]*

This is why so many U.S. politicians decline nomination as vice president, and why number twos must have a firm constitution and be secure in their own unique abilities if they are to contribute meaningfully. Only if so armed can they hope to maintain their positions as a subordinate, subject to the demands of an inevitably strong-willed number one.

Given the inherent tension between numbers one and two, the best and most stable of these partnerships rest on an appropriate mix of complementary personalities and skills. If appropriate candidates for a number two position exist—presumably CEOs will know them when they see them—the CEOs should bring them on board as soon as possible. Some CEOs say that while they run the company, their number two runs the business. The sheer size of many businesses today requires CEOs to divide their duties. Some CEOs focus on long-term strategy and external relations and need someone to tend to internal responsibilities and daily decision making under the CEO's overall supervision. Michael Dell has handed over considerable responsibilities to Vice Chairman, President, and COO Kevin B. Rollins. While Dell attends to customers and strategy, his lieutenant makes the day-to-day happen. Dell himself says: "I don't think you could do it with one person. It would kill him. There's way too much to be done."[40]

In addition to a number two, the discerning CEO also seeks out the opinions of independent third parties. The independent third party is usually an outside consultant who is unaffiliated with the inevitable organizational politics, beholden to no one, untainted by the past, devoid of corporate ambitions, and as free as anyone to tell it like it is—the bad as well as the good. This is how a CEO can receive an objective point of view from someone whose job does not depend on what that person says and does. In his article on CEO confidantes that was published by *Chief Executive,* Justin Martin wrote that CEOs often find it difficult to obtain objective feedback from colleagues.[41] Outside consultants such as Warren Bennis, Ram Charan, Noel Tichy, David Nadler, Michael Useem, and Jeffrey Sonnenfield, to name a few, have acted as CEO confidantes. They bring broad experience across many industries and are more comfortable making recommendations and telling the unadulterated truth. Furthermore, these advisors, who tend to be students of business, bring with them knowledge about other companies and the most relevant management research from the academic community.

Some CEOs turn to former company CEOs, current and retired CEOs from other industries, or even their spouses for independent opinions. Select organizations with membership limited to current or former CEOs facilitate such contacts. Miles White of Abbott Labs frequently seeks guidance from former CEOs of his company. "They all believe that they have a stake in what you are doing, and they all believe that they can give you some advice and coaching from their experience. The truth is that they can."[42] Not surprisingly, one of the most commonly sought independent parties is spouses, who can't be matched for ease of access, confidentiality, and deep understanding of a CEO's personal style. CEOs can share self-doubts with their spouses and discuss people issues more openly. This is especially true of younger CEOs whose spouses are more likely than older CEO's spouses to be, or to have been, employed, and who can therefore more easily identify with business challenges.

Choose Your Operational Tenet.   During the Countdown, CEO-elects foreshadow the future with broad suggestions of what is to come. During the First Hundred Days, new CEOs must set forth a few clear principles or themes, marking their tenure with a thematic stamp. By the end of the First Year, however, new CEOs must get specific, detailing in a concrete way how one specific principle may be put into practical effect. This single maxim must contain within it a specific, practical directive that employees can follow in their everyday responsibilities. This operational tenet must be the only tenet and it must be instantly recognizable by all.

By way of illustration, the CEOs of Home Depot and Gillette have adopted such operational tenets, each including within them practical directives, immediately understandable and observable. Robert Nardelli, former head of GE Power Systems and now the new CEO at Home Depot, advocated "Never Lose a Sale." This operational rule makes clear that restocking shelves during business hours takes time away from serving customers.[43] James Kilts of Gillette used "Zero Overhead Growth" to reinforce the need to cut costs, trim overhead growth, and reduce cash tied up in inventory. Each of these operational tenets, or strategic principles as denominated by Orit Gadiesh, chairman of Bain & Company, is a "memorable and actionable phrase that distills a company's corporate strategy into its unique essence."[44]

These tenets are not meaningless slogans that are followed when it is convenient, but rather are deliberately crafted canons of behavior that securely anchor organizations along a desired path. An operational tenet may endure for years (Jack Welch's "Be number one or number two in your business, or get out!" or Sam Walton's "Low prices, every day") or over time morph into different forms (Jack Welch's "destroyyourbusinessdotcom" to "growyourbusinessdotcom"). A CEO's operational tenet, if successful, may serve as the pivot about which a company turns.

Brian Kelley, former president of Lincoln Mercury, a division of Ford Motor Company, knew what his operational tenet would be even before his first employee town meeting. Lincoln Mercury's challenges included an aging product line, poorly executed new-model launches, and negative cash flow. Despite these challenges, Kelley was optimistic because he knew that Lincoln Mercury's brand strategy was effective, its heritage strong, its talent deep, and its manufacturing efficient. What Kelley needed to do was energize and empower his employees. At the town meeting, he unveiled how the company would operate: Debate. Decide. Deliver.

Such organizational tenets can also arise by accident, provided that a CEO recognizes their significance. Former CEO John Macomber of Celanese Corporation was deep in thought and somewhat frustrated during an executive board meeting. Board members were discussing the lack of progress in surpassing certain set benchmarks when Macomber suddenly blurted out: "We're at a stage where we'd rate about a 3 on a scale of 10. But I'm not as interested in where we are as in where we're going. What I'd like to know is what 10 out of 10 would look like."[45] From this meeting came what is still now referred to as the "Ten Out of Ten" document that sets the demand for excellence in everything they do and the phrase, "ten out of ten."

Articulate and Embody a Code of Ethical Conduct. When asked what keeps him up at night, Jeff Immelt of GE remarked, "It's always an integrity issue of some kind. With 300,000 people, you always worry that somebody doesn't get it. We can survive bad markets. What you can't live through is anybody who takes from the company or does something wrong in the community."[46] An employee being offered a bribe in Taiwan has to make a split-second decision and, if he or she chooses wrong, can tarnish the reputation of a company based in Indianapolis overnight. For this reason alone, the new CEO must establish and adhere to a formal ethical code, see to its promulgation, and ensure its adherence.

Goldman Sachs has for some time incorporated into its heritage and culture "14 Business Principles," which, according to senior partner John Whitehead,[47] serve as a continuing check on improper behavior. The goal is to familiarize employees with these principles so that the principles become "internal reminders,"[48] instinctive responses to any untoward temptations. These principles are central to the orientation of new employees. More important, they have continued relevance thereafter, with questions about their application being raised, according to one senior employee, on average at least twice daily. Employees have been known to memorize the 14 principles to guide them should ethical issues arise.

Consider Goldman Sachs' first three principles that are the keys to a smoothly functioning company:

1. *Our clients' interests always come first.* Our experience shows that if we serve our clients well, our own success will follow.
2. *Our assets are our people, capital, and reputation.* If any of these is ever diminished, the last is the most difficult to restore. We are dedicated to complying fully with the letter and spirit of the laws, rules, and ethical principles that govern us. Our continued success depends upon unswerving adherence to this standard.
3. *Our goal is to provide superior returns to our shareholders.* Profitability is critical to achieving superior returns, building our capital, and attracting and keeping the best people. Significant employee stock ownership aligns the interests of our employees and our shareholders.[49]

That Goldman Sachs' leadership walks the talk as well as talks the walk is crucial to making their code credible and to obtaining meaningful compliance from all employees. These principles emphasize the need for higher executives to avoid hypocritical behavior. A CEO must abide by tenets if others are to abide by them as well. Few things can be more damaging to CEO capital than hypocrisy.

Being an individual with integrity and high moral standards, however, is not enough for CEOs. They must make ethical leadership visible, not just through constant repetition, though repetition is important, but also through deliberate modeling of the right ethical behavior. A study of executives and corporate ethics officers concluded that executives need to develop a reputation for ethical leadership. Only in this way will they serve as a model of appropriate behavior for employees, the vast majority of whom never come in contact with top leadership.[50] Employees take their cues from the person at the top. A good example is BP's Lord Browne who pre-Enron put a halt to any political donations from corporate funds anywhere in the world.[51] For CEOs desiring to build CEO capital, their actions speak louder than words.

Enron's former CEO Ken Lay may well be a prime example of a CEO paying lip service to a code of conduct, but acting otherwise when it comes down to making the numbers. Should it be shown that he has acted unethically, the irony would be startling because Lay was at one time a poster child for espousing ethical responsibility. Enron's ethical code or values statement referred in all sincerity to "respect, integrity, communication, and excellence." The reality, of course, may be somewhat different: All talk, no walk. Even if the courts find that Lay is not directly implicated in unethical behavior, he still appears, according to currently reported accounts, to have produced an environment that condoned shortcuts, looking the other way, and perhaps even outright deceptiveness. If a CEO and his or her top executives permit the appearance of impropriety or do not model ethical behavior, then the company's code of ethics becomes nothing more than an empty promise.

Thus it is not surprising, given Enron's apparent lack of real commitment to ethical leadership, that no internal reminder would have prevented previous President and CEO Jeffrey Skilling, should the evidence so find, from wanting to fire Vice President Sherron Watkins, the whistle-blower, after she informed Ken Lay of corporate misdeeds. One has to wonder, even in the absence of ultimate criminal culpability, about the ethical leadership at Arthur Andersen when Houston partner David Duncan, apparently at the order of, or with the acquiescence of, Chicago headquarters (though this is a point still in dispute) shredded trunkloads of Enron-related documents. Even if evidence later demonstrates that the shredding occurred but was technically legal because it occurred before a subpoena was issued, Arthur Andersen's behavior is unlikely to translate into ethical conduct. Obstruction of justice in spirit, even if not in fact, simply comes too close to undesirable behavior.

Trust in the ethical leadership of CEOs suffered enormous damage in the summer of 2002. Corporate fiscal mismanagement and malfeasance cost CEOs public and investor confidence. The allegations against CEOs and other officers at companies such as Enron, Tyco, Adelphia Communications, Arthur Andersen, and Global Crossing altered the face of business and raised the prospect of jail terms for corporate misbehavior. The absence of appropriate CEO role models effectively undermined America's corporate culture.

Phil Condit, CEO of Boeing, is more in tune with ethical behavior. It would have been hard for Condit to miss the Lockheed scandal, one of the most far-reaching bribery scandals in postwar Japan, where former Prime Minister Tanaka received money from Lockheed to approve All Nippon Airways' purchase of Lockheed aircraft.[52] Condit has no intention of Boeing being caught unaware in a similar scandal, or for that matter having even one employee's transgression blindside him. Boeing encourages its employees, customers, and suppliers to take an online "ethics challenge" to test how they would solve difficult and compromising business situations. For example, one such situation describes a "business courtesy" payment that is a commonly accepted business practice in third-world countries but is more inclined to be considered bribery or a kickback in the United States. These tests educate employee test takers and set appropriate business standards, advising employees and those who work with Boeing of the company's ethical expectations. Most important, the tests allow employees to apply ethical standards to real-life situations. Applications to real-life situations is no easy task, and practice is well worth it.

Beware, the Close of the First Year Is upon You; Consider the Five-Quarter Rule. With the close of the First Year, stakeholders will be expecting results, if not now, then soon. At the very least, they will be seeking a convincing articulation of the CEO's strategic vision and some evidence that if the company is nonperforming, it will be facing a turnaround. Although Jack Welch asserts that it should take at least 10 years minimum for CEOs to impact an organization,[53] a new CEO should expect that at the end of year one, whether reasonable or not, stakeholders will be looking for substance. Year two will usher in what *Business Week* dubbed "The CEO Trap."[54] "Once those barely seasoned executives take over top billing, they must perform immediately . . . to overpromise and underdeliver eventually shreds an exec's reputation, infuriates Wall Street, and quite possibly costs the CEO the job."[55]

Thus, as year one ends, a CEO should be able to show that a new comprehensive strategy is in the works. Sometimes, the well-prepared CEO goes even further. On his first anniversary, Compaq's former CEO Michael D. Capellas synthesized his strategic vision. The company would focus on providing the computing infrastructure for the Web, such as server computers, PCs, and the next generation of access devices. "You are going to see us continue to drive a strategy of owning control of the Web."[56] He set his direction. Thereafter the new CEO needed to be concerned only with the far more difficult task of delivering on his vision.

Phil Condit, chairman and CEO of Boeing, gave evidence of his strategic vision to diversify Boeing during one of his major year-one speeches to management. In an attempt to envision what Boeing would be like in the year 2016 when the company celebrated its 100th anniversary, Condit suggested that the company should and would become more geographically diverse. That speech, which became known as Vision 2016, eventually evolved into a full-blown strategic vision. In accordance with its precepts, nearly five years later, Condit moved Boeing headquarters from Seattle to Chicago. "As I turn around and look back today, we are very geographically diverse. I am not sure that I understood how important that statement was at the time. I had this idea years before we actually moved headquarters."[57] But important it was.

Just as the CEO should pay increasing attention to pinning down a strategic vision, so too should the CEO, especially a CEO of a nonperforming company, attend to producing strong financial results. As Burson-Marsteller's research clearly demonstrates, stakeholders ultimately give CEOs up to five poor earning quarters to make a positive impression. These stakeholders, in particular Wall Street and the media, abide by this five-quarter rule with surprising consistency. By the end of a CEO's first year, some indication of a turnaround, some sense of momentum, must be in place to maintain high levels of CEO capital. At this juncture, if things are not going well, board members and perhaps a predecessor CEO will predictably ask questions and apply pressure to obtain results—or else. More on these matters is discussed in Chapter 7.

THE CLOSE OF THE FIRST YEAR

Twelve months come to a close fast. By now, the CEO's reputation within the organization should be fairly established. Employees and senior managers should be able to see what is around the corner and what is required of them individually and collectively. The CEO's name should stand for something knowable, meaningful, and inspirational. As a result, the company's stock should be at least stable or preferably rising, employment applications increasing, turnover slowing, and crises passing. Credibility should be on the upswing and the media should be paying somewhat more positive attention to the company. By following the steps outlined in this chapter and performing them well, the CEO's capital should be solidifying within the organization and within the industry.

REFLECTIONS ON THE FIRST YEAR: THE CEO PERSONA

The effective CEO who follows the guidelines set forth in this chapter will and should develop a CEO persona—an image, a reputation that transforms into CEO capital when used on the company's behalf. When consistent with the company's goals, this persona is a highly useful tool to be used for the company's benefit, a means by which to motivate employees, encourage ethical behavior, build confidence, attract the best managers, and facilitate the advancement of the best practices recommended here.

From the viewpoint of a company's employees, suppliers, customers, and other stakeholders and industry peers, when a CEO has properly established a CEO persona, the CEO's identity merges with that of the company. The CEO embodies the company's soul and becomes its alter ego. Think about those CEOs who have become household names. These CEOs have become so associated with their companies that they are almost brand names in their own right. Consider some of them: Bill Gates, Steve Jobs, Jack Welch, Warren Buffet, Lou Gerstner, Richard Branson, Sandy Weill, Michael Eisner, John Chambers, Meg Whitman, Michael Dell, Charles Schwab, Lord John Browne, Marjorie Scardino, Jürgen Schrempp, and Carly Fiorina. Even President Bush, CEO of

America Inc., has merged with his office. These men and women are all but synonymous with their companies, at least until they retire or are replaced.

These household names, of course, are just the tip of the iceberg because most successful CEOs are neither *Fortune* cover subjects nor a topic of discussion on CNBC. Yet, they too have personas. As far as employees, customers, and industry peers are concerned, for all intents and purposes, they too are the company, just as Bill Gates is Microsoft, Michael Eisner is Disney, and Warren Buffet is Berkshire Hathaway. Non–household name CEOs have leadership styles that typically are antithetical to self-importance and external self-promotion. Truly successful CEOs are, as Jim Collins states in his heavily and thoroughly researched landmark book, *Good to Great*,[58] "a paradoxical blend of personal humility and professional will. They are more like Lincoln and Socrates than Patton and Caesar."[59] And like Lincoln and Socrates, they too attract the best and the brightest, draw numerous followers, and, are leaders.

Not every CEO is a Caesar who seeks power and renown and attains it as opposed to a Socrates who seeks knowledge and by attaining it becomes renown. For some CEOs, including most from companies not on any *Fortune* or *Forbes* list, their names are barely recognizable to the general public, if at all. Rarely must the CEO morph into a star and become a celebrity to be successful and to carry weight with those who count—the company's stakeholders.

Of course, being identified so closely with a company has its responsibilities and drawbacks. As CEOs achieve this mutuality of identity with their companies, they become in effect surrogates. CEOs must take responsibility not just for the good but also for the bad. Johnson & Johnson's Chairman and CEO James E. Burke publicly stood behind the Tylenol brand, whether he was comfortable in the public role or not, during the tampering crisis of the

1980s. CEOs are now expected to draw fire away from the company brand when damaged, namely to take the hit for the company. As a consequence, CEOs are called on to suffer and are as likely to be recalled as their products. For example, British Airways CEO Robert Ayling departed abruptly after being held responsible for several blunders such as eliminating the Union Jack flag from the redesign of its airplanes' tail fins, as well as ignoring economy-paying customers.[60] When rumors of tainted Coca-Cola in Belgium temporarily undermined the world's most famous soft drink brand, influentials concentrated on the company's CEO Doug Ivester. When Coca-Cola was recalled in that market, Ivester could not sustain the blow and, several months later, Coca-Cola recalled Ivester too.

Notwithstanding the drawbacks of being a corporate alter ego, a CEO who has developed a positive CEO persona is in a position to do far more for his or her company, and do it far more efficiently, than without one. A CEO armed with a well-developed and favorable persona can do many things and do them better because the executive's reputation and the confidence it instills adds luster. Consider the positive effect that a successfully developed CEO persona has on the following: differentiating the company from competitors, attracting talent, binding customers, exciting employees, raising capital, and attaching meaning to work. CEOs with well-developed personas can distinguish themselves by standing for something unique that resonates deeply throughout the organization and ultimately in the marketplace.

One caveat: a CEO with a fully developed persona is not the same as a celebrity CEO, the hobgoblin of many commentators and, if truth be told, many CEOs as well. Jim Collins bemoans society's and the media's fascination with the CEO cult of personality:

> *[O]ur problem lies in the fact that our culture has fallen in love with the idea of the celebrity CEO. Charismatic*

*egotists who swoop in to save companies grace the cov-
ers of major magazines because they are much more interesting to read. . . . This fuels the mistaken belief held
by many directors that a high-profile, larger-than-life
leader is required to make a company great.*[61]

Being high profile and larger than life is not by itself an inherent
good. A CEO persona develops meaning only if it attains worth,
not by winning mere media attention, but by standing for something that is believable and knowable and that embodies a company's values, beliefs, and operating tenets. The CEO persona
must grow from within and must be sustainable.

Many CEOs understand that they cannot base their persona on
media fluff or hype. Most CEOs would prefer to maintain low
profiles, and many do. As noted before, meaningful CEO capital is
built on performance, not fans. Yet the Information Age drags
many of these low-profile business leaders, kicking and screaming,
out from the protective shade of public anonymity into the often
harsh glare of public exposure. For instance, Bridgestone/Firestone
CEO John Lampe found himself making headlines when he termi-
nated the historic partnership between Ford and Firestone after
questioning the safety of Ford Explorers. Some of the best-run
companies, such as United Technologies, Colgate-Palmolive, and
Emerson Electric, have contented CEOs who have been able to
limit their personas within the confines of their companies and industries. But would this remain the case if, for example, a government agency investigated Emerson Electric, like it did Exxon, for
undermining an entire coastline's ecosystem, or if someone had
tampered with a Colgate-Palmolive product, as was the case with
Tylenol? The truth is, being thrust into the limelight is often beyond a CEO's control.

Notwithstanding the distinct, almost inherent, dislike that most
CEOs have for the spotlight, forces beyond their control all too

often demand that they nevertheless publicly perform. Too often they have to explain their policies and actions to constituencies, differentiate their companies from competitors, attract and retain quality managers, offer a corporate position on environmental or social issues, and defend themselves against attacks from powerful special interest groups, dissident shareholders, rumors, or regulators. Most CEOs would prefer to avoid public image making and revert back to the years before 24/7 television, intrusive journalists, proliferating cable stations, the Internet, and an increasing number of trade publications. Reality, however, cannot be ignored.

This is especially true when public issues arise, when the government and national and international media call out to CEOs to communicate their positions and defend their companies. Should a CEO, who acts responsibly on behalf of his or her company's and the public's welfare, avoid the limelight when food is tainted, financial statements need to be restated, sweat shops are tolerated, or funds are embezzled? I think not. So even though public exposure and celebrity for its own sake should be avoided, CEOs must prepare for when they may be forced to take the bully pulpit. At such times, CEOs may well wish to extend their persona beyond company borders. A known name and a reputation for integrity will serve these CEOs well, provided that the CEOs and their personas, like that of a Lincoln or a Socrates, stand for integrity, humanity, quality leadership, public concern, and honesty—and not just hype.

Two such non-self serving CEOs with finely developed personas stepped forward to speak out publicly about corporate reform in the ill-omened summer of 2002. To restore investor confidence, chairman and CEO Henry Paulson Jr. of Goldman Sachs addressed the National Press Club calling for changes in corporate governance, accounting standards, and investment research. The reserved, even introverted CEO, who rarely speaks out publicly, realized earlier than most that ethical leadership required standing up and being counted when events demanded so.[62] Similarly, non-executive chairman of Intel Andy Grove publicly entered the debate over the deductibility of stock options. He argued that classifying options as a business expense did not effectively respond to the primary issue of exorbitant executive compensation. His reason for speaking out: "I think corporate America has acted less forthrightly and aggressively under attack than one might wish. What I'm hoping to achieve is for some of our colleagues to come out of their shell-shocked state and speak up and debate and discuss this as well as other issues."[63]

Moreover, celebrity is sometimes the inevitable product of a job well done. Sometimes celebrity and public exposure befall a CEO even when the CEO does not seek it—and the CEO rarely does. The mere fact that a CEO is well-known and has a name that has become a publicly acclaimed persona, say a Gates or a Bezos, does not mean that the CEO is necessarily effective or ineffective. Harold Burson, founding chairman of Burson-Marsteller, counselor to many well-known CEOs, and with his own acclaimed persona, has this to say about celebrity CEOs: "I don't think that there are celebrity CEOs. I think there are CEOs who *achieve* celebrity status."[64]

Finally, the importance of developing a CEO's persona is not, as many believe, a peculiarly American phenomenon. Europe and Asia also believe in developing CEO personas. Continental CEOs are becoming global, ever eager to participate in trans-Atlantic mergers and acquisitions, focusing intensely on obtaining shareholder wealth, networking, and penetrating American markets. Daimler Benz's Jürgen Schrempp developed a hefty persona at home in Germany, and then successfully transported it, at least initially, overseas during his takeover of Chrysler. Similarly, the persona of Chairman and CEO Daniel Vasella of the Swiss pharmaceutical giant Novartis has captured the attention of the media and other influential stakeholders as an innovator and one of the top 25 managers to watch in 2002.[65] Strong international personas buy CEOs time to make things right and access to more global markets. Investors are more apt to watch and invest in those multinational companies where the CEO persona reflects an ambition for growth and profit, coupled with credibility.

⟫━◦━⟪

The clock is ticking. By now, it is evident to all that CEOs have only a limited time in which to prove themselves. Stakeholders are increasingly aware of how long a CEO has been in office and, as described in Chapter 7, will defer judgment on the CEO's fitness to continue holding office for almost a year. CEOs know this. In a conference call with analysts in March 2001, Charles C. Conaway, former chairman and CEO of Kmart Corp., explained away Kmart's 40 percent fall in fourth quarter net income by reminding analysts of his brief time in office: "We've got a long way to go. Kmart is a dramatically different competitor than it was 215 days ago."[66] Conaway was quite conscious of how many days had passed and strongly hinted, in effect, that he deserved more of a chance. Since he had not yet reached the end of his third quarter, he held on to his position, his time was not yet up. But one year later it was.

As year one closes, it is hoped that CEOs have done their job well. They should have learned from others, cultivated a CEO persona, and developed a plan of action. As they enter year two, the days of reckoning are upon them.

CHAPTER 7

THE TURNING POINT: LEADING THROUGH THOUGHT

I always would have characterized Year Two as harder than Year One because this is when the change really gets binding.[1]

—Carly Fiorina, chairman and CEO of
Hewlett-Packard

You don't realize it at the time, but your first year is spent trying to establish a pattern and trying to meet with all the different constituencies. When you have gone through a second cycle, you have begun to put your plans or agenda into action and you ought to be able to see whether or not the alignment is good."[2]

—Miles D. White, chairman and CEO of
Abbott Laboratories

With the first year behind them, both CEO and company are no longer newlyweds. The glow of the wedding has long past. Akin to a husband and wife who are moving from an apartment to their first new home with a car in the garage, a baby on the way, and a mortgage to be paid, the CEO and company are now getting serious—establishing roots, committing to a vision, planning for the future, and nurturing new ideas. This is the time of truth. Can the couple work together? Can they build a future together? They better because the stakeholders are watching.

This stage, a period ranging from 13 to 22 months, is perhaps the most consequential of stages: the turning point in a CEO's tenure. According to Burson-Marsteller's research, influential stakeholders consider 15 months on average to be the point at which CEOs must prove themselves by adding to the bottom line. This five-quarter rule can be extended somewhat when a talented CEO has earned credibility and the trust of the board and key stakeholders. Give or take several months, however, this is the time of truth. The CEO must garner every bit of knowledge gained in past stages, gather the best elements, and forge a vision for the company. Stakeholders are now expecting that the company have direction, that the senior team be in place and functioning well, and for the first time, that the CEO show leadership that has born fruit. These months make or break CEOs because it is now that CEOs truly begin earning their reputations as winners, losers, or somewhere in between.

Stage four is the time for a CEO to articulate firmly and repeatedly a strategic vision that motivates and earns the company's cooperation and commitment. The CEO must convey a sense of urgency, collaboration, and conviction—and must produce and produce now. The CEO who has developed a strong persona will have a significant advantage. Rallying the troops will be less difficult and, if needed, the CEO will have built enough credibility to buy time, thus keeping stakeholders sufficiently content with the company's leadership so that they defer final judgments until closer to the end of stage four (22 months) rather than its start (13 months). In effect, the CEO with a developed persona may be able to extend the five-quarter rule perhaps an additional quarter or more. This may not seem like much, but it can be a benefit for a CEO on the hot seat. In any event, once CEOs have passed successfully through this stage, they can truly be said to have generated substantial and meaningful amounts of CEO capital.

BEST PRACTICES: FORGE A VISION, PUT STAKEHOLDERS AT EASE, AND PLAN THE FUTURE

During this stage, the first priority is to satisfy the critically important stakeholders, in particular, the financial community and board of directors, assuring them that the company is in good hands. Only by keeping these stakeholders satisfied will the CEO have the opportunity to further develop ideas and plans for the company. In many ways, the best practices necessary to keep these stakeholders at bay and confident in a CEO's leadership are a continuation of those practices set forth in prior stages. What occurs now is the culmination of what has gone before: producing results, establishing a proper direction for the company, and forming a cohesive management team. If all has gone according to plan—if the CEO is confident that stakeholders have responded favorably to the company's leadership and do not require extensive relationship-repair—the CEO should then focus further on the company's development and adopt additional best practices. These additional steps include taking measures to further the CEO's vision and strategic plan, seeking independent counsel, minding special interest groups, networking, and harnessing technology.

Exhibit 7.1 provides a shorthand description of how this chapter's best practices build the CM factors necessary for sustained formation of CEO capital.

EXHIBIT 7.1 CM Factor Analysis: The Turning Point

| | | | RESULTS | | |
Action	Credibility	Conduct	Communication	Motivation	Mgmt.
Forge A Strategic Vision					
Show them direction, forge a vision.	X			X	X
Put Stakeholders at Ease					
Show them the money.	X			X	
Show them a collaborative management team.	X		X	X	X
Plan the Future					
Seek input from independent parties.	X	X	X	X	
Mind your NGOs.	X	X			
Start networking.	X		X		
Digitize, be Internet savvy.				X	
Lead through Thought.	X	X	X	X	X

154

Credibility: At this turning point in a CEO's tenure, credibility provides smooth passage past the 15-month point of final judgment. The CEO must articulate repeatedly a strategic vision, put stakeholders and board members at bay by delivering results, and coalesce a management team. By establishing a dialogue with independent parties and peers, CEOs can monitor the business environment for rapid change and earn the trust of critical influencers. CEO-led thought leadership dimensionalizes the CEO persona and transcends the company's role beyond the confines of its industry.

Conduct: Principled leadership springs from open dialogues with outside parties and special interest groups. Listening to challenges to your company's business fundamentals stimulates thought and leads to meaningful action.

Communicating internally: Setting the vision, communicating collectively from the top, and planning the future reinforces a CEO's straightforwardness.

Motivating employees: Employees rally behind CEOs who shape a vision, deliver results, embody the future, and set the pace.

Building a management team: The team must be finalized. Establish ground rules.

Forge a Strategic Vision

Show Them the Company Has Direction. During year one, the CEO sets the operational tenet, a straightforward call to action that employees immediately and practically apply. Now the CEO must do more—much more. Based on everything learned over the first year, the CEO must finalize a strategic vision during this stage. Unlike the operational tenet, the strategic vision is forward leaning and more inspirational than the practical operational tenet. It is the rallying cry around which the CEO's company will mobilize: an objective toward which the company and every employee will work toward achieving.

Articulating that vision is not an easy task and, perhaps, it has more to do with the CEO's insight into the company and how it relates to its industry than anything else. As explained by Phil Condit, chairman and CEO of Boeing, a nonlinear approach is necessary:

> *I think the ability to think strategically into the future is a critical capability. There have been articles written about what is the appropriate horizon needed for a first level supervisor (where it's a couple of days) to a mid-level manager (where it's a year) to a senior executive (where it's a couple of years) to a CEO (where it's 15–20 years). Embedded in this ability is something that I don't even know quite how to describe. It is the ability to see nonlinear fundamental shifts. It is hard to see the twists and turns. It is hard to see what is driving those changes and then to position the company to take advantage of those fundamental shifts.[3]*

Thus, the ability to forge a strategic vision is almost spiritual.

Jay Conger, an internationally recognized leadership expert, describes vision as "an idealized future goal that the leader wishes the organization to achieve."[4] The CEO and team must identify where they want the company to be in the years ahead (the vision) and how they are going to get there (the strategy). Thus a strategic vision is a plan for the future, based on a profound understanding of the company's place in its industry and society, combined with a strategy for pursuing that plan.

Scott McNealy, chairman and CEO of Sun Microsystems, provides a classic example of a CEO with a dynamic strategic vision. In 1982, three Stanford University students and a Berkeley programmer began the Stanford University Network (SUN), which was soon to morph into the celebrated Sun Microsystems. McNealy was one of those students. The Sun vision was simple and compelling: that all computers will and should be networked. This commitment to network every product that the company manufactured never wavered. McNealy said, "Sun as a company was born to be an Internet company almost 20 years ago. Every computer we've ever shipped has been an IP [Internet protocol] computer. Every single one since 1982."[5]

McNealy's vision of the "network is the computer" evidences some of the elements that Conger attributes to designing a successful strategic vision[6] (e.g., "keep it simple," "challenge the status quo," "find thy enemy," "idealize it," "take it to the future," "expose yourself to risk," and "do not underestimate timing"). The McNealy vision is elegantly clear and concise. Moreover, the networked computer stood in sharp juxtaposition to Bill Gates's rival vision—putting a computer on every desk. Going one-on-one against Microsoft was risky business at the time, but McNealy did not hesitate. His commitment to this strategic vision was passionate; he embraced it with almost religious fervor as the wave of the future. Although the verbal sparring between the two companies has diminished somewhat (McNealy called Windows a "hairball"), Sun's anti-Microsoft, David versus Goliath, position energized McNealy, his troops, and even some of his corporate partners, such as Oracle Corporation. By making such a commitment, which was certainly contrary to conventional thinking, McNealy risked his reputation and the company's market position. At first, for much of the early 1990s, McNealy was regarded as an outsider, a brash maverick trying too hard to call attention to Java, his new programming language. His vision, however, was perfectly timed and ready-made for the emergence of the Internet—almost as if Sun had been waiting for the Internet to be invented.

McNealy's vision increasingly bore fruit. The company entered into a groundbreaking partnership with AOL, won in court over Microsoft's use of Sun's programming language, witnessed Sun's high-end servers become quick-sellers in the late 1990s, and saw its Java software take root.[7] In addition, McNealy's embodiment of strategic and visionary leadership earned him a seat on GE's prestigious board in 1998. Despite the high-tech sector slowdown, McNealy's reputation remains relatively intact. In 2000, *Fortune 500* CEOs ranked him among the top five CEOs.[8]

As typified by McNealy, a vision is in many ways the corporate expression of a CEO's passion. Passion lies at the heart of successful strategic visions. Without it, a strategic vision will amount to no more than an empty string of words. As David Pottruck, co-CEO of Charles Schwab, points out, the passion for adding meaning to people's lives drives the Schwab vision:

> *If you don't have something that gives you meaning, then you probably end up solely focusing on the money. And I think that people will work really hard for money but they will devote their lives to meaning if they find meaning. And to me, if you can work in a field that provides meaning to employees and you can inspire them to have passion, to really love coming to work every day, the money is the reward for doing the job well.[9]*

The wonderment of strategic vision is that it is inspirational. That inspiration and the ideals that accompany it give the company a direction. It is less important that the vision be absolutely, perfectly accurate than that it be inspirational. To inspire, the CEO and those responsible for implementing the vision must sincerely believe that the vision is right, that it absolutely represents the future—at least until such time as proven otherwise, whereupon, as pointed out in Chapter 8, it can be modified and then embraced once again.

The company looks to the future so that it can be successful in the present. Phil Condit of Boeing suggests looking far out into the future, a horizon of 15 to 20 years.[10] A lot can happen in 15 to 20 years to change a vision. So when forging a strategic vision, the means may be more important than the end. Thinking untraditionally, being passionate, articulating an idea, challenging the status quo, taking reasonable risks, having others share the vision—all of these elements build CEO capital. They also make a strategic vision important to a company and allow stakeholders to believe that the CEO is in control and that the company has purpose.

Being right? Well, that's okay. It's better than being wrong. But not all visions will be accurate. It's okay to be wrong as long as the CEO is wise enough and aware enough to modify a strategic vision that is going sour well before it damages the company's reputation and goodwill. A case in point: In 1993, CEO Gerald Levin of Time Warner announced the launch of the Full Service Network (FSN) and called it "the keystone of Time Warner's vision and strategy."[11] Levin claimed that FSN, to be piloted in 4,000 homes in Orlando, Florida, would change consumers' lives by providing them with limitless movies on demand, long-distance telephone services, high-speed electronic access, online shopping, video games, and cable television.[12] Expectations for FSN were never realized, and in 1996, Levin scaled back the ambitious but failed venture.[13] Confidence in Levin's leadership did not drop precipitously and even rebounded as the economy lifted and Time Warner joined the rush to the Internet.

Put Stakeholders at Ease

Show Them the Money.   As Michael Dell said so poignantly, "Ideas are wonderful but show me the money."[14] As discussed at the beginning of this chapter and the end of Chapter 6, Wall Street typically gives CEOs up to five consecutive poor earnings quarters, or about 14 to 17 months, to lift share price. When it comes to pleasing the Street, CEOs are operating on borrowed time (see Exhibit 7.2).

Surprisingly, chief executives are not quite in tune with Wall Street's timetable, mistakenly giving themselves between 17 and 19 months to show financial progress, appreciably more time to leave a good impression than the five-quarter rule actually permits. This

EXHIBIT 7.2   *Amount of Time for New CEO to Accomplish Goals by Stakeholder Group*

Average Number of Months	CEOs	Execs.	Wall St.	Gov't.	Media
To develop strategic vision	8.63	8.06	7.94	6.85	6.44
To win support of employees	9.66	9.05	8.59	8.46	7.38
To develop quality senior management team	14.35	14.34	12.48	11.34	12.31
To earn credibility with Wall Street	17.47	17.16	14.80	17.40	16.27
To increase share price	19.01	18.79	17.06	17.50	18.40
To turn company around	20.45	20.60	20.56	20.72	21.60
To reinvent how company does business	22.26	21.91	21.63	21.77	22.31

Note: Sample consists of CEOs, senior business executives (Execs.), financial analysts/institutional investors (Wall St.), government officials (Gov't.), and business media (Media).

Source: Burson-Marsteller, *Building CEO Capital*, 2001.

discrepancy of one to three months is an alarming disconnect at a crucial time, when a month or two of poor performance can mean the death knell to a CEO's future. Making matters worse, senior executives tend to offer similarly generous estimates, compounding the perceptual error. Accordingly, CEOs and their teams may need to accelerate their timetable for delivering results or at least adopt an early strategy to buy themselves additional time if they wish to mollify the financial crowd and their boards, whose impatience in the absence of firm results will inevitably mount by the middle of year two.

Charles C. Conaway's time as Kmart Corporation's CEO ended abruptly in his 22nd month. Initially, stakeholders positively viewed Conaway's turnaround plan to reduce inventory, close stores, install better technology, partner with Martha Stewart, and improve customer service. But then Kmart reported poor sales results after the 2001 holiday season, even though its competitors—Wal-Mart and Target—both reported sharp sales increases during the same period. At the start of Conaway's 20th month, Kmart issued a profit warning and the stock sunk 71 percent. Time ran out for Conaway. Stakeholders' excitement about his initial plans could not save him, and he lost credibility. The market and board no longer had confidence in his leadership, and the company went into a free fall. In a matter of weeks, the board installed a new chairman.

For most stakeholders, one of the best indicators of whether a company is producing is its share price. Near the end of year two, the share price should reflect increasing financial strength and, for a company that had been nonperforming, indications of a turnaround. If under the CEO's watch the company cannot deliver substantive results, the CEO's tenure will be in jeopardy. Conaway is not alone in missing his second anniversary for exactly this reason. He joins several other executives who could not hold onto their titles past 22 months: Leo J. Hindrey, Jr. of Global Crossing, G. Richard Thoman of Xerox, Lloyd D. Ward of Maytag, Robert Nakasone of Toys 'R' Us, Charles R. Perrin of Avon Products, Durk I. Jager of Procter & Gamble, and Michael C. Hawley of The Gillette Company.

As discussed in Chapter 6, when first meeting analysts and discussing financial goals, CEOs must not overcommit. They must be disciplined and avoid talking too much, because loquaciousness all too often leads to overpromising. This is easier said than done when investor confidence hangs on every word. Yet no reason exists to fall into the trap of spouting overly optimistic or excessively specific predictions. Far better to follow Warren Buffet's Noah Rule, "Predicting rain doesn't count; building arks does."[15] The consequences of failing to heed this advice during the first year will now be apparent. Even if the company does reasonably well, a failure to meet previously articulated unrealistic goals could be disastrous. Although a positive performance might ordinarily have been deemed satisfactory or even praiseworthy, once goals are stated, only meeting or bettering those goals will likely be labeled a success. Anything less, even if better than every other competitor, amounts to little more than a failure to meet expectations.

Show Them a Collaborative Top Management Team without Dissidence and Discord.   According to Burson-Marsteller's research, by 14 months on average, CEOs are expected to have their senior team in place. The right team must be positioned to drive performance. Stakeholders expect no less. The time for attracting and building a management team is essentially over. Throughout the first year, the team had their chance to coalesce, and the CEO had the opportunity to replace nonperforming members or those who cannot commit to the CEO's strategic vision and direction.

Failure to assemble a talented team that is skilled at inspiring, leading, and implementing can be catastrophic. Stakeholders are well aware that even a CEO with highly developed CEO capital cannot run a company alone. Every CEO needs a team. Shortly after George W. Bush's election, the press reported that Russia's President Putin had little regard for the new president. When questioned, Putin deflected the inquiry, noting that when it comes to leadership, "the retinue makes the king."[16] The absence of a sufficient retinue or the presence of one in which internal dissension prevails might therefore undermine all that a CEO hopes to achieve.

One such instance occurred when a communications company CEO failed to put a collaborative management team in place before he passed his one-year anniversary. At monthly executive meetings, the CEO's words landed on deaf ears. Everyone continued to say one thing to the CEO and then do another as soon as he departed. The otherwise talented chief executive could not resolve the conflicts or diminish the enmity among executive team members. Half the team—those who had prior ties to the CEO and who had the CEO's attention—felt protected and lacked a sense of urgency to perform. As word eventually reached the board about the team's lack of harmony and the CEO's refusal to dismiss nonperformers, the board dismissed the CEO and shortly thereafter the remainder of his executive team.

Top management teams model appropriate corporate attitudes for the rest of the company. The team and the CEO shape the culture that becomes part and parcel of the CEO's strategic vision. "The culture of a company is the behavior of its leaders,"[17] remarks Richard Brown, CEO of computer-services giant EDS. "Leaders get the behaviors they tolerate."[18] Managers serve as an alternative means of CEO communication as well as a pathway of authority. It is essential that management act in line with the CEO's direction and that they appear united and cooperative. These managers are armed with the power to immediately reinforce daily behavior, whether through outright rewards such as spot bonuses and increased responsibilities, or more often and perhaps most effectively, through simple verbal praise. Without a top management team exhibiting behaviors and articulating objectives consistent with the CEO's strategic vision, without superiors modeling appropriate behavior for employees and those employees passing on similar direction to their direct reports, all the CEO communications in the world are not likely to produce tangible results. The failure to establish a collaborative top management team without dissension will inevitably have disastrous consequences. Progress will grind to a halt.

EDS's Brown is a good example of a chief executive who reshaped management to build a new culture based on accountability and collaboration. When Brown arrived from Cable and Wireless, EDS found itself sadly trailing IBM Global Services and on a losing streak. Brown unleashed massive change, starting at the top with the dismissal of several executives who had been working in the lap of luxury, commonly referred to as the "God Pod."[19] He then used a framework developed by management guru Ram Charan to further his operational tenet—the company's commitment to "action, urgency, excellence." "The dialogues, beliefs, and behaviors of the CEO and his or her change agents," Charan explains, "will become the models for all others . . . [and these agents will] design rewards and sanctions to enforce them."[20] Brown and Charan set forth a three-part structure to modify management and make it a tool for culture change:

1. *Triannual, in-person, general policy meetings.* Top managers meet face-to-face at least three times each year to share

information, focus priorities, and analyze the competitive marketplace. By keeping top leadership informed of what is required of them on a regular, scheduled basis, the company ensures that managers speak to their team members with a single voice.

2. *Monthly performance meetings.* At EDS, 125 senior managers from around the globe participate in monthly early morning conference calls to review progress in meeting financial objectives, sales targets, and service excellence. As Brown comments on these calls, "there is no shade."[21] Senior executives must participate—vacation plans or not. Managers share the good, the bad, and the ugly. Again, accountability, collaboration, and honesty—the qualities Brown emphasizes.

3. *Forced rankings or quartiling* (ranking employees into quarters and linking compensation to rank). EDS judges employees against their peers, compensates them accordingly, and offers them feedback.[22] Feedback is honest and clear and is provided at regular intervals, so as to reinforce all who are doing well and to give those who are not an opportunity to improve. The company rewards those who rank high and ultimately counsels out those who do not. Forced rankings (GE also uses this performance-based model) emphasize that the EDS culture measures and rewards people on merit. The effect is often profound and particularly useful in a company that is fat with "dead wood." As Brown noted, the system rewards energy providers and redirects or removes the energy drainers.[23]

These structural changes among top leadership echo Brown's mantra of "action, urgency, excellence." According to Brown, once the senior team embraces the mantra, the culture of top leadership would change, eventually affecting the culture of the broader organization too. At EDS, the culture did change, shifting decisively toward action, urgency, and excellence. Although EDS profits have recently plummeted, EDS produced $21.5 billion in revenues in 2001—its best ever. Moreover, employee turnover sank below 10 percent and client satisfaction ratings rose sky high.[24]

Plan the Future

Seek Input from Independent Parties.   During year one, the CEO sought self-edification to learn about the company from a variety of sources, including customers, analysts, current and former employees, and research. The prudent CEO should also have established, if possible, a confidante in the form of an aide de camp and, ideally, independent counsel as well. During the Turning Point stage, the CEO goes further, applying these same practices to the company at large. The goal is to institutionalize two kinds of input from external sources that benefit the company as a whole: (1) a checks and balances system—input from third parties to ensure that the company remains aware of outside developments and is subject to independent evaluation; and (2) creative intake—outside ideas that stimulate thought and encourage original solutions to company problems. Independent, outside parties, who are beholden to no one for job security, are excellently positioned to challenge accepted policies, procedures, and thought processes and to prompt innovation. By initiating discussions with such third parties, the company communicates its openness to untraditional channels and promotes a team ethic, a sense of joint ownership over company strategy.

Andy Grove, chairman and co-founder of Intel Corporation, wrote in his acclaimed book, *Only the Paranoid Survive*,[25] how important it is for a CEO to be aware of the forest as well as the trees—that is, not to get caught up in the minutiae of running a company, and in the process, lose sight of how a CEO's strategy fits into general industry and societal trends. Grove advised constant monitoring of the marketplace for so-called "strategic inflection points,"[26] indications that business fundamentals are about to change. In the mid-1980s, Grove faced one of those strategic inflection points when Japanese manufacturers of memory chips, which were Intel's flagship product, began offering stiff competition. Aware of Intel's weakening position in the marketplace, Grove avoided disaster by steering Intel into an entirely new line of business—microprocessors—which Intel manufactures today and which positions the company at the top of its industry.

Unlike Intel, Prodigy Services, the first online service launched in 1990, was not so attuned to industry trends. The company paid undue attention to the trees, not enough to the forest, and suffered accordingly. By way of illustration, even though almost any Web surfer would have been able to confirm that free speech, community interaction, and free, ready access were the Internet's principle allures, Prodigy's parent companies Sears Roebuck and IBM banned discussion groups about sex and AIDS. They then compounded the error by imposing a 25-cent surcharge for each e-mail over 30 e-mails per month.[27] Prodigy subscribers lobbied to change the edict, but the company—curiously impervious to the burgeoning success of H&R Block's CompuServe and America Online, each of which aligned themselves with the forces of free speech on the Internet—resisted. Prodigy lost its lead.

Bringing in opinions and voices from outside the company is one way to ensure that a company will go the way of Intel and not the way of Prodigy, and that the company will be aware of both the forest and the trees. It is also a means to encourage discussion, avoid insularity, and generate creative solutions to company problems. Some ways of utilizing independent third parties include the following:

- *Invite futurists, industry experts, academics, consultants or non–industry-specific change agents to speak.* To stimulate discussion, invite a speaker with a partisan point of view—the more partisan, the better. Typically, the forum chosen for these speakers is an offsite gathering, but rolling breakfasts or lunches will suffice. Christopher B. Galvin, chairman and CEO of Motorola, for example, held "strange idea" meetings as an excuse to brainstorm about the future.[28] Some CEOs also bring in other chief executives to speak with their management teams (Ford Motor Company brought in Lord Browne of BP) or visit other companies to obtain a better handle on their best practices. Similarly, senior teams from various companies regularly visit many most-admired companies for pointers.

- *Ask university groups to discuss specific business topics.* Former CEO Thomas Whitford of PNC Advisors used Wharton's Executive Education Program to provide a series of seminars for his top 25 senior executives and then expanded the seminars to include middle management. The program addressed industry drivers, business theory, high-performance teaming, and financing trends. CEO Whitford said: "We all have a better understanding of and stronger commitment to the strategic choices we have made. There is joint accountability."[29] Not only did the Wharton team stimulate thought, but it also helped develop a sense of collective ownership over company direction.

- *Create special work groups.* In the early 1990s, Shell Oil Company produced $0 in profit on $26 billion in gross revenues. Under the leadership and vision of President and CEO

Philip J. Carroll, Shell created the Business Transformation Team (BTT) to stir management's thinking. Sixtus J. Oechsle III, a former Shell vice president, reported how Shell structured the BTT:

> *The idea was that these teams (made up of a variety of highly rated employees from a very wide range of management and line positions) would spend approximately one-tenth to one-third of their time for 6 to 12 months benchmarking other companies and developing recommendations . . . on how to move Shell to "best of breed" in specific business arenas. During the first year, for example, five teams were set up in the following areas: Strategy and Planning, Human Resources, Growth, Brand/Identity, and Information Technology. Over the next few years topics included such areas as Benefits, Diversity, and Virtual Organizations.*[30]

Crucially, BTT sought third parties to stimulate ideas. According to Oechsle, the BTT team met with distinguished experts such as Professor Noel Tichy at the University of Michigan, learning theorist Peter Senge, and organizational developmentalist Stan Nabozny of the Gestalt Institute of Cleveland, Ohio. BTT concept workshops eventually led to the adoption of Shell's core purpose: "Helping people build a better world with an unwavering commitment to be the best."[31] From this purpose developed the pioneering concept of the "triple bottom line," that financial, social, and environmental success are all important. Oechsle concludes that BTT helped Shell discover its "beating heart."[32]

Mind your NGOs. The CEO who is keen on maintaining a long tenure should also take stock of special interest groups or nongovernmental organizations (NGOs) such as CARE, the Parents Music Resource Center, Oxfam, Medecins Sans Frontieres (Doctors without Borders), Helen Keller International, Interfaith Center on Corporate Responsibility, Amnesty International, Greenpeace, The Sierra Club, and World Wildlife Fund. That companies can exist, indeed flourish, in glorious isolation from governmental regulation and free of social obligation has long been an outdated concept. Today, social responsibility is no longer a matter of corporate discretion. NGOs demand that CEOs hear them, pay attention to their position, and change their company ways with regard to the issues they advocate. CARE, for example, asks companies to partner with them to eradicate poverty; Amnesty International works to protect human rights; and the Interfaith Center on Corporate Social Responsibility presses pharmaceutical companies to make life-saving HIV/AIDS medicines accessible and affordable in third-world countries. Better to recognize the inevitable and deal with social and environmental issues sooner rather than later in a spirit of cooperation rather than confrontation.

Recent surveys evidence the rising influence of NGOs and the issues they espouse. The public simply does not believe that NGOs are the wild-eyed fanatics that some naysayers imply. In a study by public relations firm Edelman Worldwide,[33] European opinion leaders report trusting NGOs twice as much as they trust government and substantially more than they trust companies. In the United States, trust in NGOs is somewhat more moderate, but still significant. The trust that American opinion leaders place in NGOs approaches parity with their trust in business and government. With globalization increasing, refuge can no longer be found by simply staying within national borders.

For example, the European campaign against non–genetically modified foods eventually influenced the U.S. market. Just ask Robert Shapiro, former chairman and CEO of Monsanto, who believes that genetically modified crops were "the single most successful introduction of technology in the history of agriculture, including the plow."[34] Genetically modified foods were at the start a success in the United States. Introducing such products in Europe was another story altogether. Many Europeans were against genetically enhanced seeds for crop protection, particularly coming on the heels of mad-cow disease and anti-American sentiment in Europe. Monsanto became a target. Greenpeace actively campaigned against the company, and crops were destroyed. Even Prince Charles joined the protest. Eventually the European campaign affected U.S. opinion. Americans also began criticizing Shapiro and referring to Monsanto as killers of monarch butterflies and purveyors of "frankenfoods."

Notwithstanding the increasing influence of NGOs and their growing credibility among the public, CEOs all too often underrate the significance of NGOs, failing to give them their due consideration. According to a 2002 PricewaterhouseCoopers study conducted in conjunction with the World Economic Forum, a mere 1 percent of worldwide CEOs believes that NGOs have any influence on the making of corporate strategy.[35] CEOs seem tradition-bound, turning first for guidance to customers and board members, seemingly insentient to wider societal concerns. Yet the court of public opinion, represented at least in part by NGOs, is becoming a more divisive voice on corporate actions that have social and environmental impact.

Today's NGOs, unlike yesterday's activists, are not powerless against even large multinational companies. Improved technology and communications enable most NGOs to investigate corporate social or antisocial behavior on a global level. Moreover, NGOs have become adept at using the media masterfully. Headlines broadcasting NGO complaints are not rare. Websites challenging corporate environmental practices are growing at an

unprecedented pace (e.g., corpwatch.com, mcspotlight.com, rag-
ingbull.com, and yahoo.com). Corporate Watch alone boasts more
than 100,000 user sessions per month.[36]

CEOs should expect to be brought into the NGO scuffle sooner
or later. Engaging NGOs in a dialogue before conflict arises rather
than after will lessen risk and safeguard credibility. Such dialogue
seems to be the wave of the future. In a survey of U.S. and European opinion leaders, no less than a startling 80 percent want business to partner with NGOs on tough issues.[37] Engaging in dialogue
with NGOs is no longer a rarity. Ford Motor Company, for example, held talks with worldwide environmental groups in August
2000. Chairman Bill Ford participated in a "Dialogue on Emerging Issues in Corporate Citizenship," a two-day private meeting
that brought together top Ford executives with environmentalists
so that they could address the fuel emission levels debate.[38]

Another such dialogue occurred in August 1995. Birds Eye
Wall's, a Unilever brand, asked Burson-Marsteller's London office
to evaluate an anticipated Greenpeace campaign. Greenpeace was
concerned about the depletion of stocks in the world's fisheries.
Because Unilever is one of the world's largest industrial users of
fish stocks (e.g., cod, hake, hoki, Alaskan pollack, and saithe), it
was, not surprisingly, an ideal target for any protest. With the help
of Burson-Marsteller's Corporate Social Responsibility Practice,
Unilever voluntarily established an innovative partnership with the
World Wildlife Fund for Nature (WWF) to establish the Marine
Stewardship Council (MSC). Unilever and WWF joined forces to
create a certification program that promoted responsible, environ-
mentally appropriate, socially beneficial, and economically viable
fisheries practices. In fact, Unilever announced that all of its fish
products would be 100 percent sustainability compliant by 2005.

Unilever's commitment to MSC certification was an important
achievement. The partnership succeeded in removing the company

from public scrutiny, enhanced Unilever's public image, provided brand differentiation, pleased employees, and most important, helped ensure a long-term sustainable fish supply. Unilever became part of the solution, not the problem. Now, Antony Burgmans, chairman of Unilever NV, regularly meets with NGOs and antiglobalists. He firmly believes that the two sides have plenty to learn from one another, regardless of their objectives. Burgmans has not abandoned his role as a representative of his company because he engages in these discussions. To the contrary, these discussions offered Burgmans the opportunity to explain Unilever programs:

> *I am called to account by the media and by the share-holders. So I am automatically a spokesman and how I formulate my message does matter. I think that companies must be transparent and that CEOs have to set the example in that. I feel very comfortable explaining it, as I know that our policy, our projects and our reports are well put together. When I talk about agriculture or fisheries, that is based on real projects, it's not just bland, non-committal words. I also go and find out for myself.*[39]

Thus Burgmans remains a spokesperson for the shareholders, but at the same time fosters his company's transparency even if it means meeting with NGOs.

As Burgmans discovered, cooperating with NGOs often does not hurt a company's bottom line all that much, and in many ways it helps. A growing body of evidence indicates that consumers vote with their pocketbooks, and those votes are in favor of socially responsible corporate policies. The Millennium Poll on Corporate Social Responsibility reports that nearly half of American consumers say they reward or punish companies' actions by buying or not buying their products or speaking out against the company.[40] The same study found that this attitude is even more pronounced among influential opinion makers around the world.

Start Networking.   Few activities are more time consuming for the typically overworked and time-pressured CEO than public speaking. Yet, at times, speaking engagements, especially before other CEOs and leaders, are highly desirable, if not essential. The more select the audience, the better. The companies of these peer CEOs and leaders might very well be the next merger partner, joint venturer, or new customer. Face-to-face contact is essential. Sizing up other leaders and achieving a sense of their rhythm can only be done in-person. Even in this age of huge, complex, multinational companies and burgeoning virtual communications and communities, personal contact among leaders is still important and supplies the lubricant that builds goodwill and eases negotiation. Personal contact among CEOs has brought together many corporate marriages.

Given a CEO's time pressures, selectivity in speaking engagements is a must. Prime engagements might include, for example, the Economic Club of Detroit, the Microsoft CEO Summit, or a *Fortune, Business Week, Forbes,* or *The Economist* CEO Forum. Some of these events are invitation only. However, the World Economic Forum, the jewel in the crown of all CEO gatherings, is typically held in Davos, Switzerland. Because of the forum's sheer size, exclusivity, and importance, a newcomer CEO might first wish to merely participate and only later, at a subsequent gathering, give a keynote speech or play another high-visibility role. Other key venues for speaking and networking include Herb Allen's Sun Valley event, *Chief Executive's* CEO conferences, the annual Business Roundtable conference, and George Gilder's Telecosm.

In addition to these premium events, whose intrinsic value emanates from their high-level networking potential, CEOs should select other engagements carefully, choosing only those that allow the CEO to reinforce the company's strategic objectives before an appropriate audience. One efficient way to accomplish this goal is for CEOs to orchestrate their own corporate conferences. These conferences build CEO capital, equity in the company's name, and provide a platform to enhance the company's specific expertise.

Bill Gates began his CEO Summits several years ago. He invites approximately 150 multinational CEOs, many of whom are customers, to Redmond, Washington to discuss business technology. Accenture, the leading management and technology services organization, holds top-level conferences categorized by industry and service type and highlights them on its website. Other management consulting firms also hold conferences on selected topics that interest customers and prospects.

Alternately, CEOs can pinpoint the niche they want to reach through an exclusive company-sponsored seminar, where the guest list can be handpicked. In June 2000, General Motors invited 65 top automotive journalists and financial analysts to meet with top GM executives over several days in Italy. The company flew the invitees and their spouses to a 15th century villa in the Italian Lake region to candidly discuss the future of the automotive business. President and CEO Richard Wagoner led the on-the-record meetings. Alex Taylor III, an automotive journalist for *Fortune*, reported that the seminar's value for GM was not to be found in media promotion but rather in providing a forum that developed the CEO's capital and provided an opportunity for the new CEO to meet people and, more important, for people to meet the new CEO:

> *Did GM get its money's worth? No favorable newspaper stories emerged in the days after the seminar, and no analyst raised his rating on GM stock. But the event did focus attention on the square-shouldered, energetic Wagoner, who became CEO on June 1.*[41]

Taylor's assessment of Wagoner was fairly positive, which was as much as GM could have hoped for. Meeting leading journalists and financial analysts can be worth the time, effort, and cost.

Another means of networking is for the CEO to accept a position on a board of a major institution, such as a community-driven organization (e.g., the Metropolitan Museum of Art, Lincoln Center, or Chicago Symphony Orchestra), a business-oriented forum (e.g., Business Roundtable, Junior Achievement, or Chicago's Commercial Club), or an industry-driven association (e.g., Chemical Manufacturers Association, Pharmaceutical Manufacturers Association, or American Medical Association). Joining organizations provides forums for building relationships and obtaining introductions to community and industry influentials.

A word of caution: A penchant for speaking engagements can overwhelm. Selectivity is the goal. CEOs, especially those who become well known, can easily become bogged down with speaking engagements. Michael Dell reportedly had 100 speaking requests in 1997, 800 the following year, and 1,500 by the first half of 1999. The number grows from there. Obviously he must turn down most requests. Many of Dell's engagements are personal, small-group meetings with top executives at companies interested in obtaining Dell's advice. For example, he spoke to the top 11 executives at Eastman Chemical and the top 300 executives at Ford Motor Company.[42] For Dell, key customer events get an automatic "yes." All evidence indicates that Michael Dell has no difficulty managing a full schedule while running a company. Whether most other CEOs should maintain a similar workload is questionable. In any event, before becoming a mainstay on the lecture circuit, CEOs should carefully weigh the benefits against the costs of excessive appearances.

Another caution about CEO speaking engagements: If the company is not performing as well as it should, employees and board members may take offense at the CEO devoting time, energies, and possibly resources to speaking opportunities. To many, the value of speeches and networking is simply not obvious and may be viewed as showcasing the CEO and drawing the CEO's attention away from more pressing company needs.

Digitize, Be Internet Savvy.   CEOs are hardly unaware of the technology revolution in business. In *On the Minds of CEOs*, a research investigation undertaken by Burson-Marsteller and the marketing arm of *Fortune*, 91 percent of worldwide CEOs reported using the Internet.[43] Most notably, CEOs use the Web at extraordinarily high levels—96 percent exchange e-mail, 94 percent visit online news and information sources, 87 percent visit their own company Web sites, and 75 percent monitor the competition online.

For those CEOs who have not yet entered the Information Age, they should reassess, and reassess quickly. Chairperson and CEO Daniel Vasella of Novartis Ag, for example, was one such convert. Novartis was preliminarily testing breakthrough drug STI-571 (marketed under the name Gleevec) that showed remission rates greater than 95 percent for sufferers of chronic myelogenous leukemia (CML). A Web site dedicated to accelerating clinical trials became a beacon for victims of the disease, eventually accelerating an intense online appeal to Novartis AG by more than 4,000 sufferers for more of the breakthrough drug. Almost immediately, Vasella ordered a vast increase in production, notwithstanding clear financial risks. Vasella had learned the Internet's power firsthand. A single patient had created the Web site, and through his initial efforts, had organized patients online, eventually influencing the pharmaceutical company's policies. "Before that I'd never had any contact with the power of the Internet."[44] Now Vasella knows that logging on can be a matter of life and death.

Failure to embrace the Internet can lead to setbacks, as W. Howard Lester, now chairman of the upscale retail outlet Williams-Sonoma, Inc. learned. Despite being headquartered in San Francisco, a stone's throw from Silicon Valley, Lester dragged his heels at committing to an online presence for retail chain and catalogue operations for Pottery Barn, Williams-Sonoma, Hold Everything, Chambers, and Gardener's Eden. He feared that going online would amount to competing against oneself, cannibalizing sales from stores and catalogues. "I just can't imagine that people are going to sit in front of a computer screen," Lester remarked in late 1997, "and buy our merchandise. Right now, I think it is way over hyped."[45] Two years later, however, Lester came to the realization that the Internet, acting in conjunction with outlets, could help build the brand and increase sales. The Williams-Sonoma Web site went live in November 1999. Although Lester had embraced the Internet late, his new Web venture soon exceeded revenue expectations.[46]

REFLECTIONS: LEADING THROUGH THOUGHT

The quintessential circumstance under which thought leadership arises is when a CEO finds it beneficial to address a broad audience, usually including representatives from a wide spectrum of different industries, on a topic of the CEO's choosing. What should the CEO discuss? What does the leader of this enterprise have to say that is meaningful? A discussion on meeting business targets or a rising share price won't suffice. Such a speech would amount to no more than shoptalk. Even articulating a CEO's vision may well fall short if its appeal is primarily company- or industry-specific. What outside and inside audiences are interested in learning is something that will have meaning to them as listeners, something with communitywide or societal implications. The CEO must offer words of wisdom, some meaningful idea about how the company makes a difference and is distinguishable from all the rest.

Thought leadership encompasses the development of new ideas—ideas that keep a company at the forefront of change. It transcends sectors and geographic borders, may amount to a broadly applicable vision or even an operational tenet, or may simply reinforce current corporate beliefs. What is perhaps most significant about thought leadership is that it distinguishes and differentiates a company from its competitors—proclaiming, in effect, "Look at us if you wish to know what a company with a purpose looks like and acts." Thought leadership often breaks with business or industry convention, astonishes if not startles. Thought leadership reflects on the company and builds CEO capital. Given its far-reaching consequences, it may often, although not always, fit within the category of socially responsible corporate behavior. Typically, a leading thought amounts to an epiphany of graceful simplicity, a seemingly self-evident assertion of the "Why didn't I think of that" variety, which is capable of eliciting an Ah-hah! acknowledgment of sudden clarity.

Thought leadership, even when socially oriented, should not be inconsistent with financial common sense. Take, for instance, Carly Fiorina's World e-Inclusion program at HP. Started in October 2000, the program (sometimes called B2-4B or "business to four billion" of the world's poor) has HP selling, leasing, or donating products and services to governments, development agencies, and nonprofit organizations in developing countries. By providing low-powered HP products, HP facilitated villagers' educational training, income opportunities, health care resources, and financial services. Fiorina's commitment to "doing well by doing good" is bold, inventive, and startling. As David Kirkpatrick of *Fortune* explained, "I see HP, with operations already in 120 countries and a long tradition of community engagement, as a laudable pioneer."[47] Self-interest clasps hands with admirable purpose: "At last, a so-called global corporation is facing up to what much of the world really is: a place of abject poverty."[48] Despite HP's merger with Compaq, Fiorina's commitment to e-inclusion continues.

Crucial to thought leadership is the willingness to flout convention, a willingness to rethink commonly held assumptions. On May 19, 1997, BP's Lord Browne broke ranks with other leading oil companies and acknowledged concern over global climate change at a speech given at Stanford University. He remarked: "It is a moment for change and for a rethinking of corporate responsibility."[49] Although, technically speaking, the link between greenhouse gas emissions and an increase in temperature is still unproven, according to Browne, the risk was great enough to "take precautionary action."[50] Browne's Stanford University speech alarmed oil industry leaders. One industry leader remarked: "He's out of the church."[51]

Browne outlined five steps that BP would take to alleviate global warming: controlling its own emissions, funding scientific research, jointly implementing programs, developing alternative fuels, and participating in the effort to find global answers.[52] The speech also laid out his position on corporate responsibility and obligation, which, he believed, was entirely consistent with profit: "No company can be really successful unless it is sustainable. . . . Real sustainability is about simultaneously being profitable and responding to the reality and the concerns of the world in which you operate. We're not separate from the world. It's our world as well."[53] Under Browne's watch, BP would help take "responsibility for the future of our planet."[54]

A critical element of BP's thought leadership is increased investment in solar power. Browne intends to make solar power competitive within 10 years. He estimates that replenishable energy sources such as solar power could meet 5 percent of the world's energy needs in 20 years and 50 percent by 2050. Actions BP takes today will, according to Browne, reap benefits 20 to 30 years down the road. Browne has also added another aspect to the challenge of global climate change: the development of clean fuels that contain no lead or have minimal levels of sulphur. BP offers these fuel alternatives in 40 cities worldwide to combat air pollution. Like so many of his initiatives, Browne manages his push to combat climate change strategically, methodically, and for the long term.

Browne sets clear and specific metrics for BP's global anti–climate change efforts just as he does for any other company program. He makes it clear that there are good business reasons for this position. In a 1998 speech at Yale University, Browne presented the targets BP set for itself: by 2010, to reduce greenhouse gas emissions by 10 percent from a 1990 base. BP's target was twice the 5 percent cut that 35 nations agreed to at a United Nations conference on global warming. Fred Krupp, executive director of the Environmental Defense Fund, expressed astonishment that BP was willing to "follow forward and cut emissions on the same timetable as the Kyoto agreement but independent of whether it is ratified is an example of corporate leadership that is historic."[55] Not only was BP willing to commit when others were not, not only was BP willing to set targets at rates far in excess of those being discussed, but in March 2002 the company announced that it had far exceeded expectations. BP was eight years ahead of its target, having reduced greenhouse gas by more than 9 million tons.[56] The BP CEO is a firm believer in the view that whatever gets measured gets managed.

Browne never seems to miss a beat or an opportunity to explain BP. In each speech and interview, he repeats BP's position on the global climate change debate, emphasizes specific targets, and describes why BP's commitment is good for shareholders.

For Browne, BP's commitment to the environment provides competitive distinctiveness. Browne talks frequently about the importance of being distinctive. Browne's responsibility to the planet is now an integral part of the company's business strategy and growth and is deeply integrated into the company's culture and performance ethos. "And none of this is about public relations. It isn't about applying a coat of green paint."[57] As viewed by Lord Browne, "It is no good just being another decent company with decent results."[58]

Browne has built a deep cache of CEO capital. He has received numerous awards in admiration of his environmental position and leadership. Browne has worked hard at taking his message to some of the world's most significant audiences. His public leadership on behalf of BP has been a role model for other 21st-century CEO-led initiatives. Browne and BP stand for something distinctive—something that has a positive, measurable impact on the company and the environment—which is no easy task in this oversaturated world. Not surprisingly, he continuously ranks among the top 10 CEOs in the *Financial Times'* "World's Most Respected Leaders" survey.[59]

Thought leadership is expected of companies today, especially in matters of social concern. Nancy Adler, management professor at McGill University, sees the future corporation assuming many of the larger societal issues that governments currently manage. "In 2020, I would see a third of a CEO's time being spent on issues bigger than the company—world education, world health, world peace, the environment."[60] Harold Burson, founding chairman of Burson-Marsteller, also sees change in corporate attitude toward greater public responsibility: "The corporation has a societal role to play, and CEOs are being held accountable for their social performance."[61]

So how then does a CEO develop thought leadership? Surely gathering research and being open to various thoughts and ideas from a variety of sources is part of it. For the CEO who follows the suggested practices set forth in this book, this type of information gathering and issue raising should have started as early as the Countdown and become institutionalized by the Turning Point stage. What is needed, however, is something more than information gathering: an attitude, a willingness to question convention, the strength to buck the trend. Playing it safe won't suffice. So, when gathering information and analyzing situations, the CEO who wishes to contribute beyond the bottom line must think untraditionally, assume no givens, and be aware of societal changes that present implications for the way the company does business. The type of epiphany that leads to thought leadership is not always so apparent. When the circumstances occur that create the possibility of an Ah-hah! solution, the CEO must have an open enough mind to recognize and act on it.

J. Michael Cook, retired chairman and CEO of Deloitte & Touche, had such an open mind when he visited his eldest daughter at college in the late 1980s, a time when the female presence in his industry had made little headway and for all intents and purposes, the "good ol' boy network" was alive and well.[62] Cook noticed that his daughter's dorm room was inundated with business cards and recruiting brochures. He also realized that his daughter, and undoubtedly other young women her age, were as determined as any man to establish a career. That so many young women would aggressively seek paths other than one that led without serious deviation toward motherhood and domesticity was new to Cook, who had come of age in prefeminist America.

This initial observation regarding the changing role of women made a strong impact on him, and a few years later, after becoming chief executive of the U.S. consultancy, he noticed that Deloitte was losing female accountants. The implications of all those business cards and brochures in his daughter's room came rushing back to him—an Ah-hah! moment was about to happen. "I couldn't in good conscience be head of an organization that offered less to women than I would expect for my daughters," he stated.[63]

Cook subsequently formed a task force on the retention and advancement of women in his firm. This task force evolved into the

Initiative for the Retention and Advancement of Women. Deloitte & Touche soon became widely recognized as a leader in women's advancement and won numerous awards as a result: Columbia Business School Botwinick Prize in Business Ethics (1998), *Fortune*'s "100 Best Companies to Work for in America" (2001, 2000, 1998), *Working Mother*'s "100 Best Companies for Working Mothers" (1994–1999), and The Catalyst Award (1995).[64]

By the late 1990s, an expanding role for women became an accounting industry standard, with more than 60 percent of accounting graduates being women. Cook articulated two reasons for his company's championship of the woman's role in the workplace: one because it was socially correct, the other because it was fiscally correct:

> *The first reason is that it's the right thing to do. We as an organization are committed to providing our people with the opportunity to realize their full potential to succeed to the extent of their abilities. . . .The second reason for being committed to the advancement of women is the business imperative.[65]*

As is more often than not the case, such recognition of societal change can be linked to clear business goals, grounded in a profit motive. Cook realized that if Deloitte & Touche was going to be an attractive employer to a new and growing pool of female talent, Deloitte & Touche had to become more hospitable to professional women. Social responsibility and business purpose once again dovetailed nicely.

Being a thought leader requires companywide commitment, not just executive lip service. Such an initiative usually carries a high price tag. Furthering a concept with societywide implications, as in the case of changing a company's processes and environmental practices, as in the case of Lord John Browne's, and Cook's Women's Initiative, requires considerable investment. Steve Case,

CEO of AOL before its merger with Time Warner, adopted as his thought initiative eliminating online child pornography and enforcing family-friendly online options. Apart from contributing much of his own time and effort to the initiative, Case had AOL fund several lawsuits against spammers (individuals or companies who send unsolicited e-mail) who promoted pornography and developed educational brochures and parental controls aimed at helping parents regulate their children's use of the Internet.

Once a CEO focuses on a thought leadership position, and goes public on that position, the CEO owns that thought. With ownership of a thought initiative comes the responsibility to do something about it; hence the CEO's time and effort, and the company's financial support, inevitably follow if the CEO's and the company's credibility are to be maintained.

One way to promote a thought initiative is to create partnerships and affiliations with outside organizations, typically NGOs or governmental or quasi-governmental groups. Partnerships and affiliations with nonprofits and other like-minded organizations signal the CEO's earnestness and willingness to join with others to develop solutions to pressing problems. These affiliations also lend legitimacy to CEO's efforts by providing third-party endorsements to their corporate initiatives.

Under the aegis of Cisco Systems, CEO John Chambers partnered with the United Nations Development Programme to form Netaid.org in an attempt to use the Internet to eradicate extreme poverty. Fiorina's World e-Inclusion similarly seeks to partner with like-minded local organizations having extensive experience and credibility in the Third World, such as the Foundation for Sustainable Development of Costa Rica and the Grameen Bank in Bangladesh. BP works on low carbon technology with the Batelle Institute, the Electric Power Research Institute, and the U.S. Department of Energy. The petroleum giant also supports environmental research at MIT in Cambridge, Massachusetts, and the Royal Society in London.

Steve Case of AOL partnered with several organizations to promote his anti–child pornography platform, including the Federal Bureau of Investigation, the National Center for Missing & Exploited Children, and the Family Research Council; Michael Cook partnered with Catalyst, the women's independent research firm, to develop his women's workforce initiative; and Gerald Levin of Time Warner worked with literacy organizations as part of his broader value initiative. In fact, Time Warner's "Time To Read" volunteer initiative is the country's largest corporate-sponsored literacy program. Finally, Intel—whose chairperson Andy Grove has championed science education for decades—has partnered with the Science Talent Search Awards, offering scholarships to high-achieving high school students. These awards have been compared in prestige to "mini" Nobel Prizes.

Thought leadership differentiates a company's standing in its industry, providing it with a strategic and competitive advantage. The CEO is the perfect channel for delivering a differentiating and "leaderful" thought. Without commitment from the top, the platform will not realize its full potential and sustainability. Of course, the rhetoric of thought leadership must accurately reflect reality.

During the fifth stage of the CEO Capital model, both the strategic vision and the formation of a thought-leadership platform go a long way in building CEO capital and in differentiating a company and its management. Often such initiatives are just being introduced during the last few months of year two and may not yet have debuted internally or in the marketplace. That will come soon enough, and selection of a thought leadership position should be strategically based. Many stakeholders such as Wall Street and the media may, in the short term, express more interest in increased share price than with doses of social good. Yet, even where the social element overshadows the business implications of a thought-leadership position, CEOs must persevere, offering relevance to the societies in which they operate while enhancing employee pride, attracting newcomers, and driving financial performance.

------➤◦◄------

If all has gone well, the CEO has sharply reshaped the enterprise by the close of the second year. As the company's leader, the CEO has acted responsibly by building a strategic vision and infusing the senior team and organization with a sense of urgency in pursuit of a vision, a promise, and numerous other possibilities.

Critical stakeholders expect CEOs to meet financial targets; excuses are not tolerated. Even so, as important as running a financially viable company is, the success of a CEO, at least one who aspires to have his or her company rise above the multitude, is measured by more than just dollars and cents. Not that economic success is unimportant. To the contrary. It is an essential CEO responsibility. Without achieving financial performance, a CEO can hardly be said to have followed his or her prime directive and is hardly in a position to develop thought leadership. Yet simply raising share price or otherwise evidencing large returns for shareholders is not enough for the CEO who wishes to accomplish something that surpasses the ordinary and to fully develop CEO capital. To reach this higher level of business achievement, the CEO must not be just a bottom-line leader, but also a leader in thought. Chairperson Robert Haas of Levi Strauss & Co., a company known for its socially responsible thought leadership, skillfully states: "I don't want my tombstone to read: 'He shipped a billion pair of jeans.' "[66]

CHAPTER 8

REVISION AND REINVENTION: RECASTING THROUGH SUCCESSION, LEAVING A LEGACY

The vision phase is full of excitement, vim, and vigor. Everything looks big and rosy. At that stage, we don't know what we don't know. Then you get into the patience stage, and that's tough.[1]

—Steven A. Ballmer, CEO of
Microsoft Corporation

The primary task of leadership is to communicate the vision and the values of an organization. Second, leaders must win support for the vision and the values they articulate. And third, leaders have to reinforce the vision and the values.[2]

—Frederick Smith, chairman and
CEO of FedEx

The fifth and final stage of building CEO capital begins at approximately 23 months and continues into the fourth year. Describing this stage, one CEO said he felt as if he was "herding cats." As soon as one cat escapes—that is, as soon as the CEO realizes that an approach fails to work—the CEO must go and catch it, bring it back to the fold, find out where the opening was, and then build a better enclosure to prevent that cat from escaping again. This fifth stage parallels Harvard professor John Gabarro's consolidation stage where senior executives "typically take corrective measures,"[3] modifying what did not previously work and reinforcing what did. Focus is first and foremost on efficiently executing on the central tenets of the CEO's strategic vision, ensuring that what the CEO intends to happen does happen, and correcting what does not happen. It is a time neither to coast nor to rest on previous triumphs. Rather it is a time to engage in the nitty-gritty aspects of management, moving forward with the best practices of previous stages and getting the job done.

Although revising and reinforcing the CEO's vision and focusing on execution requires much of the chief executive's attention during this stage, the seeds of a new or altered vision sprout near the end of year four. Change sweeps through business today with increasing speed, and no CEO can realistically expect that even the most well-crafted vision will retain its validity or vitality free of some modification for more than a few years. A seemingly internal contradiction must thus be maintained. To be effective, a CEO must forge a vision that looks far into the future. Yet the CEO must be flexible enough to tolerate modifications to that vision, even total makeovers, after only a few years as industries and markets change, and as technological and global advances alter our concept of what tomorrow will bring. CEOs must reinvent their organizations to keep them competitive and fresh. They must change direction, sometimes moderately, sometimes drastically, near the end of year four.

By keeping the CM factors on the agenda, CEOs can continue to fine-tune their CEO capital building. As Exhibit 8.1 illustrates, CEOs amass capital by implementing the strategic vision, reinventing the future, and casting a legacy.

BEST PRACTICES FOR REVISION

Execute to Deliver

Having made it through stage four, a CEO is likely to conclude that matters are well in hand. The CEO must resist that urge. The best practices in this stage amount to nothing other than more of the same—that is, to do what the CEO has been doing and not to slacken the pace, to stay focused, to execute on the plan. To rest on one's laurels leads to disaster. As chairman and CEO Gordon Bethune of Continental Airlines observed, "I can't emphasize it enough. A company can't just stay good. It has to keep getting *better*."[4] Stage five may not be the most creative part of a CEO's tenure, but that does not mean it is unimportant. The emphasis is on operations and management, making plans a reality, and improving what has already been achieved.

Repetition of the vision and taking action is characteristic of this period. To be sure, CEOs are by now undoubtedly growing weary of their mantra. Jack Welch, former chairman and CEO of GE, described this feeling well: "Like every goal and initiative we've ever launched, I repeated the No. 1 or No. 2 message over and over again until I nearly gagged on the words."[5] Weary or not, CEOs must maintain interest, communicate the message repeatedly and vigorously, remain hands-on, and not be diverted from the primary directive—putting their company's strategic vision into action.

EXHIBIT 8.1

CM Factor Analysis: Revision and Reinvention

			RESULTS		
Action	*Credibility*	*Conduct*	*Communication*	*Motivation*	*Mgmt.*
Revise					
Execute to deliver.	X	X	X	X	X
Execute. Keep it burning.			X	X	X
Execute. Put the customer front and center.		X		X	X
Reinvent					
Leave a legacy.	X	X	X		X

Credibility: This is a time to engage in the nitty-gritty of management, continuing with best practices and achieving goals. Focus is first and foremost on efficiently administering the central tenets of the CEO's strategic vision. Time should be set aside to reflect on leaving a lasting imprint, a final tribute to the CEO's beliefs and values.

Conduct: The actions by which the CEO shepherds the organization to execute and calibrate customer satisfaction calls attention to CEO principles. Perceptions of CEO conduct during this stage endure.

Communicating internally: Reiteration of the strategic vision to internal constituencies reinforces the urgency of delivering on promises. Employees will pass along lessons of this stage to future generations.

Motivating employees: Employees must be motivated to stay focused, to put the customer first, and to do the hard detailed work of getting the job done. Keeping up the company's spirit and keeping employees on task is therefore critical.

Building a management team: The CEO must work closely with the management team to fine-tune and execute. By the end of stage five, the CEO and the management team should consider new ideas for reinventing the organization, formulate a new vision, and transform the company once more. The CEO should give serious consideration to bequeathing CEO capital to a worthy successor.

For David Pottruck, co-CEO of Charles Schwab, role modeling, training, and attending to details are also an important part of execution. CEOs must model appropriate behavior by sweating the details, coaching, and having their managers coach direct reports. Pottruck says:

> That's how Schwab got to be the company it is. We had some good strategies but we really executed well. I mean it's like hitting a golf ball. You don't watch Tiger Woods on television swing a golf club and say, "That's all" or "I can do that" and go out to a golf course and pick up a club and ball and swing it. It doesn't mean you hit like Tiger Woods or even anything close. It takes someone to coach you and teach you because there's a lot of subtlety in the execution. Swinging a club is not just swinging a club. It's all in the subtleties.[6]

Thus, the devil is in the details, or more accurately, attending to the details. After adopting and pursuing best practices, the CEO must not wander and must remain focused, making sure that each practice has its desired result.

The CEO must relentlessly hold the senior team accountable for executing and delivering on promises made and remind the organization that the most inspirational visions amount to nothing without superior execution. The CEO's job is to make sure that the plan is executable and executed. Management must ensure that employees understand how the CEO's vision fits into their daily responsibilities, actions, and decision making. CEOs must charge managers with reinforcing appropriate employee behavior and winning the support of their colleagues to enhance the company's vision.

For the most part, CEOs do not make speeches, write books, or attend conferences to discuss execution. People want to hear about the vision, not how to execute it. The vision is motivating and inspirational; execution is dry and dull. The nuts and bolts of getting work done constitutes the hum-drum activities of running an organization. Former AlliedSignal/Honeywell International chairman and CEO Larry Bossidy and management consultant Ram Charan agree. They have written one of the few, if any, books on the art of executing, *Execution: The Discipline of Getting Things Done.*[7] Bossidy believes that the CEO plays a central role in this stage, "intensely evaluating people, making sure strategies can be implemented, and making sure operating plans are sufficiently detailed so that they can be executed. The CEO must lead that charge and, above all, must always remain realistic."[8]

We've just discussed reiterating past practices, repeating messages, modeling, coaching, holding employees accountable—all of which emphasize detail and are routine. Steve Ballmer, chief executive of Microsoft, describes the hum-drum of this stage as tweaking strategy and being patient while change falls into place. Not exactly sexy activities. He says that the hardest part is, "Always being mindful of the amount of patience we have to show toward the things that we engage in. It means sticking with things even when they are not going well, and it also means that you are decisive enough when you do really need to make change."[9] Such efforts are dogged detail work.

A chief executive who ignores the dogged detail work required in this stage does so at considerable risk. In a Burson-Marsteller study among CEOs, financial analysts and institutional investors—often the most impatient group—rate a CEO's inability to execute as the single most important reason for failure.[10] As far as these market movers are concerned, being able to execute makes or breaks a CEO. According to management guru Ram Charan and *Fortune*'s Editorial Director Geoff Colvin, 70 percent of CEO failures are caused by poor implementation: "It's bad execution. As simple as that: not getting things done, being indecisive, not delivering on commitments."[11]

During the fifth stage of the CEO Capital model, the most effective CEOs are operational watchdogs who closely monitor how the work gets done. Jeff Bezos, CEO of Amazon, it is said, makes decisions before breakfast. Part of Lou Gerstner's makeover at IBM was getting the right things done right. When he inherited IBM in 1993, there were many meetings, many "yeses," and many task forces. Yet, IBM's products never went to market on time or as planned. Even in an industry that changes constantly and so dramatically, Gerstner concluded that if IBM could only execute more effectively, the going would be easier:

> The single biggest challenge at IBM is making it all happen. . . . It's making execution. We are arguably the most complex company in the world. . . . The real issue is how do we execute in a company of 300,000 people across 17 countries . . . in an industry that changes as dramatically as ours does. When we can execute what we want to do in front of the customer, we're unique. We win almost every time. It's a huge managerial challenge.[12]

In 2000, Gerstner reached what he termed the "third turn of the wheel."[13] He reorganized his senior management team to bring execution front and center.[14] He argued that the e-business strategy they had put into place was working, but the deciding success factor rested on execution. Gerstner concentrated on developing "a very, very focused execution capability within the company."[15] And develop he did. He set strategy, made the hard decisions, motivated people, and rewarded those who met their goals. IBM received its reward, too—it was the most admired company in its industry in the *Fortune* 2001 America's Most Admired Companies survey.[16]

Recently, a former CEO of a *Fortune* 100 company offered advice similar to that of Gerstner's—emphasize the importance of execution. The CEO confirmed that stage five was definitely different and more difficult than the others, a time when there is no room for excuses or mistakes: "[The emphasis] changed from the formation of a strategy and a vision to a very intense focus now on . . . flawless implementation. So it is a change. It is just as exciting but in a different way . . . But it's tough. It's tough."[17] As recent advertising by management consulting giant Accenture reminds us, "It's not how many ideas you have, it's how many you make happen."

Execute: Keep It Burning

The issue facing CEOs is not what to do during this stage. Presumably, most CEOs who have made it thus far have already isolated those best practices that are most useful to them. For the most part, they need to do little more than what they have already done, making sure, however, to stay focused on the job at hand and to stay diligent. They need to do the hard detail work required to get the job done and done well. Motivating and maintaining the company's spirit, along with keeping employees productive and focused, are critical responsibilities during the third and fourth years. CEOs must spice things up, keep the fire burning. According to David Pottruck of Charles Schwab: "[E]xecution is about detail. It's a lot of hard work. But the phrase 'hard work' is a tricky one because it can be seen as either daunting or inspiring. And I think CEOs need to look their employees straight in the eye and say, 'Everything we're going to do is hard but it can be fun, fulfilling and inspiring.' "[18]

Larry Bossidy, former chairman and CEO of AlliedSignal and later Honeywell International, insists that one of the best ways to keep an organization on track is to ensure that every employee senses the urgency for change. As master of "the burning platform," Bossidy believes that it is too easy for an organization to turn its back on the hard work of implementation and that nothing will happen without that sense of urgency: "The leader's job is to help everyone see that the platform is burning, whether the flames are apparent or not. The process begins when people decide to take the flames seriously . . . a brutal understanding of reality."[19] To make employees feel the heat of the flames, the CEO and senior managers have to narrate clearly and forcefully why the status quo no longer works and convince employees that if the strategic vision is not achieved, the company and each employee's job will in effect be engulfed by flames.

The burning platform is of course a figure of speech, and not all employees need actually be burned, even figuratively speaking, to get things done. Gordon Bethune of Continental Airlines, for example, kept the fires burning by selectively using rewards. After accomplishing a stunning turnaround at an airline that had been slipping dangerously low in the industry, Bethune faced the archetypical problem of a stage-five CEO: "It gets harder and harder to keep it up, and that's the next challenge."[20] With competitors nipping at his heels, Bethune's keep-it-burning solution was to raise the bar of what was acceptable and then keep on raising it even higher.

When Bethune first assumed leadership of Continental Airlines and saved it from bankruptcy, he told employees that for each month that the airline's on-time performance placed it among the top-five airlines nationwide, the company would demonstrate appreciation by including an extra $65 in every employee's paycheck, costing the company $2.5 million per month. To ensure that the organization did not become complacent once the goal was met, Bethune raised the bar even further one year later. On-time performance then had to place among the top three. To raise the bar even higher, Bethune finally offered to increase monthly bonuses to $100 if Continental took best in show in the Department of Transportation's on-time competition. It worked.

Bethune's approach has two critical elements worth noting: (1) a CEO should seriously consider using rewards as an incentive to encourage employees to meet major company goals, and (2) a CEO should recognize the importance of measurement to reach those goals. What gets measured gets managed.

Execute: Put the Customer Front and Center

We have said that the best practices of the revision and reinvention stage amount in many ways to little more than doing what the CEO has done before. One such practice, however, deserves special mention. In the first 18 months, the CEO Capital model emphasizes the need to learn from customers and seek input from external constituencies. As always, these practices are good advice, but now the focus on customers must be ratcheted up to yet another level. To fight internal myopia, successful CEOs inevitably emphasize, to an extreme, the importance of customer satisfaction.

By way of illustration, former Chairman and CEO Herb Kelleher insisted that all Southwest Airlines' communications capitalize the word *customer*. Of course, accenting customer service is almost always good in its own right and it usually leads to a better company. But seriously focusing on customers at this stage furthers an additional end as well. Most CEOs are convinced that closely monitoring customers is the best way to obtain meaningful feedback on company performance, which can then be used to determine what needs to be done and to improve what has already been done. The customer is the ultimate looking glass. Customers' attitudes toward the company and its performance will reflect both beauty marks and blemishes and typically provide the most reliable indication of the company's performance.

Customer focus is so important at this stage that CEOs can often recount exactly how many customers they have seen during the previous months. Customer visits of up to 300 in one year are not uncommon. During these visits, customers are more than willing to rate the services they receive and to offer suggestions on how a company can improve.

To organize customer feedback, Chairman and CEO Dick Brown at EDS instituted the Service Dashboard,[21] a Web-based program built on client surveys that charts service performance and client satisfaction. The easily accessible dashboard—available 24/7—provides all employees with immediate feedback on the quality of EDS services, making any customer service problems instantly identifiable. Armed with this tool, senior leadership can quickly respond and fine-tune any practices hindering execution.

Another customer-oriented approach is EMC's customer advisory councils, which Chairman Michael Ruettgers holds twice a year. These councils are a type of advanced focus groups that consist of two days of intense discussions with carefully selected customers. EMC's top product management and engineering executives attend. EMC uses the councils "to methodically extract product requirements from customers, to test the validity of concepts we are considering for future products, and in general to create a climate of collaborative innovation." [22] At these councils, EMC describes its vision and how it intends to respond to anticipated changes in the marketplace. EMC then uses the feedback, as did Dick Brown of EDS, to fine-tune company practices, reaffirming what works and correcting what does not.

BEST PRACTICES FOR REINVENTION

Dogged detail work, repetition, perseverance, progress, motivation, customer feedback—all of these things characterize getting the job done in stage five. After keeping these goals in motion, the astute CEO should look back at the company's progress and smile with satisfaction, but not for too long. The CEO must now also consider the extent to which the world has changed since the original vision was forged, avoid becoming outmoded or outpaced, and forge a new or revised vision. The CEO should start rebuilding, in effect tearing down much of what has been so painstakingly constructed but is no longer relevant to the company's future. Revision followed by reinvention.

If recent history is any indication, the marketplace is subject to profound shifts in most industries every three to five years. The fast pace of technological change accentuates these cycles, requiring that the CEO stay attuned to the changes that will inevitably occur. By the end of stage five, the CEO and top management should mull over new ideas for reinventing the organization, formulating a new vision, and transforming the company once more.

The word *reinvention* can barely be spoken without bringing to mind Jack Welch, the champion of reinvention and a legend in his own time. These two words—*Welch* and *reinvention*—are nearly synonymous in business circles and form the foundation for Welch's vast supply of CEO capital. Former Chairman and CEO Welch reinvented GE no fewer than five times in his impressive 20-year reign. Consider his visions: be number one or two in your business, globalization, boundarylessness, zero-defect Six Sigma, and near the end of his tenure, utilize the Web or grow your business dot-com. Welch reinvented on average every three to four years.

Michael Ruettgers, chairman and former CEO of EMC, is another master of reinvention. EMC boasted one of the past decade's best performing stocks, although like most other technology firms it has struggled since 2001 with the general devaluation affecting almost all technology stocks. Before ceding the CEO title,

Ruettgers changed the company's direction nearly four times in nine years. As Ruettgers stated: "The letters E-M-C could stand for 'everything moves constantly.' During this decade . . . we've reinvented EMC about every two years . . . by forcing ourselves to jump to a new growth curve . . . before the one we're on begins to turn down."[23]

Then there is another legend, Lou Gerstner. In 1993, the fabled IBM, one of the world's most revered institutions, was in a state of near collapse. The former perennial favorite of the *Fortune* Most Admired Companies survey found itself placing 354 out of 404 companies.[24] The former Chairman John Akers resigned in shame. Three months later, in walked Lou Gerstner, a nontechnology turnaround artist from a food products and tobacco company. The news shaved $3 off IBM's stock. What people did not readily realize was that Gerstner was well-suited to the job. He had been an IBM customer for years as CEO of RJR Nabisco Holdings and as president of American Express. His outsider perspective was particularly appropriate to rebuilding a company plagued with myopia.

The new CEO quickly learned that IBM excelled at coming up with grand information technology theories. IBM was the aging track star of a former, more staid technological age. One who was living on past Olympic glories, but perhaps now too arthritic to act quickly, much less to run a hundred-yard dash at breakneck pace against its more nimble, youthful competitors. IBM's culture, it seemed, emphasized the "elegance of the definition of the problem rather than the actual execution of an action plan."[25]

Gerstner acted decisively and drastically. He discarded Akers' federation plan to divide the company into 13 smaller divisions. In lieu of a culture that tolerated unending discussion over theoretical issues and then waited for general agreement among management,

Gerstner infused IBM's culture with the need for speed, urgency, financial discipline, and no-nonsense achievement. Although he kept most of his predecessor's senior team, he laid off 35,000 employees. Gerstner reinvented IBM's vision by focusing on customers and providing services and solutions that met customers' needs. As the world approached the millennium, technological advances had wrought much change, creating a complex and sometimes confusing, uncertain business environment. Gerstner's reinvention allowed IBM to adapt to, and even flourish in, this environment, and customers were soon seeking out IBM to help them manage the new technology age.

By ridding IBM of its infamous political infighting and too-heavy reliance on consensual decision making, Gerstner positioned the organization to take advantage of the Internet boom. Gerstner launched his e-business strategy with a $200 million advertising campaign describing how the now fast-moving IBM was ready to network companies and their customers through intranets, extranets, and the Web. Instead of pursuing dot.coms, Gerstner focused on IBM's traditional customers. The strategy worked, and with Gerstner's flawless execution, commentators widely hail it as a stunning success. His relentless effort to change IBM's slow, traditional, homogeneous white-shirt culture into a high-octane, rolled-up-sleeves one made the transformation possible. Gerstner had reinvented that icon of technology, that darling of coupon clippers, the very blue chip IBM. If even Big Blue, the epitome of early 1990s technological sluggishness, can be reinvented to meet the needs of a morphing marketplace, then no company can say it can't be done.

Reinvention requires an element of restlessness. A CEO's mere receptiveness to emerging opportunities or a willingness to change is insufficient. Something more edgy and intense is required: a deep awareness that no successful company can be static for long and that success requires constant adaptation. Gerstner confirms the wisdom of reinvention: "I've been absolutely convinced that you've got to blow things up and start over again every few years, and that puts a whole new face on people's jobs. It gets people focused externally rather than internally."[26]

The reinventing CEO must affirmatively search for ways in which to encourage a company to change. Because change is an inevitable given of business life, reinvention must become a deeply ingrained mindset. In short, the reinventing CEO must acknowledge that the CEO's job is never finished and that aiming for a goal is often as important as reaching it.

REFLECTIONS (PART I): REINVENT THROUGH SUCCESSION

Asking CEOs to be so flexible as to reinvent what they have built every several years, to change focus and restructure anew, is asking a lot. Perhaps too much. Not everyone can be a Jack Welch or Lou Gerstner. Each of these champions of reinvention had the foresight to recognize the value of change for change's sake and embraced the belief that business is a dynamic in which corporate practices are not immutable.

Far more typical are the CEOs who cannot change in midstride, who cannot, after initial successes, continue to transform and adapt as the world changes around them and their companies. Therefore, it is not surprising that the average tenure of chief executives is now at most five to seven years,[27] just about the length of a complete cycle of the CEO Capital model. Not surprisingly, many CEOs find it difficult to extend their tenures long enough to encompass successive visions, to lead a company through successive reinventions, and to pass through successive cycles of the five CEO capital stages. Being able to steer a company through one vision is an accomplishment in its own right, but steering a company through more than one reinvention is even more remarkable.

When CEOs run out of steam and share price reflects the lack of a renewed vision, boards sense the CEO's waning attention and seriously begin to consider successors. No wonder then that decade-long tenures are so rare today. Indeed, it is almost expected that a company will have two or three CEOs during that time. Thus, the business community's tolerance for ever-changing leaders is part and parcel of the need to reinvent and adapt. In many ways this is a good thing because in the absence of a Jack Welch, periodically appointing a successor is one way to spark and enforce reinvention.

That even successful CEOs find it difficult to span multiple visions and that a company must deal with multiple successions is not the disaster that it may initially appear, even when the outgoing CEO has amassed a high level of CEO capital. After all, presidents retire from office every four to eight years without catastrophe. As much as we may identify a president with his office, even a Lincoln or an FDR is not the United States. Much the same is true in the business world. CEOs, even immensely popular CEOs, may be alter egos of their companies or otherwise embody the company in character or in culture, but they are not the companies. We may revere them and the company might not have succeeded without them at that particular time, but they are replaceable. Capable CEOs, even ones who have amassed substantial CEO capital on behalf of their companies, leave their companies stronger, not weaker, and in a better position to be run by a successor. Chief executives can personify a company's vision and voice. Yet companies, like nations, endure beyond their leaders and beyond their founders.

After guiding companies through the one or two cycles of the CEO Capital model, many CEOs may wish to look for new challenges, leaving the next wave of reinvention to a worthy successor. They may, like Andy Grove of Intel, move on to a non-executive chairman position, leaving the daily running of the business to a successor. Succession planning is essential. As Gerald Levin of AOL Time Warner said upon choosing Richard Parsons as his successor: "I have always believed that your timing should not be how long you think you can contribute but if you have succession in place."[28] Thomas Stemberg of Staples, like many recent retiring CEOs, leave functioning companies in able hands for which reinvention is not likely to be due soon (as did Lou Gerstner with Samuel Palmisano of IBM, Geoffrey Bible with Louis Camilleri of Philip Morris, James Kelly with Michael Eskew of UPS, Jack Welch with Jeffrey Immelt of GE, Harvey Golub with Kenneth Chenault of American Express, and Herb Kelleher with Jim Parker of Southwest Airlines). Other retiring CEOs are relinquishing companies in need of change because of changing market forces. To turn the tide, their successors will face a more pressing need for immediate reinvention (e.g., David Komanksy with Stan O'Neal of Merrill Lynch, and Gerald Levin with Richard Parsons of AOL Time Warner). In all of these cases, the board, the outgoing CEO, or both have attempted to establish a smooth transition with carefully selected CEO-elects.

History has shown that few CEOs have had the stamina or prescience to successfully start over with new visions every few years. If the board of directors is doing its job right, it will be aware of the need for adaptive change. Hopefully, both directors and outgoing CEOs will plan for an heir apparent with the strength, values, and experience to handle the next stage of the company's evolution.

REFLECTIONS (PART II): LEAVE A LEGACY

During stage five, many CEOs begin thinking about leaving a lasting legacy. Wanting to leave a legacy is only natural. What constitutes an appropriate legacy is a matter of individual preference and can vary from CEO to CEO. As noted in the previous section of this chapter, most tenures do not last long after stage five. Accordingly, near the end of this stage most CEOs should consider what matters most to them. Once they make this determination, they then should consider how to express that personally significant matter in a meaningful way that is likely to leave a lasting imprint.

Although such legacies almost invariably benefit companies immensely, CEOs choose legacies primarily as a matter of personal preference, by highlighting past deeds, programs, or positions about which they care deeply and for which they wish to be remembered. The legacy is a personal statement. Sometimes CEOs are fortunate to be able to intentionally select their legacies from an array of possibilities and then go about purposely crafting one. More often, however, what will constitute legacies is largely chosen for them by events. In most cases, a few highlights of their tenures are likely to have stood out among the rest. From these few, they must choose one, stress it, and then imbue it with symbolic importance. Thereafter, these CEOs must define themselves and their tenure primarily by references to these legacies.

This is not to suggest that CEOs select a legacy on the basis of personal preference simply for the sake of self-promotion or for any other reason that is inconsistent with corporate culture. To the contrary, legacies must be beneficial to the company—that is, they may assist in attracting new hires, strengthening the brand, promoting a sense of belonging among employees, and serving to motivate. Otherwise, legacies will never outlast the departing CEO. Still, there is nothing improper about CEOs who isolate some quality leadership facet of their tenure and then seek to hold it out as a symbol of their tenure. Such legacies are beneficial to both the CEOs and the companies. CEOs who have worked long and hard on behalf of their company will have merited no less. Carefully selected legacies are akin to what companies have always done when they hang oil paintings of their CEOs on the walls of the boardroom. The difference is that true legacies are akin to living paintings that carry far more meaning. Presumably, a legacy, unlike a mere canvas, carries with it a symbolic essence that transcends personal aggrandizement and adds to a company's culture. In effect, it institutionalizes a CEO's capital, allowing the company to use it even after a CEO's tenure has ended.

A legacy's goal can take many forms. It might focus on a values-based thought-leadership platform (Merck's Roy Vagelos's donating Mectizan to cure river blindness in Africa), a set of values (Time Warner's Gerald Levin's defense of First Amendment rights), or some other deed of which a CEO is proud (L'Oreal's Lindsay Owen-Jones' Women In Science achievement program). What is important is that a CEO be able to point to at least one accomplishment of his or her tenure that stands out. For instance, the reinvention of HP by way of the HP–Compaq merger will undoubtedly remain part of Fiorina's legacy, whichever way the wind eventually blows on evaluating her overall effectiveness. Similarly, retired Chairman and CEO Lou Gerstner has left behind a legacy: a vibrant, new culture for IBM that is focused squarely on the customer.

For CEO Craig Barrett of Intel Corporation, the legacy he hopes to leave is for "people to say, 'By golly, Craig was able to keep Intel in the center of action in computing; Intel is still a high-tech growth company; Intel is still one of the most valued companies in the world; Intel does great work; Intel is a great place to work.' That's the legacy I want."[29] For William "Bill" W. George, the former chairman of Medtronic, leaving a legacy during his tenure meant leading a company that meshed with his personal values. His legacy goal, stated in Vision 2010, was for Medtronic to be a provider of medical services, not just products. It is a legacy that he dreamed about as a young man. George likened Medtronic to a place "where a company could become a kind of symbol for others where the product that you represent is doing good for people."[30]

Two years before retirement, Chairman and CEO Jerry Choate of The Allstate Corporation wanted to accentuate how deeply he and the company cared about its employees. He organized a major communications effort around The Allstate Partnership, an informal covenant between company and employee outlining what employees can expect from the company and what the company can expect in return. When Edward Liddy became Allstate's chairman and CEO in 1999, he continued espousing Choate's contract of mutual expectations. Even today, Allstate imbues prospective and new employees with the spirit of Choate's Plan, referring to it on the company's Web site[31] and during employee orientation.

Where businesses are strongly associated with their founding families, legacies often become part of a continuing family tradition of corporate contribution, a family persona that transcends individual CEOs. Bill Ford, grandson of Henry Ford, instituted a bold advertising campaign in February 2002 in an attempt to repair the automotive company's battered image after the Firestone tire recall fiasco and Jacques Nasser's fall from grace. The advertisements reminded consumers of the Ford family tradition and heritage. Two advertisements, aptly referred to as "Family" and "Legacy," stressed the Ford family's emotional connection to the Ford Corporation. As Bill Ford states in the opening of the "Family" advertisement, what "is special about Ford is, we're not just another nameless, faceless company. We're a company that has a soul. There is a sense of family here."[32] The family's legacy lives on.

⟹•◦•⟸

During most of the final stage of building CEO capital, CEOs must fine-tune their strategic visions and take corrective action to ensure that their visions are implemented. Near the end of Revision and Reinvention, CEOs must evaluate how the future will require not just fine-tuning, but perhaps modification or even total overhauls of their original vision. The timing of reinvention ironically seems to parallel the relatively brief tenures of most CEOs today. In search of continuous reinvention, boards will be increasingly on the lookout for successors to CEOs who are ready, willing, and able to start the process of building CEO capital anew. In turn, as CEOs contemplate a future out of the spotlight, many will want to leave legacies, a lasting imprint of an accomplishment that reflects highly on their tenures and that benefit companies for years to come.

This completes the full cycle of building CEO capital—the very core of CEO stewardship, which can only be extended further if CEOs successfully reinvent their vision. In doing so, the stages in the cycle need repeating. This cycle, however, is no more than a reflection of current reality. It too, like the visions of reinventing CEOs, must remain fluid, as the world evolves, taking business along with it. No doubt, the CEO Capital model will also in time require reinvention to maintain relevance in a changing world.

Chapter 9 takes a look forward at emerging CEO trends.

IMPLICATIONS
FOR CEOS

OVER THE HORIZON: FUTURE TRENDS AND SUGGESTIONS

I have seen the future; and it works.[1]

—Lincoln Steffens, American reformist

Modern CEOs are all things to all people: turnaround artists, coaches, globalists, strategists, branders, recruiters, ethicists, negotiators, communicators, consensus builders, technophiles, customer advocates, wealth creators, and, among many other things, clairvoyants. Modern CEOs also face a business climate encumbered by an accelerating number of challenges and complexities. The traditional, steadfast company, populated by unvarying hordes of white-shirted, blue-suited males—the almost mythological, seemingly changeless bedrock of yesteryear's CEOs and 1950s cinema—is no more. In its place is an ever-morphing entity, populated at all levels by both sexes, graced with flextime, home-office commuting, onsite day care, and casual Fridays.

The need for such endless adaptations and transformations subjects CEOs to intensifying pressures and growing challenges as technological, political, and social changes impinge on corporate behavior. Consider for instance the anticipated wide-reaching consequences of recent post-Enron, WorldCom and Tyco demands for greater financial transparency and executive accountability. Then consider, too, the political and social impact of the rise of the increasingly powerful, global multinational organization. These companies' net worth dwarfs the total national product of some nation states and their expanding economic supremacy has reawakened concerns about undue corporate influence over society, culture, and the environment. By requiring CEOs to play so many roles and adapt to so many changes, companies are asking much from CEOs and will ask even more tomorrow.

New problems and new concerns will without doubt greet future CEOs. Old problems and old concerns will oftentimes reappear, but in altered form with new wrinkles and twists. All this will occur at an increasingly rapid pace. Few things are more obvious than this: In coming years, the corporate world will face change upon change. Nothing will be permanent.

Notwithstanding this ever-shifting future, we can draw a few conclusions about the ebb and flow of various business currents and where they seem to be heading. Several currently recognized trends remain credible, while a few previously heralded trends have proved to have little, if any, staying power. In addition, a few observations are in order about the state of the corporate world today and its impact on CEO leadership.

Admittedly, this book is largely an account of the way business is—the way research has for better or worse shown it to be, not the way it should be. At the end of this chapter, we finally become judgmental with a perhaps quixotic attempt to alter two unfortunate (at least in the author's opinion) aspects of modern CEO history: (1) the penchant to give even promising new CEOs only 15 to 18 months to prove themselves, and (2) the inclination to paint the entire career of a replaced CEO with the brush of his or her most recent failure rather than that of his or her overall achievements.

CEOS SHOULD NOT AVOID THE LIMELIGHT AT THE EXPENSE OF RESPONSIBLE CORPORATE BEHAVIOR

CEOs will continue to occupy the public's attention in the years ahead. When circumstances demand that they account publicly for their companies, CEOs must ignore their natural instincts against being in the public eye and face up to their obligation in an open and free society to take the public stage. As this book goes to print, charges of gross improprieties are forcing the executives of Enron, Arthur Andersen, Tyco, WorldCom, and Global Crossing to go public within the limits of the Fifth Amendment. But CEOs should not need a black cloud over their heads before they account openly for corporate activities of public import.

The modern company no longer has the luxury of operating within a cocoon. As explained in Chapter 6, where we distinguish between mere celebrity seeking and taking legitimate actions on behalf of a company, many reasons exist for CEOs to reach out to stakeholders. CEOs reach out because of credit downgrades, dissident board members, bankruptcies, special interest groups, regulators, chatroom rumors, local community issues, and, among other reasons, the need to attract and retain first-rate employees. Most of these reasons do not require a crisis or a criminal investigation to prompt public disclosure. The CEO should be willing and prepared to fulfill this corporate responsibility and go public in the corporate interest.

There are good reasons why the public will remain interested in what CEOs have to say. With all due respect to baseball, business and financial markets are also one of America's favorite pastimes.

To feed this national pastime, the media's demand for business-related subject matter and their concomitant fascination with CEOs as embodiments of all that is good and bad in companies and in business will undoubtedly continue. Media activity is now 24/7, complete with all-business-all-the-time cable and radio news programs as well as numerous Web sites adding to the more traditional print media coverage. Given the ever-growing number of cable news stations, this superabundance of news-seeking vehicles has apparently not yet begun to satiate the public's demand for more business information. Future business coverage can be expected to grow even further.

The net result is a continuing trend toward increased business news and CEO coverage, which in turn influences corporate decision making. All that is covered by the media has become important. CEOs must now and in the future be alert to both offline and online media. As business news becomes more ubiquitous, public awareness also deepens. Any perceived controversy, incident, or corporate crisis may now be subject to the benefits and drawbacks of public exposure and examination. Where a corporate decision could once go unnoticed, no significant decision is likely to remain unobserved for long, now or in the future.

News outlets need material to fill airtime and drive ratings. In looking for stories, the company, particularly a multinational one, becomes a journalist's natural subject and target. In these reports, the CEO is more likely than not to be an integral part of the story. Because the CEO is the company's top representative and company alter ego, this is as it should be. For this same reason, investors will carefully peruse these reports and assess companies by evaluating, at least in part, their CEOs. The CEO has become a desktop icon, a quick way to search for and sift through a company's worth. For many, the CEO has become a shortcut that people rely on to make investment decisions, select employers, judge alleged transgressions, and grapple with business's role in society—all of which augments the value of CEO capital even further. There is no reason to believe that this situation will change.

The media spotlight may surprise and direct its glare on any business leader. To do their job appropriately, CEOs will have to become accustomed to conducting business in looking-glass environments where all of their deeds are on display and critiqued in real-time. As much as most CEOs will struggle to remain out of the public eye, too many forces will draw them out of the shadows.

CEOS SHOULD NOT LIGHTLY FORGO THE COUNTDOWN STAGE

A few 21st-century CEOs-elect have recently hit the ground running before the predecessor CEO has left and presumably without first making use of a Countdown stage. This trend may become more commonplace in the years ahead.

A CEO-elect who steps into the shoes of an outgoing CEO even before the retired CEO has stepped out of them must do so with the approval of the board and the outgoing CEO. For instance, within weeks of the announcement of his appointment, CEO-elect President Stan O'Neal of Merrill Lynch, heir apparent to CEO David H. Komansky, drove out two rivals, cut costs, pulled the company back from further expansion in Japan, and reorganized the executive team.[2] As CEO-elect, Richard Parsons of AOL Time Warner reassigned COO Robert Pittman to AOL's headquarters to reignite that former online powerhouse and lured CNN founder Ted Turner back into the fold, even though retiring CEO Gerald Levin had previously shunted aside the mercurial and often outspoken Turner. To act this swiftly, CEOs-elect must have the unanimous support of the board and the confidence of the outgoing CEO.

Were this apparent trend to continue, that is, CEOs-elect acting as CEOs even before formally taking office, the Countdown stage in the CEO Capital model would soon look not much different from the First Hundred Days; however, appearances are deceiving. As previously alluded to in Chapter 4, many CEOs-elect have known of their selection well before the public announcement of their appointment and have in fact been planning for months in advance for their upcoming tenure. Accordingly, they have benefited from a Countdown stage, albeit a *sub rosa* one, well before having taken upon themselves the role of CEO, an act that would otherwise seem precipitous, if not presumptuous. Thus the shift toward CEOs assuming leadership responsibilities well before formally taking office is mostly a matter of form over substance.

In any event, whether or not *sub rosa* Countdowns become more commonplace, they are unlikely to infringe substantially on the more traditional methods of transferring leadership. Human nature is unlikely to change. Undoubtedly most incoming CEOs will still play by the rulebook, quietly preparing in the shadow of the retiring CEOs, paying homage to their predecessors' legacies, and being careful not to enrage the two-headed monster before the formal transfer of power. The truth is that corporate cultures are not totally devoid of sensitivity. CEOs-elect, employees, customers, and other loyalists still expect the pomp and circumstance surrounding an outgoing leader's rightfully earned farewell.

CEOS SHOULD BE THEIR COMPANY'S FIRST CITIZEN

Christopher Komisarjevksy, president and CEO of Burson-Marsteller Worldwide, has become convinced that multinational companies sincerely realize that they share a common bond and must act to promote the world community's welfare. According to Komisarjevsky, international corporate cooperation will give rise to what he calls The Responsible Century. Therefore, discussions about social responsibility played a prominent role at the 2002 World Economic Forum. If, as Komisarjevsky predicts, greater social awareness is inevitable, more parochial CEOs will find it increasingly difficult to avoid some of the day's larger political, social, and economic issues.

Corporate social responsibility is neither a passing, activist-driven fad nor an image-polishing tactic for CEOs. Rather, it is being institutionalized internationally and becoming a legitimate and permanent feature of the business landscape. The consequences of these changes are real and will surely multiply over time. Leaders recognize that the international business community, as well as the developed world at large, will be judging them and their companies on integrity and social reputation. Corporate social responsibility has shifted from the realm of "nice to do" to "need to do," and is now an essential part of corporate reputation management.

Much of the impetus behind these changes is a mix of corporate culture, constituency relations, and the good intentions of CEOs and other corporate players, however, as with most things, when you give you often get as well. At least in part, companies also gain from socially responsible behavior. As noted in Chapter 7, a growing body of evidence indicates that consumers vote with their pocketbooks. People regard corporate social responsibility as fundamental to the kind of society in which they wish to live, work, and raise their families.

As a company's first citizen, the CEO must be the driver of social responsibility. CEOs need to walk the talk and behave as the guardians of their company's social behaviors and attitudes. The international movement on behalf of corporate responsibility requires no less. The 2002 World Economic Forum challenged chief executives, chairmen, and boards of directors to develop socially responsible programs, making them happen and executing them in a manner that is transparently open.[3]

As discussed in Chapter 7, social responsibility is both morally right and good business. With the increasing dialogue among world leaders about promoting social responsibility, good corporate citizenship will undoubtedly increase and in the future become a given on most companies' agendas. The words of Lord Browne, group chief executive of BP, on social stewardship hold immense meaning for all CEOs: "Companies can't thrive in isolation. We are part of society and we are dependent on its success. We have to invest in the development of society if we want to ensure that we can do business successfully over 30 years or more."[4]

CEOS MUST HEED THE RATINGS

As I've noted throughout this book, media coverage and public interest in business are increasing. Part and parcel of the greater attention being paid to business is a fascination with corporate ratings that compare various companies against each other and to various benchmarks. Keeping a scorecard on the corporate world has become a popular diversion and investment guide. True, keeping scorecards has its drawbacks. The scorekeepers are not always reliable, and the process used when developing the ranks is not always statistically valid. Even so, each day it seems more such rankings arise. A Google.com search located no fewer than 3,430,000 "Top 10 Company" lists.[5] Fair or not, scorecards are here to stay. Just as sports fans study their team's league standings, so do influentials and investors study business ratings. In both cases they pay particular attention to who is on top and who is challenging the leader for top billing.

CEOs must not entirely ignore these rankings. The number one– or number two–ranked companies are more likely to have their messages heard, draw capital, attract and retain employees, and earn the benefit of the doubt if crisis strikes. Such rankings have the legitimacy, real or imagined, of objective, independent third-party evaluations. High rankings amount to highly believable and marketable endorsements. Stakeholders usually perceive these endorsements to be credible evidence of good management and strong market position. Accordingly, rankings play a particularly effective role in swaying opinion. Some rankings can turn out to be a reputation creator, breaker, or builder.

Although many of these rankings may seem superfluous and possibly flawed, they do serve the salutatory purpose of helping people sift through and make sense of the maze of available information. For these people, of which there are many, knowing which companies are the 10 most diverse or which are the top 10 best places to work is immensely helpful. Followers of scorecards include the general public, as well as investors and other key stakeholders. Board members are also followers and are sure to note how their companies fare on their favorite rankings. They will also be quick to demand explanations if the company's rank slips.

Some of the more notable scorecards that CEOs should heed are the Malcolm Balridge National Quality Award, *Fortune*'s Most Admired Companies and Best Places To Work surveys, J.D. Powers & Associates' customer satisfaction surveys, the *Financial Times*' Most Respected Companies, the Ron Brown Award for Corporate Leadership, the Lawrence A. Wien Prize in Corporate Responsibility, the Domini Social Index, *Business Ethics*' 100 Best Corporate Citizens, *Institutional Investor*'s All-America Research Team, Interbrand's World's Most Valuable Brands, and *Chief Executive*'s and *Business Week*'s best and worst boards. Ranking at the top of one of these best-of scorecards adds luster and enhances a company's and its CEO's capital. Ranking at the bottom raises questions and can even result in disaster.

Chief Executive Ewald Kist of ING, one of the world's largest Dutch banking and insurance companies, spoke for all present and future CEOs when he stated: "We want to stay in the top 10 in the United States and the world. Others are growing bigger and bigger. We need to keep building through acquisitions and internal growth, or we might be kicked out of the top 10."[6]

CEOS MUST DO PENANCE FOR SHORTFALLS

As CEOs grow increasingly comfortable with their roles as corporate alter egos and become more accustomed to going public when necessary, so too will they become more accepting of their role as chief apologist when the company errs or otherwise falls short.

The watershed of all corporate apologies is, of course, the Tylenol tampering episode of the 1980s. When Johnson & Johnson CEO James Burke was faced with a product laced with cyanide that had caused seven deaths, he acted quickly and decisively by recalling more than 30 million bottles. The Tylenol incident was significant because Burke was extraordinarily open and accessible to the media, took full responsibility, ceased all production of the product, and replaced the product with tamper-resistant capsules. The public readily accepted the CEO's willingness to place customers' safety before financial gain and viewed Tylenol's position as evidence of the company's goodwill and sincerity. In time, sales recovered. Contrast the public's response to Tylenol with the negative reaction to Exxon Chairman Lawrence Rawl's stonewalling during the *Valdez* oil spill.

Since the Tylenol recall, the number of corporate apologies has multiplied. The messenger for these apologies is, of course, the CEO. Former CEO Joe Berardino of Andersen signed his name to a letter included in full-page advertisements in national newspapers acknowledging " . . . an error in judgment that had been made with respect to the accounting on one of Enron's partnerships."[7] Nor is it uncommon to see CEOs on primetime television programs apologizing to customers for poor service or other problems. Standing front and center when a problem arises is what we expect from CEOs. Former United Airlines' CEO James Goodwin apologized for his airline's mishandling of a rash of delays in the summer of 2000. Immediately after the November 2001 crash in New York City of an American Airlines Dominican Republic–bound flight that killed all on board, CEO Don Carty raced to New York to address the nation and express his sorrow over the heavy loss of life.

The awareness of the CEO's role as not just a seeker of profit but as the embodiment of the company on all matters, including matters of deep sentiment and emotion, is reflected by more than their willingness to atone publicly for error. Following September 11, numerous CEOs expressed sympathy and support and urged calm in advertised notices throughout the United States. Some of the first advertisements came from companies most stung by the destruction—Merrill Lynch, AON, Bank of New York, Cantor Fitzgerald, and Morgan Stanley. Soon after, however, other CEOs joined, including chief executives from Lehman Brothers, Charles Schwab, American Express, Citigroup, Credit Suisse First Boston, Goldman Sachs, UBS Warburg, and the Securities Industry Association. These gestures serve as symbolic reminders that financial leaders have accepted their expanded roles as more than mere purveyors of profit and have embraced additional responsibilities—being stewards of the nation's prosperity and well-being.

CEOS AND HIGHER MANAGEMENT SHOULD NOT NEGLECT TRAINING

Current opportunities for prospective chief executives to obtain leadership training, and for CEOs to refresh established skills and learn new ones, are surprisingly limited. A handful of top-echelon programs exist such as management experts RHR International's Top Talent Leadership Development and the CEO Academy, a one-day seminar taught by distinguished CEOs and corporate experts.[8] These programs appear to be on the right track, but more programs are needed. As discussed in Chapter 6, CEOs primarily educate themselves not through formal instruction but through advice from consultants and retired CEOs, and by the trial-by-fire approach. The same opportunity for on-the-job training, however, will not be available in the future. Beginning in 2010, the number of candidates from whom the upper echelons of corporate officers will be chosen is expected, because of demographics, to be far fewer, almost 20 percent less.[9] To fill the void in qualified candidates, companies will have to seek out younger prospects than they do now, candidates with substantially fewer years of experience. The only way to address this significant deficit in experience is through training programs.

A new emphasis on more thorough leadership training that is appropriate for new or prospective CEOs has already begun and is likely to continue as CEOs realize that effective training requires more than just a few business school classes, well-intentioned mentoring, or an occasional off-site seminar. CEOs will also need to recognize that such higher-level leadership training may often require their active participation including teaching classes, setting curricula, and imparting their unique perspective to others. Leadership training facilities such as the famed GE Crotonville facility where Jack Welch taught, and where Jeffrey Immelt now teaches, will become more common. The Boeing Institute opened its doors in March 1999 to provide training, including instruction by CEO Phil Condit, for all employee levels, including the most senior executives. Scott McNealy, CEO of Sun Microsystems and a GE board member, has started Sun Microsystem's Leadership Institute, a leadership training facility that is modeled after GE's.[10]

Although formal leadership instruction by CEOs and others will never completely substitute for on-the-job practical experience, it will nevertheless ensure that future executives are at least exposed to a full gamut of issues and challenges. This training becomes particularly important in light of the higher ethical and financial standards that companies must meet today. The need to prepare future CEOs for the moral and ethical dilemmas they will face when barreling down the highway of their careers will be profound. To trust such matters exclusively to hit-or-miss learning that is so prevalent in the school of hard knocks is simply too risky.

SHARING LEADERSHIP DOES NOT WORK

Some things never change. Over the past decade, we have seen several attempts at forging a communal leadership structure where two CEOs are charged with running a company. Typically, such job-sharing arrangements arise following a merger or other business combination where both companies are eager to seal a deal but can't quite agree on a CEO. Rather than surrender power to another, all too often the two negotiating CEOs arrive at an ego-saving, but simplistic, solution—let both of them serve as CEO.

As noted in Chapter 6, the CEO job is more than one individual can usually handle. Hence we have urged CEOs, if possible, to select a trusted number two to shoulder a portion of the burden.

Thus, the related concept of co-CEOs where two executives share responsibility has superficial appeal. Two co-equal number ones, however, are not the same as choosing a number two who serves at the command of a single CEO. As noted in Chapter 4, companies led by two-headed monsters often encounter trouble even when job sharing is brief and one head has at least technical authority over the other. Not surprisingly, experience shows that job sharing between equals works only as a convenient way to a deal quickly, but it hasn't succeeded long term as a means of running a company. Business influentials no longer expect those kinds of arrangements to work either: One Burson-Marsteller survey found 87 percent of the executives reporting that co-CEOs do not serve the interests of the company and shareholders.[11]

Only a few job-sharing leadership arrangements have worked. In Europe, joint-chairmen Antony Burgmans and Niall FitzGerald of Unilever, PLC have worked together since 1999. Similarly, co-Chairmen and CEOs' Hasso Plattner and Henning Kagermann of SAP AG have jointly, and successfully, led the world's leading provider of e-business software. In the United States, Charles Schwab and David Pottruck have acted as co-CEOs for more than five years, with Schwab and Pottruck holding chairman and president titles, respectively. Other than Unilever, SAP AG, and Schwab, however, almost all other co-CEO experiments in major companies, especially where U.S. companies are involved, have failed (e.g., Sandy Weill and John Reed of Citicorp; John Mack and Philip Purcell of Morgan Stanley Dean Witter & Co.; and David Mahoney and John Hammergren of McKesson HBOC).

Attempts by founding families to share power with outsiders have similarly failed (e.g., Thomas Middelhoff of Bertelsmann and the Mohn family; and Walter Hewlett and Carly Fiorina of HP). We have seen litigation arise when a European CEO's sharing of power with an American CEO has been dismissed as a ploy after the European CEO, in effect, summarily wrote off the supposedly co-equal American CEO (e.g., Jürgen Schrempp and Robert Eaton of DaimlerChrysler). Whether more recent attempts at co-leadership will prove successful (e.g., Betsy Holden and Roger Deromedi, co-CEOs at Kraft Foods; and Jim Parker and Colleen Barrett, CEO and president at Southwest Airlines) remains to be seen. Should they overcome the odds, they will deserve special examination, in particular with respect to whether cross-gender pairing somehow makes sharing leadership more palatable.

For a short time at Microsoft, people held high hopes for a troika arrangement with Bill Gates (chairman and chief software architect), Steve Ballmer (CEO), and Richard Belluzzo (president and COO) running the company; however, Belluzzo resigned in April 2002 mentioning that he wanted to run his own show.[12] What was left was a twosome, where Gates has stepped back into almost a mentoring role, while Ballmer for all intents and purposes runs the company. A similar situation arose at Intel where Andy Grove has, like Gates, stepped back into a counselor role while Craig Barrett runs the company. In each case, we at least superficially think of the companies as jointly led. We think this because one of the co-leaders is a founder of the company. Both founder and company have all but merged identities and it is almost inconceivable that the founder would no longer play a role. Yet in these cases the founder and former CEO has truly stepped back, not sharing power but rather contributing in the manner of a respected elder. Again, there remains only one number one, and it is no longer the founder or prior visionary.

In any event, despite ambitious attempts to invent a co-CEO office, few have succeeded. Although the chief executive position may be too overwhelming for any one individual, the fact is that single-leader companies have outlasted all attempts at other arrangements, for better or for worse. Although sharing power more equitably may seem more desirable, fairer, and more in accord with our democratic instincts, we still keep returning to square one, namely, one CEO alone seems to work best. The buck stops at one door only, in the past, present, and undoubtedly, in the future.

INFUSING A COMPANY WITH MEANING

We do not have to delve too deeply into pop psychology to realize that human beings want to belong. Despite waves of layoffs, job infidelity, and the appeal of freelancing and flexible schedules, it remains a basic human need to be part of something larger than oneself. This essential yearning has not disappeared despite networked computers and the triumph of the Internet. In fact, the events of 9/11 have demonstrated just how much people still hunger for and appreciate community. Although much of this longing to belong has already become less visible as times have returned to normal, the hunger undoubtedly will always remain just below the surface, ready to reappear in a more obvious form during crises. This employee need will not diminish, regardless technological or social forces that may emerge in the future.

Effective CEOs can reinforce that longed-for employee bond. By building a CEO persona that captures the human spirit and character of the organization, CEOs can—in the course of building CEO capital—build an environment that fulfills employees' yearning for meaningful lives at work. By motivating employees and instilling the company with a common purpose, the CEO further encourages a sense of community in the pursuit of worthwhile goals. Max DePree, the exemplary former chairman of Herman Miller and author of *Leadership Is an Art*, sums it up this way: "Leaders owe a covenant to the corporation or institution, which is, after all, a group of people. Leaders owe the organization a new reference point for what caring, purposeful, committed people can be in the institutional setting."[13] CEO commitment in the 21st century should be no less.

TWO APPEALS

Extending the CEO Timetable

The trend toward increasingly short CEO tenures is undermining business productivity and focus. In light of the shortened time frames and abrupt ousters (some clearly deserved) that were all too characteristic of the past decade, we'd have to agree with Alice in Wonderland, who might have been referring to boards of directors when she said: "They're dreadfully fond of beheading people here: the great wonder is that there's anyone left alive!" Fewer CEOs seem to make it past the five-quarter mark and even fewer beyond their three-year anniversary. Such instability irrevocably and adversely affects a company's reputation and destiny. Chief executive departures have substantially adverse consequences, affecting too many employees, customers, partners, and investors. Organizations become paralyzed months before an expected exit as rumors swirl, and months, if not years, afterward as the organization adapts to new leadership.

As this book makes abundantly clear, the CEO's responsibilities are almost mind-boggling. That a CEO must take command of all these duties and must produce within 15 to 18 months seems a Herculean task. Hence our repeated references to the need for a CEO to buy time through building CEO capital and, in particular, developing a persona in an effort to slow down the rush to perform.

I propose a possible solution to this problem: A more involved and engaged board of directors will create a leadership dynamic that is more resistant to simplistic time frames such as the five-quarter rule. With a more hands-on attitude, better CEO selection criteria, a greater willingness to ask the tough questions, and more involvement in company operations and strategy, boards may well develop a greater tolerance for a promising CEO who appears on track but has not yet crossed the finish line when the fifth quarter arrives. Perhaps a well-informed, insightful board will do more to help a CEO buy time so that a CEO's daunting task may be completed.

This is not to say that all CEOs deserve to stay in jobs when they are not performing. For instance, CEOs who lose sight of their accountability to stakeholders and bypass ethical standards to meet bottom-line expectations serve no one's interests and deserve to be quickly dismissed. Yet, CEOs who display a vast supply of the critical CM factors (i.e., credibility, conduct, communications, motivation and, management building), coupled with financial performance, should earn our trust and support. Companies should not be deprived of the skills of these talented CEOs, even if more time is necessary before judgment day. Boards, in particular, are in the strongest position to extend the CEO timetable. Their support, involvement, and resistance to short-term pressure from Wall Street, the media, and other powerful constituencies can lengthen a CEO's time in office and extend the time to fulfill the CEO's mandate.

Taking the Long View

In addition to an appeal for more time for CEOs to deliver, I also submit another plea that I raised earlier in this book. By the time this book goes to print, some of the CEOs mentioned will have left office for one reason or another. All CEOs leave their successes and failures as their mark. As spectators, we must not judge CEOs solely by their most recent failure but by both their conquests and their collapses. We remember Richard Thoman at Xerox for the defects associated with his sales reorganization, but his on-target strategy to sell management solutions was never in question. George Fisher of Kodak accurately and with foresight laid down the fundamentals for a digital transformation of his company even though his failure to execute eventually compelled him to leave the company sooner than expected. Percy Barnevick of ABB shaped a global powerhouse from a merged Asea and Brown Boveri before harsh criticism for collecting an outsized pension depleted the value of his CEO capital. After soon-to-be retired Millard "Mickey" Drexler successfully filled the coffers of the Gap for years, his prior successes appeared long forgotten when retail sales plummeted. Unfortunately, all of these chairmen and CEOs are re-membered more for their frailties than their feats, a what-can-you-do-for-me-today attitude—the past be damned.

Just as we beseech boards to take the long view of CEO perfor-mance and not prematurely dismiss promising CEOs, so must we all take a panoramic view of a CEO's performance—successes as well as failures. Not to do so is to discourage risk taking and cre-ativity. In setting forth the various best practices in each stage of the CEO Capital model, we have urged CEOs to encourage col-leagues to speak freely and not to kill the messenger. CEOs should be allowed to take reasonable risks, to be allowed to make mis-takes that do not have significant implications for the company. As industrialist and inventor Charles Kettering pointed out, "Mis-takes are the practice strokes of progress."[14]

Even where a CEO's record has not been perfect, because of the executive's own failing or because of circumstances beyond his or her control, imperfection does not vitiate the ways in which a leader has otherwise contributed significantly to a company's welfare. Much can be learned from a leader's successes, even if a CEO has gone wrong from time to time.

CEO Capital provides a blueprint for chief executives intent on making a difference and doing the job well. The guidelines in each chapter are meant to remind CEOs about what matters, especially what matters to stakeholders. Just as people pass through different stages in their lives, CEOs pass through leadership stages, but far more quickly. Work imitates life. Each stage—from the first hundred days to the last hundred hours—has its own distinctive highpoints and disappointments.

In closing, I am reminded of one question that always stumped CEOs when asked: "If you were going to leave a note on your desk for your successor, what would it say?" At first I could not understand how this question could be such a showstopper. Did they think that they would live on forever? Did they have trouble visualizing that a final day would come? Now I understand their sudden speechlessness. There's just too much to say. Too much to share. Perhaps this book will aid retiring CEOs in leaving a note on their successor's desk, even if it is an unusually long note. Perhaps this book will hold those few words of wisdom on which new CEOs, watchful of their stocks of CEO capital, will build better, stronger, and more purposeful companies.

NOTES

Preface

1. John J. Gabarro, *The Dynamics of Taking Charge* (Boston: Harvard Business School Press, 1987).
2. Donald C. Hambrick and Gregory D.S. Fukutomi, "The Seasons of a CEO's Tenure," *Academy of Management* 16, no. 4 (1991): 719–742.
3. Robert B. Reich, "The Company of the Future," *Fast Company*, November 1998, 132.

Chapter 1   The CEO Effect

1. David S. Pottruck, *Clicks and Mortar* (San Francisco: Jossey-Bass, 2000), 94.
2. Ram Charan and Geoffrey Colvin, "The Right Fit," *Fortune*, 17 April 2000, 228.
3. David Greising, *I'd Like the World to Buy a Coke* (New York: John Wiley & Sons, Inc., 1998), 131–132.
4. Id., 68–81.
5. [Internet]. Available from: *www.amazon.com/exec/obidos/search-handle-form/103-1763137-1635000* (accessed August 31, 2001).

6. G. William Dauphinais and Collin Price, *Straight from the CEO* (New York: Simon & Schuster, 1998).
7. G. William Dauphinais, Grady Means, and Colin Price, *Wisdom of the CEO* (New York: John Wiley & Sons, 2000).
8. Joseph L. Badaracco, Jr., *Leading Quietly* (Boston: Harvard Business School Press, 2002).

Chapter 2   CEO Reputation: A Capital Investment

1. A.J. Vogl, "The Car Guy," *Across the Board*, February 1999, 34.
2. Burson-Marsteller, *Maximizing CEO Reputation*, 1997 and 1999.
3. Burson-Marsteller, *Maximizing Corporate Reputation*, 1998.
4. Burson-Marsteller proprietary research, *Importance of CEO Reputation in United Kingdom*, April 1999.
5. David Larcker, Conversation with author, 12 April 2000.
6. Burson-Marsteller, *Building CEO Capital*, 2001.
7. Id.
8. "Measures that Matter: The Importance of Non-financial Measures," The Cap Gemini Ernst & Young Center for Business Innovation [Internet]. Available from: *www.cbi.cgey.com/research/current-work/valuing-intangibles/measures-that-matter.html* (accessed August 31, 2001).
9. Anthony Bianco, "The 21st Century Corporation: The New Leadership," *Business Week*, 28 August 2000, 61.
10. Steve Einhorn, "For Capital Results, Clean Up Your Company's Image," Burson-Marsteller, 1996.
11. John M. Broder, "Microsoft Tries Another Court: Public Opinion," *The New York Times*, 21 June 2000.
12. "Home Straight," *Financial Times*, 29 January 2002.

13. Lord John Browne, Group Chief Executive of BP, "The 1998 Elliott Lecture," St. Anthony's College, Oxford, 4 June 1998 [Internet]. Available from: *www.bp.com/pressoffice/default-story.asp?PressReleaseID=737* (accessed February 25, 2001).

14. Drake Beam Morin, *CEO Turnover and Job Security*, draft report, 18 April 2000, 5.

15. Diane E. Lewis, "When Baton Passes, Handoff Is Key: Replacing a CEO Requires Long-Term, Strategic Plan," *The Boston Globe*, 13 January 2002.

16. Booz Allen and Hamilton, "Study Reveals CEO Job Security is Declining Throughout World," Press Release, 17 June 2002.

17. Kathleen Nagel, "Route to the Top," *Chief Executive*, February 2000, 48.

18. *See* note 6.

Chapter 3   How CEO Capital Is Built

1. Jack Welch with John A. Byrne, *Jack: Straight from the Gut* (New York: Warner Books, 2001), 394.

2. Dr. Rory F. Knight, "Recovery from Tragedy," *Financial Times*, 3 August 2000.

3. Id.

4. Id.

5. Charles Farkas and Suzy Wetlaufer, "The Ways Chief Executive Officers Lead," *Harvard Business Review*, May–June 1966, 110.

6. Michael Useem, *The Leadership Moment* (New York: Random House, 1998), 204.

7. "Senior Executives Advise CEOs To Make Communications a Top Priority," Burson-Marsteller, press release, 5 February 2002.

8. John P. Kotter, "Leading Change: Why Transformation Efforts Fail," *Harvard Business Review,* March–April 1995, 63.

9. Human Capital conference brochure, Hunt-Scanlon, 7 February 2001.

10. Amy Kover, "Dick Kovacevich Does It His Way," *Fortune,* 15 May 2000, 300.

11. John J. Gabarro, *The Dynamics of Taking Charge* (Boston: Harvard Business School Press, 1987).

12. Thomas A. Stewart, "Why Leadership Matters," *Fortune,* 2 March 1998, 72.

Chapter 4   The Countdown: Beware the Two-Headed Monster

1. Matt Murray, "Challenges Loom as Immelt Prepares to Take Over Welch's Job at GE," *The Wall Street Journal,* 25 April 2001.

2. Stephen W. Quickel, "A Delicate Operation," *Dun's Business Month,* June 1988, 42.

3. Miles White, Interview by author, tape recording, Chicago, Illinois, 2 May 2001.

4. Paul Beckett, "American Express CEO Announces 2001 Retirement and Successor," *The Wall Street Journal,* 27 April 1999.

5. John Huey, "Outlaw Flyboy CEOs," *Fortune,* 13 November 2000, 246.

6. Ram Charan and Geoffrey Colvin, "Making a Clean Handoff: Picking Your Successor Is Only Part of the Challenge," *Fortune,* 17 September 2002, 72.

7. Jennifer Steinhauer, "Initial Steps by Bloomberg Show Contrast with Giuliani," *The New York Times,* 10 November 2001.

8. Bernard Marcus, 1998 Letter to Shareholders, Home Depot Annual Report, *http:/com/www.homedepot/HDUS/EN_US/ compinfo/financial/annual/1998/letterto.html* (accessed April 20, 2002).

9. Robert P. Bauman, Peter Jackson, and Joanne T. Lawrence, *From Promise to Performance: A Journey of Transformation at SmithKline Beecham* (Boston: Harvard Business School Press, 1997), 242–243.

10. Carol Kennedy, "The First 100 Days," *Director* 48, no. 8 (1995): 34.

11. Dan Ciampa and Michael Watkins, "The Successor's Dilemma," *Harvard Business Review*, November–December 1999, 163.

12. Anthony Bianco, "A Talk with Harvey Golub of Amex," *Business Week* Online, *www.businessweek.com/2000/00_50/ b3711007.htm* (accessed January 21, 2002).

13. *See* note 3.

14. Diane E. Lewis, "When Baton Passes, Handoff is Key: Replacing a CEO Requires Long-Term, Strategic Plan," *The Boston Globe*, 13 January 2002.

15. Id.

16. Bruce Pasternack, Karen Van Nuys, and Donald Perkins, "It's Not A Coronation," *Across the Board*, October 1998, 17.

Chapter 5   The First Hundred Days: CEOs under the Magnifying Glass

1. Gerald Levin, *Business Week*'s Captains of Industry, 92nd Street Y, New York, NY, 19 October 2000.

2. Matt Murray, "As Huge Companies Keep Growing, CEOs Struggle to Keep Pace," *The Wall Street Journal*, 8 February 2001.

3. Miles White, Interview by author, tape recording, Chicago, Illinois, 2 May 2001.

4. Id.

5. Phil Condit, Interview by author, tape recording, New York, New York, 27 March 2001.

6. John Helyar and Joann S. Lublin, "The Portable CEO: Do You Need an Expert on Widgets to Head a Widget Company?" *The Wall Street Journal*, 21 January 1998.

7. David Gergen, *Eyewitness To Power: The Essence of Leadership, Nixon to Clinton* (New York: Simon & Schuster, 2000), 166–167.

8. Mort Meyerson, "Everything I Thought about Leadership Is Wrong," *Fast Company*, April 1996, 10.

9. Reed Abelson, "A Leader's-Eye View of Leadership," *The New York Times*, 10 October 1999.

10. Dan Ciampa and Michael Watkins, *Right from the Start: Taking Charge in a New Leadership Role* (Boston: Harvard Business School Press, 1999), 16.

11. Raymond V. Gilmartin, New Leadership Conference co-sponsored by *Harvard Magazine*, New York, 20 October 1998.

12. Noel M. Tichy and Ram Charan, "The CEO as Coach: An Interview with AlliedSignal's Lawrence A. Bossidy," Leadership and Change, *Harvard Business Review*, March–April 1995, 70.

13. Quentin Hardy, "All Carly All the Time," *Forbes*, 13 December 1999, 143.

14. Wirthlin Worldwide Executive Omnibus, Burson-Marsteller proprietary research, April 1999.

15. Leslie Gaines-Ross, "The First 100 Days," *Across the Board*, September 2000, 45.

16. Burson-Marsteller/*Forbes* CEO Conference, proprietary research, May 1998.

17. Larry E. Greiner and Arvind Bhambri, "New CEO Intervention and Dynamics of Deliberate Strategic Change," *Strategic Management Journal* 10 (1989): 74.

18. Thomas D. Bell, Conversation with author, 18 November 1999.

19. Matt Murray and Emily Nelson, "New P&G Chief Is Tough, Praised for People Skills," *The Wall Street Journal*, 9 June 2000.

20. William C. Symonds, "Basic Training for CEOs," *Business Week*, 11 June 2001, 103.

21. Editors, "Agenda for the Future," *Chief Executive*, February 2001, 71.

22. *See* note 3.

23. *See* note 6.

24. William M. Bulkeley, "Unisys, Back from the Edge, Stresses Service, Comfort—CEO Weinbach Cuts Costs, Offers Off-the-Shelf Solutions, Boosts Morale," *The Wall Street Journal*, 22 April 1999.

25. David S. Pottruck and Terry Pearce, *Clicks and Mortar* (San Francisco: Jossey-Bass, 2000), 127.

26. David Pottruck, Interview by author, tape recording, San Francisco, California, 20 June 2001.

27. "To the EDS Worldwide Team," Richard Brown, electronic communication, 9 August 2001.

28. *See* note 2.

29. Steve Lohr, "He Loves To Win. At I.B.M., He Did." *The New York Times*, 10 March 2002.

30. Marcia Stepanek, "How to Jump-Start Your E-Strategy," *Business Week,* 5 June 2000, EB 98.

31. Gordon Bethune with Scott Huler, *From Worst to First* (New York: John Wiley & Sons, 1998), 36.

32. "Measures that Matter: The Importance of Non-financial

Measures," The Cap Gemini Ernst & Young Center for Business Innovation [Internet]. Available from: *www.cbi.cgey. com/research/current-work/valuing-intangibles/measures-that-matter.html* (accessed August 31, 2001).

33. Constance L. Hays, "Chief Is Out as Kmart Tries To Get Footing for Comeback," *The New York Times*, 12 March 2002.

34. *See* note 31.

35. Gordon Bethune, "Leading People for Results," *Chief Executive Digest* 4, no. 2 (2000): 7.

36. Wendy Zellner, "Meet the 'Completely Different EDS,' " *Business Week*, 18 December 2000, 206.

37. Matt Andy Pasztor and Joann Lublin, "Skeptics Query Honeywell CEO's Fitness," *The Wall Street Journal*, 21 February 2002.

38. Alex Taylor III, "Gentlemen, Start Your Engines," *Fortune*, 8 June 2000, 138.

39. Lisa Bannon, "Mattel's New Boss Promises a Leaner and Meaner Firm," *The Wall Street Journal*, 10 August 2000.

40. Erin White and Alessandra Galloni, "WPP's Sorrell Shines Amid Gloom," *The Wall Street Journal*, 21 August 2002.

41. Burson-Marsteller proprietary CEO media analysis 1990–2001, March 2002.

42. Burson-Marsteller proprietary CEO media analysis in more than 50 select European newspapers and business sources, 1999.

43. Jonathan Sprague, "The AsiaWeek POWER 50: When Creators Arise," *AsiaWeek*, 26 May 2000, 32.

44. *The National Credibility Index: Making Personal Investment Decisions*, The Public Relations Society of America Foundation and the Center for International Business Education, Columbia University Graduate School of Business and School of

International and Public Affairs (New York: The Public Relations Society of America Foundation, 2000).

45. John J. Havens and Paul G. Schervish, "Millionaires and the Millennium: New Estimates of the Forthcoming Wealth Transfer and the Prospects for a Golden Age of Philanthropy," Boston College Social Welfare Research Institute, 19 October 1999.

46. Randolph P. Beatty and Edward J. Zajac, "CEO Change and Firm Performance in Large Corporations: Succession Effects and Manager Effects," *Strategic Management Journal* 8 (1987): 305–317.

47. Editors, "CEOs," *Worth*, May 1999, 104.

48. Holman W. Jenkins Jr., "Exporting the Jack Welch Way," *The Wall Street Journal*, 10 March 1999.

49. Rachel Emma Silverman, "CEO Turnover Slows as Boards Seem Tolerant in a Cool Economy," *The Wall Street Journal*, 24 April 2001.

50. Vivian Marino, "Chiefs' Departures Decline From 2001," *The New York Times*, 7 July 2002.

51. Kathleen Nagel, "Route to the Top," *Chief Executive*, February 2000, 48.

52. Booz Allen and Hamilton, "Study Reveals CEO Job Security Is Declining Throughout World," press release, 17 June 2002.

53. *See* note 51.

54. Richard W. Oliver, "CEO: Long-term Strategist or Short-term Hired Guns?" *Journal of Business Strategy*, 1 September 2001.

55. Editors, "It's Your Choice," *Fast Company*, January–February 2000, 208.

56. Elizabeth Lesly Stevens, "Making Bill," *Brill's Content*, September 1998, 103.

57. Id., 104.

58. Tom Peters, *Reinventing Work: The Brand You 50* (New York: Alfred A. Knopf, 1999), 46.

59. Catherine Gourley, *Wheels of Time: A Biography of Henry Ford* (Brookfield, CT: The Millbrook Press, 1997), 38.

60. N.T. Feather, "Attitudes Towards High Achievers and Reactions to Their Fall: Theory and Research Concerning Tall Poppies," in *Advances in Social Psychology,* ed. M.P. Zannd (New York: Academic Press, 1994), 1.

61. John Carreyrou, "A French CEO's Taste for America Is Hard To Swallow Back Home," *The Wall Street Journal,* 18 March 2002.

62. Ellen Joan Pollock, "Twilight of the Gods: CEO as American Icon Slips Into Down Cycle," *The Wall Street Journal,* 5 January 1999.

63. Diana B. Henriques, "Business Reporting: Behind the Curve," *CJR,* November–December 2000, 18.

64. John A. Byrne, *Chainsaw: The Notorious Career of Al Dunlap in the Era of Profit-At-Any-Price* (New York: Harperbusiness, 1999).

65. Mark Maremont and Laurie P. Cohen, "Executive Privilege: How Tyco's CEO Enriched Himself," *The Wall Street Journal,* August 7 2002.

Chapter 6   The First Year: From Pupil to CEO Persona

1. Dean Fourst and Gerry Khermouch, "Repairing The Coke Machine," *Business Week,* 19 March 2001, 87.

2. Robert Slater, *Saving Big Blue* (New York: McGraw Hill, 1999), 111.

3. Donald C. Hambrick and Gregory D.S. Fukutomi, "The Seasons of a CEO's Tenure," *Academy of Management Review* 16, no. 4 (1991): 728.

4. Noel M. Tichy and Ram Charan, "The CEO as Coach: An Interview with AlliedSignal's Lawrence A. Bossidy," *Harvard Business Review*, March-April 1995, 72.

5. David Sable, Interview by author, telephone, 5 April 2002.

6. Burson-Marsteller proprietary analyst research, 2000.

7. Mark Maremont, "Gillette Chief Says Cost-Cutting Plan Will Take Time," *The Wall Street Journal*, 7 June 2001.

8. Greg Winter and Reed Abelson, "The Optimist Leading Bristol-Myers," *The New York Times*, 12 May 2002.

9. Miles White, Interview by author, tape recording, Chicago, Illinois, 2 May 2001.

10. Id.

11. Phil Condit, Interview by author, tape recording, New York, 27 March 2001.

12. Burson-Marsteller/*Forbes,* CEO Conference Survey, May 1998.

13. Jessica Sung and Christopher Tkaczyk, "Who's on Top and Who Flopped," *Fortune*, 4 March 2002, 75–82.

14. Charles J. Fombrun and Naomi A. Gardberg, "Who's Tops in Corporate Reputation?" *Corporate Reputation Review*, no. 3 (2000): 13–17.

15. Daniel Goleman, "What Makes a Leader?" *Harvard Business Review*, November–December 1998, 94.

16. Daniel Goleman, "Primal Leadership: The Hidden Driver of Great Performance," *Harvard Business Review*, December 2001, 44.

17. Mort Meyerson, "Everything I Thought about Leadership Is Wrong," *Fast Company*, April 1996, 6.

18. Id., 10.

19. David S. Pottruck and Terry Pearce, *Clicks and Mortar: Passion Driven Growth in an Internet World* (San Francisco: Jossey-Bass Inc., 2000).

20. Jeffrey Sonnenfeld, *The Hero's Farewell* (New York: Oxford University Press, 1988), 47.

21. Associated Press, "Paper Company Helps Burned Churches: Seventeen Arson-Destroyed Southern Churches Are Being Supplied with Wood Products Donated by International Paper Co. So They Can be Rebuilt," *Portland Press Herald,* 24 March 1997.

22. "Personal Histories," *Harvard Business Review,* December 2001, 38.

23. Elie Wiesel, *The Gates of the Forest* (New York: Holt, Rinehart and Winston, Inc., 1996).

24. Howard Gardner, *Extraordinary Minds* (New York: Basic Books, 1997), 108.

25. Gordon Shaw, Robert Brown, and Philip Bromiley, "Strategic Stories: How 3M Is Rewriting Business Planning," *Harvard Business Review,* May–June 1998, 44–45.

26. Warren Buffet, "Letter to Shareholders," 1995 Berkshire Hathaway Annual Report [Internet]. Available from: *www. berkshire hathaway.com/letters/1995htm.html* (accessed 27 August 2000).

27. Don Cohen and Laurence Prusak, *In Good Company: How Social Capital Makes Organizations Work* (Boston: Harvard Business School Press, 2001), 112.

28. Eileen Roche, "Words for the Wise," *Harvard Business Review,* January 2001, 27.

29. Peggy Noonan, "Return to Normalcy," *The Wall Street Journal,* 15 December 2000.

30. Carly Fiorina, "Strategy and Execution for the Digital Renaissance," Chief Executives' Club of Boston, 27 September 2000 [Internet]. Available from: *http://hp.com/hpinfo/deo/speeches/ceo ceclub 00.html* (accessed December 3, 2000).

31. David P. Hamilton, "Inside Hewlett-Packard, Carly Fiorina Combines Discipline, New-Age Talk," *The Wall Street Journal*, 22 August 2000.

32. Id.

33. Patricia Sellers, "The 50 Most Powerful Women in Business: Secrets of the Fastest-Rising Stars," *Fortune*, 16 October 2000, 132.

34. Thomas H. Davenport and John C. Beck, "Getting the Attention You Need," *Harvard Business Review*, September–October 2000, 120.

35. Id., 119–126.

36. "Why John Chambers Is the CEO of the Future," *Chief Executive*, July 2000, 34.

37. "Supporting Your CEO," Best Practices In Corporate Communications, Conference Call Transcript, The Public Affairs Group, 28 February 2002.

38. Jerry Useem, "Boeing Vs. Boeing," *Fortune*, 2 October 2000, 152.

39. Jeffrey Tarter, "The Role of the COO," *Softletter*, Volume 16, no. 8 (February 2000): 1.

40. Matt Murray, "As Huge Companies Keep Growing, CEOs Struggle to Keep Pace," *The Wall Street Journal*, 8 February 2001.

41. Justin Martin, "Wanted: CEO Confidante," *Chief Executive* [Internet]. Available from: *www.chiefexecutive.net/mag/165/index.html* (accessed May 27, 2001).

42. *See* note 9.

43. Chad Terhune, "At Home Depot, Nardelli Taps Ex-Colleagues," *The Wall Street Journal*, 5 June 2001.

44. Orit Gadiesh, Rob Markey, and George Vassilaras, "A Strategic Approach," worldlink, [Internet]. Available from: *www.worldlink.co.uk/stories/storyReader* (accessed March 7, 2001).

45. Nancy L. Breuer, "The Power of Storytelling," *Workforce*, December 1998, 39.

46. Jeffrey Immelt, *Business Week*'s Captains of Industry, 92nd Street Y, New York, 15 January 2002.

47. Lisa Endlich, *Goldman Sachs: The Culture of Success* (New York: Simon & Schuster, 2000), 88.

48. Id.

49. "Business Principles," Goldman Sachs [Internet]. Available from: *www.gs.com/about/principles.html* (accessed March 9, 2002).

50. Linda Klebe Trevino, Laura Pincus Hartman, and Michael Brown, "Moral Person and Moral Manager," *California Management Review*, Summer 2000, 128–142.

51. Lord John Browne, "Whitehead Lecture," Royal Institute of International Affairs, Chatham House, London, 27 February 2002.

52. Andrew W. Malcolm, "Airline Chief Is 7th Held by Japan in Payoff Case," *The New York Times*, 8 July 1976.

53. Anthony Bianco and Louis Lavelle, "The CEO Trap," *Business Week*, 11 December 2000, 91.

54. Id., 90.

55. Id.

56. Gary McWilliams, "Compaq Is Trying To Get Web Act Together," *The Wall Street Journal*, 20 July 2000.

57. *See* note 11.

58. Jim Collins, *Good to Great: Why Some Companies Make the Leap . . . and Others Don't* (New York: HarperCollins, 2001).

59. Id., 13.

60. Grant Ringshaw, "City: The Ousting of Ayling Last Week," *The Sunday Telegraph*, 12 March 2000.

61. Jim Collins, "The Misguided Mix-Up of Celebrity (And Why It Imperils Our Institutions)," The Conference Board 2001 Annual Essay and Report, 5.

62. Henry M. Paulson Jr. "Restoring Investor Confidence: An Agenda For Change," The National Press Club, Washington D.C., 5 June 2002.

63. Don Clark, "Contrary Intel Won't Expense Options," *The Wall Street Journal*, 8 August 2002.

64. Harold Burson, Interview by author, tape recording, New York, 25 September 2000.

65. "The Top 25 Managers of the Year," *Business Week*, 14 January 2002, 53.

66. Amy Merrick, "Kmart Net Falls 40% on Overhaul Costs, but Beats Analyst Expectation by Penny," *The Wall Street Journal*, 14 March 2001.

Chapter 7   The Turning Point: Leading through Thought

1. Peter Burrows, "The Radical," *Business Week,* 19 February 2001, 73.

2. Miles White, Interview by author, tape recording, Chicago, Illinois, 2 May 2001.

3. Phil Condit, Interview by author, tape recording, New York, 27 March 2001.

4. Jay A. Conger, *The Charismatic Leader* (San Francisco: Jossey-Bass Publishers, 1989), 29.

5. Brent Schlender, "The Odd Couple," *Fortune* Online [Internet]. Available from *www.fortune.com/fortune/2000/05/01/ wel5.html* (accessed December 29, 2000).

6. *See* note 4, 38–47.

7. Robert D. Hof, Kathy Rebello, and Peter Burrows, "What's That Glow Around Sun's Stock? The Internet," *Business Week* Online [Internet]. Available from *www.businessweek.com/1999/03/b3612007.html* (accessed December 27, 2000).

8. "On the Minds of CEOs," Marketing Division of *Fortune* and Burson-Marsteller, 2000.

9. David Pottruck, Interview with author, tape recording, San Francisco, California, 20 June 2001.

10. *See* note 3.

11. Mark Robichaux, "The Players: Big Money, Big Ideas, Big Egos: Here Are the People and Companies to Watch," *The Wall Street Journal*, 21 March 1994.

12. Id.

13. Eben Shapiro, "Time Warner Expands Plans for Cost Cuts," *The Wall Street Journal*, 10 October 1996.

14. Michael Dell, *Business Week*'s Captains of Industry, 92nd Street Y, New York, 3 April 2001.

15. Warren Buffet, "Letter to Shareholders," 2001 Berkshire Hathaway Annual Report [Internet]. Available from: *www.berkshirehathaway.com/letters/2001pdf.pdf* (accessed May 5, 2002).

16. Patrick E. Tyler, "Putin, Sizing Up Bush, Says the Retinue 'Makes the King'," *The New York Times*, 3 September 2001.

17. Ram Charan, *Action Urgency Excellence* (Houston, TX: Southwest Precision Printers, 2000), 7.

18. Id., 62.

19. "Fast and Unafraid," *The Economist*, 8 January 2000, 68.

20. *See* note 7, 70.

21. Richard Brown, Executives' Club of Boston, Boston, Massachusetts, 14 March 2002 [Internet]. Available from: *www.eds.com/thought/thought_speeches_brown031402.shtm* (accessed March 23, 2002).

22. *See* note 19.

23. *See* note 21.

24. Id.

25. Andrew S. Grove, *Only the Paranoid Survive* (New York: Doubleday, 1996).

26. Id., 3.

27. Eric W. Pfeiffer, "Start Up; The Story of a Prodigy; Whatever Happened to America's First Cutting-Edge Online Service?" *Forbes,* 5 October 1998, 19.

28. Quentin Hardy, "Motorola Struggles to Regain Its Footing," *The Wall Street Journal,* 22 April 1998.

29. Michael Useem, "Leadership Development: Building the Top Team at PNC Advisors," *Wharton Leadership Digest 5,* no. 3, December 2000.

30. Sixtus J. Oechsle III, Electronic message to author, 4 April 2002.

31. Sixtus J. Oechsle III and Tom Henderson, "Identity: An Exploration into Purpose and Principles at Shell," *Corporate Reputation Review* 3, no. 1 (2000): 76.

32. Sixtus Oechsle, "Identity: An Exploration into Purpose and Principles at Shell" (speech at the Corporate Reputation Conference, Puerto Rico, 9 January 1999).

33. "An Independent Minded Individual," *IPRA Frontline,* March 2002, 29.

34. David Barboza, "Monsanto Faces Growing Skepticism on Two Fronts," *The New York Times,* 5 August 1999.

35. "Uncertain Times, Abundant Opportunities," PricewaterhouseCoopers in conjunction with the World Economic Forum, 5th Annual Global CEO Survey, 2002, 16.

36. Available from: *www.corpwatch.org/press/PPO.jsp?articleid=913* (accessed April 12, 2002).

37. James Burnett, "NGOs Are Catching up with Business in Approval Poll," *PR Week*, 11 February 2002, 7.

38. Jeffrey Ball, "Ford Contacts Environmentalists behind Scenes," *The Wall Street Journal*, 12 May 2000.

39. Antony Burgmans, "Business Principles," 13 March 2002 [Internet]. Available from: *www.unilever.com/news/speeches/EnglishSpeeches_3819.asp* (accessed March 22, 2002).

40. "The Millennium Poll on Corporate Social Responsibility," Environics International in collaboration with the Prince of Wales Business Leaders Forum and The Conference Board, September 1999.

41. Alex Taylor III, "GM Tries To Woo Skeptics with Food and Chardonnay," *Fortune*, 24 July 2000, 54.

42. Del Jones, "When Dell Computer CEO Michael Dell Talks, Older CEOs Listen," *USA Today* Online, 15 April 1999 [Internet]. Available from: *www.dell.com/us/en/gen/corporate/michael 011 press.html* (accessed November 5, 2000).

43. *See* note 8.

44. Stephen D. Moore, "Blood Test: News about Leukemia Unexpectedly Puts Novartis on the Spot—Promising Trial of New Drug Spurs Demand, the Chairman Steps in—an Outcry on the Internet," *The Wall Street Journal*, 6 June 2000.

45. Daniel Galvin, "E-Commerce at Williams-Sonoma," Harvard Business School, 9-300-086, 25 October 2000.

46. Id., 1–20.

47. David Kirkpatrick, "Looking for Profits in Poverty," *Fortune*, 5 February 2001, 175–176.

48. Id.

49. Lord John Browne, "Addressing Global Climate Change," Stanford University, 19 May 1997 [Internet]. Available from: *www.bp.com/speeches/sp 970519.asp* (accessed January 20, 2001).

50. Id.

51. Id.

52. Id.

53. Id.

54. Id.

55. Alex Barnum, "BP Honoring Pledge to Slow Global Warming," *The San Francisco Chronicle*, 18 September 1998.

56. "BP Beats Greenhouse Gas Target by Eight Years and Aims to Stabilise Net Future Emissions," BP Press Release, 11 March 2002.

57. Lord John Browne, "Advancing Energy Technology: Meeting Growing Global Needs," Houston, Texas: World Energy Congress, 18 September 1998.

58. Lord John Browne, "Learning to be Distinctive," Goldman Sachs, London, 27 February 2000.

59. Michael Skapinker, "Admiration for Those Doing It Their Own Way," *Financial Times*, 17 December 2001.

60. Anthony Bianco, "The 21st Century Corporation: The New Leadership," *Business Week*, 28 August 2000, 61.

61. Harold Burson, Interview by author, tape recording, New York, 25 September 2000.

62. Pamela Mendels, "Role Model Daughters: Both Fathers and Daughters Agree That a Daughter Leads to More Aware CEO Dads," *Newsday*, 23 April 1995.

63. Id.

64. Deloitte & Touche, "Women's Initiative, What We Believe," October 3 2000 [Internet]. Available from: *http://us.deloitte. com/Women/women5g.html* (accessed December 17, 2000).

65. J. Michael Cook, Economic Club of Detroit, videotape, 22 February 1994.

66. Karl Schoenberger, "Levi Strauss Stitches Together Turnaround Plan," *The Globe and Mail*, 4 July 2000.

Chapter 8   Revision and Reinvention: Recasting through
             Succession, Leaving a Legacy

1. Roberto Parada, "Steve Ballmer's Big Moves," *Fast Company*, March 2001, 144.

2. Harris Collingwood and Julia Kirby, "All in a Day's Work," *Harvard Business Review*, December 2001, 57.

3. John J. Gabarro, *The Dynamics of Taking Charge* (Boston: Harvard Business School Press, 1987), 31.

4. Gordon Bethune, *From Worst to First* (New York: John Wiley & Sons, 1998), 155.

5. Jack Welch with John A. Byrne, *Jack: Straight from the Gut* (New York: Warner Books, 2001), 109.

6. David Pottruck, Interview by author, tape recording, San Francisco, California, 20 June 2001.

7. Lawrence Bossidy and Ram Charan, *Execution: The Discipline of Getting Things Done* (New York: Crown Books, 2002).

8. A.J. Vogl, "The Way It Is," *Across the Board*, May/June 2002, 34.

9. Adam Hanft, "The Best CEOs," *Worth*, May 2001, 79.

10. Burson-Marsteller, *Building CEO Capital*, 2001.

11. Ram Charan and Geoffrey Colvin, "Why CEOs Fail," *Fortune*, 21 June 1999, 70.

12. Robert Slater, *Saving Big Blue* (New York: McGraw-Hill, 1999), 122.

13. Steve Lohr, "Broad Reorganization at I.B.M. Hints at Successor to Gerstner," *The New York Times*, 25 July 2000.

14. Id.

15. Id.

16. Jessica Sung and Christopher Tkaczk, "Who's on Top and Who Flopped," *Fortune*, 4 March 2002, 78.

17. Unpublished interview by author.

18. *See* note 6.

19. Noel M. Tichy and Ram Charan, "The CEO as Coach: An Interview with AlliedSignal's Lawrence A. Bossidy," *Harvard Business Review*, March–April 1995, 70.

20. *See* note 4, 151.

21. "Service Excellence," [Internet]. Available from: *www.eds. com/about_eds/about_eds_service_excellence.shtml* (accessed March 29, 2002).

22. Paul Hemp, "Managing for the Next Big Thing," *Harvard Business Review*, January 2001, 134.

23. Michael Ruettgers, "Thriving in the Information Economy," The Wired Index Event, New York, 13 May 1999 [Internet]. Available from: *www.emc.com/about/management/speeches/ wired_index.jsp* (accessed April 1, 2002).

24. *Fortune*/Roper Corporate Reputation Index, 2002.

25. Steve Lohr, "He Loves To Win. At I.B.M., He Did," *The New York Times*, 10 March 2002.

26. *See* note 13.

27. Jill Vardy, "CEOs Post Some Spectacular Departures: Boards Getting More Vigilant, Less Tolerant of Mediocrity," *National Post*, 7 December 2001.

28. Matthew Rose and Martin Peers, "Levin Leaves Corporate Battles To Search for Life's 'Poetry,' " *The Wall Street Journal*, 6 December 2001.

29. Daniel Roth, "Craig Barrett Inside," *Fortune*, 18 December 2000, 247.

30. David Whitford, "A Human Place to Work," *Fortune*, 8 January 2001, 119.

31. "What's it Like to Work at Allstate?" [Internet]. Available from: *www.allstate.com/Careers/PageRender.asp?Page=culture. htm* (accessed May 15, 2002).

32. "Ford Expands No Boundaries in New Ad Campaign," Press Release, 19 February 2002 [Internet]. Available from: *http:// media.ford.com/newsroom/* (accessed 19 February 2002).

Chapter 9   Over the Horizon: Future Trends and Suggestions

1. John Cook, *The Book of Positive Quotations* (Newington, CT: Rubicon Press, 1993), 314.
2. Emily Thorton, "Shaking Up Merrill," *BusinessWeek* online [Internet]. Available from: *www.businessweek.com/maga- zine/content/01_46/b375706.htm* (accessed April 5, 2002).
3. "Global Corporate Citizenship: The Leadership Challenge for CEOs and Boards," World Economic Forum [Internet]. Avail- able from: *www.weforum.org/pdf/CSR/Final_Statement.pdf* (accessed May 3, 2002).
4. Lord John Browne, "Whitehead Lecture," Royal Institute of International Affairs, Chatham House, London, 27 February 2002 [Internet]. Available from: *www.bp.com/centres/press/s_ detail_p.asp?id=147* (accessed March 1, 2002).
5. "Top 10 Companies," [Internet]. Available from: *www. google.com* (accessed May 4, 2002).
6. Joseph B. Treaster, "Big Dutch Insurer Sizes up Potential Takeovers," *The New York Times*, 25 May 2001.
7. "An Open Letter from Joe Berardino," *The Wall Street Jour- nal*, advertisement, 29 January 2002.
8. William C. Symonds, "Basic Training For CEOs," *Business Week*, 11 June 2001, 103.
9. Michael Skapinker, "Business Heads for Too Much Room at the Top," *Financial Times*, 23 April 2002.
10. "A Talk With Scott McNealy," *Business Week*, 1 April 2002, 66.
11. Burson-Marsteller, *Maximizing CEO Reputation*, 1999.

12. Steve Lohr, "President Set to Step Down at Microsoft," *The New York Times*, 4 April 2002.
13. Max DePree, *Leadership Is an Art* (New York: Dell Publishing, 1989), 15.
14. Charles Kettering, recollection from Harold Burson.

INDEX